Big
League,
Big
Time

Big League, Big Time

The Birth of the Arizona Diamondbacks, the Billion-dollar Business of Sports, and the Power of the Media in America

LEN SHERMAN

POCKET BOOKS

New York   London   Toronto   Sydney   Tokyo   Singapore

POCKET BOOKS, a division of Simon & Schuster Inc.
1230 Avenue of the Americas, New York, NY 10020

ISBN: 0-671-00343-7

First Pocket Books hardcover printing September 1998

10 9 8 7 6 5 4 3 2 1

POCKET and colophon are registered trademarks of
Simon & Schuster Inc.

Printed in the U.S.A.

All photos are from the author's collection, unless otherwise noted.

To Betsy—
My wife, my partner, my best friend

Acknowledgments

I would like to thank Tris Coburn, my editor and friend, for his expertise and encouragement through this book's long gestation.

I would like to express my appreciation to my mom for her heroic editorial work, undertaken despite her utter lack of familiarity with baseball or sports of any kind. I would also like to thank my dad and Betsy, both knowledgeable fans and readers, for their comments and suggestions.

A special thank you to copy editor Steve Boldt, whose contribution to this work ranked above and beyond the call of duty.

A word of acknowledgment to the *Arizona Republic*, which, despite my criticism, served as my primary secondary source.

Finally, I would like to thank the Arizona Diamondbacks, and especially Bob Crawford and Joel Horn, for their cooperation and assistance.

When the One Great Scorer comes to write against your name—
He marks—not that you won or lost—but how you played the game.

—Grantland Rice
(1880–1954)

Foreword

Flying thirty thousand feet above the desert, if the night is just right, the universe appears to be once again poised on the edge of the big bang, before the stars were created, before the planets tumbled into being, before light and warmth provided relief from the darkness, before life stirred and breathed consciousness and reason into the void. From thirty thousand feet above the desert, there is no earth, no sky, only a sable blanket covering everything, swallowing everyone. Absolute, inviolable, perfect.

And then that perfect blackness explodes as the city abruptly appears in a burst of muted yellowish light, a sickly, unnatural yellow light that means that humanity has staked its claim. Come a little closer and discover that the yellow light is divided into huge blocks of avenues and streets defined by streetlamps, giant squares extending flat to the utterly black horizon. Glide yet nearer and see the white and red lights of cars, the incandescent, bleached brilliance illuminating ballparks, the blue and green and purple and pink neon streaks and sprawls adorning restaurants and office buildings. Closer still and the night and the lights and the movement become homes and parks and street signs, all bits and pieces of a vast metropolis. This is Phoenix.

Phoenix exists, though not because it is blessed with a deepwater port or because it sits atop a diamond mine or because its strategic locale protects the earth from invading aliens. Phoenix exists, Phoenix thrives, because we decided it would. We (or at least some of us) decided that a city should be constructed and maintained in the middle of one of the world's most unforgiving deserts, a desert with an annual rainfall of just seven inches, a desert where daytime summer temperatures routinely reach well over one hundred degrees for weeks on end.

Phoenix thrives because determined pioneers brought the will, and the federal government brought the water. Money and power and politics made Phoenix and the entire Southwest possible. Frigid winters, crowded urban areas, and decaying industrial bases have transformed the desert into a fresh, increasingly paved, and stuccoed start for millions upon millions of discontented Americans.

Phoenix is emerging as the quintessential modern city: horizontal rather than vertical, more a gigantic suburban expanse of malls and houses and gas stations and multiplex movie theaters than a community with an identifiable city center, no central place pulling everything else toward its orbit with undeniable gravitational force.

The consequences of this outward as opposed to upward expansion are many. On the negative side, rather than bringing people together, horizontal development acts to segregate communities by social, economic, and class measures. Mass transit falls by the wayside in the rush to build more highways to more readily—and more cheaply—accommodate the distended community. On the other hand, more and more families get the chance to live in their own houses, set upon their own plots of land, maybe beside their own swimming pools, escaping all the dirt and danger and human throngs of their former existences back somewhere else.

Phoenix is the largest city in the United States in area, and the sixth largest in population. It is growing because it is what we (or at least many of us) want.

And now Phoenix wants baseball.

We each hold a baseball memory—or perhaps more exactly, a memory of baseball—within us. A catch in the backyard with dad when he got home from work. A seat in the bleachers on a lazy Sunday afternoon. A grandparent's story about seeing Babe Ruth hit one over the wall. Trading baseball cards during lunch hour.

It doesn't matter if you're a real fan, or if you even like the game. Baseball is part of our collective American soul, same as Coca-Cola or Elvis or the Civil War.

That's why baseball matters. And that's why baseball is changing.

Baseball is but one cog (albeit a massive, crucial cog) of the great conglomerate that is the sports industry. Baseball is changing because it is becoming ever more important in our society and in our lives. It is important economically, culturally, and socially. It is a billion-dollar business to the owners and players, worth billions more to television networks and shoe manufacturers and soft-drink distributors. It is the field of dreams upon which we foist many of our most cherished values and ideas. It is the arena where we teach our young people what—and who—counts.

This does not mean that its march to success has been without controversy and dissent. We've all heard the same songs. One refrain goes like this: sports are too influential, too wealthy, too strong—just too damn big. The other, a kind of countermelody, claims that sports build character ten different ways, all good and right.

Both verses are on target. Athletic activity and competition possess the power to both build and break down, inspire and corrupt.

However, through the relentless cacophony of cheering crowds and adoring media, dissenting voices are few and far between, as virtually every American city of any reasonable size engages in the perpetual chase for a limited number of professional teams. A professional sports team is regarded as a boon to the community, a good citizen of the highest order, a necessity if a town is to be regarded as Big Time and Major League.

Everybody knows it's true. Everybody says it's true. Why else would so many mayors and governors, television correspondents and newspaper editorial writers, corporate CEOs and Hollywood celebrities—*those among us who really count*—support the home team, prospective or actual?

The rewards are self-evident: financial, political, psychic, psychological, spiritual—all spread absolutely evenly and fairly throughout society.

Right?

This book is about the arrival of professional baseball in Phoenix, relating some of the highlights of the three years between the awarding of the franchise on March 9, 1995, and the Arizona Diamondbacks' inaugural opening day on March 31, 1998.

This is about major league baseball—the game—and Major League Baseball—the corporate entity.

This is about baseball and also about government and business and the media. This is about culture and society and the future. This is about what we believe and what we value.

For a lot of reasons, to a lot of people, baseball matters. And baseball is changing.

This is about baseball, but it's also about so much more.

Big League, Big Time

The Game

C louds in Arizona sweep over the land in all shapes and sizes; long, elegant, pastel swirls inside swirls; wispy puffs of pure white cotton candy; flat-bottomed, multicolored mushrooms rising into the stratosphere; gray streaks and slashes racing across the horizon; ivory froth and foam playing in the sky.

Today, however, the clouds are of a different variety, huge and black and heavy, and they are everywhere. But the threatening clouds are only one manifestation of a twilight gone bad.

A dust storm is coming from the west, a huge brown blanket rolling over first the mountains that encircle the valley and then the buildings of the city center, obliterating everything in its path. The storm is pushing a powerful gale before it, whipping the dirt into the air. It is a sight not quite like any other, awesome and overwhelming, and still far enough away to repress a burst of panic.

Directly above, a piece of the sky is still visible and making a valiant fight against the wind and the darkness and the clouds, and the sun is cutting through the celestial turmoil with rays of blue and gold and red. It is startlingly gorgeous and absolutely futile, because the approaching night and roiling storm will not be denied.

And it is hot, improbably hot, brutally, scorchingly, bone-dry hot, at twilight.

1

The stadium is in the middle of this unquiet, disorderly world, or so it appears to the few people seated inside. That is, those among that small band who look away from the game to pay momentary heed to nature's doings.

Phoenix Municipal Stadium is on the east side of town, an unexpected patch of green surrounded by massive red stones forming bare, rounded, prehistoric mountains, a panorama resembling the surface of the moon. Nestled within these stark confines is the minor-league ballpark, a miniature rendition of the big-league version, with a few thousand seats and several concession stands and advertising broadsides lined against the outfield wall.

The Diamondbacks are leading 1–0 in the second inning, with men on first and second, and one out. The Athletics manager is on the mound, conferring with his pitcher and catcher before the situation deteriorates any further.

Roland Hemond is leaning forward, watching intently. He hopes the manager keeps the pitcher in the game. He has to learn how to get himself out of these situations, Roland says, and the only way to do that is to go through it, up on that mound, alone.

The manager walks back to the dugout. The Diamondback batter digs into the batter's box. The pitcher shakes off a sign, and another, then nods his assent. He rears back and throws.

The batter smacks the ball sharply to the second baseman, who scoops it up and pivots right. He knows that the shortstop will be hurrying into position, because in baseball every act demands a specific and immediate reaction, and every player should instantly know how every other player will respond. So the second baseman grabs the ball from the pocket of his glove and tosses it underhand toward second base just as the shortstop plants his foot on the bag, seven steps ahead of the base runner launching into his slide. The shortstop catches the ball, makes the out, and leaps into the air to avoid the body hurtling toward him. At the same time, the shortstop takes the ball in hand and, in midair, hurls it toward first, where the first baseman is waiting, stretching toward the ball, shortening the distance. The second baseman has completed his role by ducking to ensure that he doesn't interfere with the flight of the ball.

The throw is straight and true, and the first baseman has the ball well before the batter, who started it all, is three-quarters down the base path. In seconds, the double play is completed and the inning is over.

Roland leans back, satisfied. "That's the way to do it," he says.

Hemond is not an Athletics' fan. Not at all. In fact, he is the Arizona Diamondbacks' senior executive vice president of baseball operations. Roland is a baseball man to the core. His career began in 1951, in the front office of the Eastern League's Hartford Chiefs, and took him to major league postings in Boston, Milwaukee, Los Angeles, Chicago, and Baltimore, winning three MLB's Executive of the Year awards along the way.

Roland is not only a baseball man, he married into a baseball family. Margo Hemond's father was John Quinn, a major league general manager for twenty-eight seasons, and her brother, Bob, had been the general manager of the San Francisco Giants.

Roland's last job before coming to Arizona was as general manager, the top front-office job on any pro baseball team, of the Baltimore Orioles. In eight years in Baltimore, he negotiated 135 trades involving 428 players. Hemond left after the 1995 season and, soon thereafter, on October 27 of that same year, he joined the Diamondbacks, one of the first people on board to assist in the arduous task of building a franchise.

After five decades in professional baseball, Roland Hemond says this will be the last baseball job he will ever have. After five decades in professional baseball, Roland Hemond is having the time of his life.

So sure, Roland wants the Diamondbacks to win tonight, because that, as the old saying goes, is why they play the game. On the other hand, the truth is, this is the Arizona Rookie League and winning isn't the real issue here. The Arizona Rookie League, like all minor leagues, is a feeding trough for the major league clubs, a place where the young are brought to train and learn and improve. And if they improve enough, they move up to the next level of the minor leagues, and then the next and the next, until they either stop improving or make the leap to the majors—to the Show.

As a true-blue baseball man—as a man who truly loves baseball—Roland wants all these young players to do their best. He wants them to succeed.

Unfortunately, the reason the young players are in the Arizona Rookie League is because they are young and prone to all kinds of mistakes; the game has its sloppy moments. The Diamondback pitcher—baby Diamondbacks, these rookies are called—hits two batters in a row.

"Stay calm," Roland says aloud. "Keep it together."

The Athletics' try to bunt the runners over, but the pitcher, who got his team into this mess in the first place, makes a nice play as he scoops up the ball, whirls, and throws out the man sliding into third.

The next batter hits a solid shot into right field and now the bases are loaded.

"This is it," Roland says. "Let's see how they do."

A grounder down the third-base line. The runner on third has a big jump and is halfway home before the third baseman has picked up the ball.

"Come on," Roland says quietly and with a touch of urgency, his Diamondback colors showing. "Come on!"

The infielder knows he can't get the man at home, so he hurls the rock to first, just nabbing the batter.

All even, 1–1.

"Okay," Roland says. "Let's get the next guy."

The next batter pops up. The side is out. The baby DBs are lucky to escape having given up only one run.

Hemond is wearing a Diamondbacks' polo shirt, as are several of the other spectators. They are scouts and other front-office personnel, taking notes on every pitch, every hit, every throw. A couple of men (one for each team) aim radar guns at the mound to calculate the speed of each pitch, ready to track the ball as it travels to home plate. They jot down the ball's speed and then aim the radar guns again.

Some of the men—and they are all men—sit together, and some sit separately. They tend to move around, chatting with one another or checking the action from different angles.

Whoever is selecting the music to play over the loudspeakers between innings has an affinity for seventies groups such as the Eagles, the Kinks, and a bit disconcertingly, the Partridge Family. It is a loud and slightly bizarre counterpoint to the weather, which is only growing more fierce. Night has fallen and the stadium lights at the top of the poles are swaying in the wind. Every couple of minutes, lightning cracks on all sides of the ballpark. Even if it does start to rain, the people in the stadium will never know, because the heat is so intense that the raindrops literally evaporate before they reach the ground.

Buck Showalter enters the ballpark in jacket and tie. He looks utterly exhausted.

Buck has come straight to the stadium off a sixteen-day trip to Korea. He shakes a few hands and takes a seat.

An old-time scout who's stopped by to exchange a few words with Roland glances over at Buck. "Can't find 'em any better," he says in a deep Southern voice.

Buck Showalter is the manager of the Diamondbacks—even though there are no major league Diamondbacks, because there is no Diamondback team, not until the 1998 season, which is two long years away. Still, Buck is most assuredly the manager of the entire Diamondback organization and all the baby DB teams, even in a double-breasted suit.

The old-timers liked Buck. He was a hardworking, straight-shooting traditionalist, a young man from the old school.

"Can't find 'em any better," the scout says again.

At a game like this, on a night like this, everybody in the stands has a solid reason for being there. Two women, one young and the other older, sit beside each other, cheering for the Diamondback—and particularly one of the Diamondback infielders.

He is at bat, and the count is one strike and two balls. The pitcher rears back and lets go.

"Stri-i-i-i-ke!" the ump roars, and theatrically shoots out his right arm in World Series style. Just as minor league players imitate major leaguers in manner and attitude, evidently minor league umpires also imitate their professional betters.

"Don't agree with that one," the batter's girlfriend mutters. "That was low."

The next pitch is a ball.

Two strikes, three balls.

"He was a good student," the batter's mother states, but then her voice trails off, concentrating.

Her baby Diamondback swings and misses. Strike three. You're out.

Both women momentarily grimace as their boy walks back to the dugout, head down.

The girlfriend can't be much more than twenty years old. She explains that she and the infielder have been together for several years now. She spots him when he lifts weights. She even tosses the ball with him on occasion.

"He was never handed anything," his mother says. She has also played more than her share of ball with her son.

"That's right," affirms the girlfriend. "He's had to earn his way onto every team he's been on. And then earn the starting job."

Hemond likes the youngster's enthusiasm and his work ethic, but says he doesn't know if he possesses the basic physical skills to make it all the way.

"But that's the thing about baseball," continues Roland. "You never know how somebody's going to ultimately develop."

"If this doesn't work out," says Mom, "he wants to go back to school and study to be a physical therapist."

But for now her son is being paid $850 a month, with an extra $10 a day for room and board, for the chance to play professional baseball.

This is a dream come true, for all involved.

But the dream returns to harsh reality when the Athletics score seven runs in the fifth and the DBs head to defeat.

Roland gets up to leave.

It has been a good night: nature has held off exploding over this precious field. The lightning has struck elsewhere, the dust storm has veered off to eradicate some other place, the wind and the rain have vanished.

It has been a good game: Hemond has watched while a score of young men made the plays, displaying some ability and a lot of hustle. Baseball is a tough business, a daily grind, a game of speed and agility and coordination and balance, of skill and persistence and patience, of hope and promise and potential. Baseball players are not made overnight, the process takes time, talent, and determination.

All in all, tonight has been a good day at the office for Roland.

And tomorrow holds the promise of another game.

PART I | The End of the Beginning

Chapter 1

Pregame at the Expansion Draft

T he organization was mobilized and operating in high gear. Kelly Wilson was stationed at the gate, making sure the invited guests received their scorecards and dog tags. The scorecards were for keeping track of the game, which on this day didn't involve strikes and balls, hits and runs, but names and positions—the names of the players who were going to man the positions on the new team.

The dog tags were a giveaway from Bank One, little aluminum tablets hanging from chains, with "Bank One" printed on one side and "Miller Time, Expansion Draft Party, November 18, 1997," along with a glass of beer and the Diamondback logo, on the other. Bank One would soon give its name to the new ballpark—an honor purchased at a dear price—and had earned the right to produce whatever trinket it preferred. Nonetheless, dog tags didn't seem to suit the style of this crowd of season-ticket holders and local notables, and one had to wonder about the marketing thought behind the promotion. Perhaps it was intended as a public service for those guests who consumed too much Miller Lite during the festivities, fell into unconscious stupors, and were robbed of their wallets and ID; the dog tags left behind would provide the police with a clue as to the origin of the crime.

In any event, the dog tags were only a tiny, shiny piece of the entire promotional puzzle waiting at the southeast corner of Monroe and Second, outside on the Phoenix Symphony Hall Terrace. The score-card and the dog tags represented more than just two random giveaways; they represented the key components of the Diamond-back story: baseball and business.

The long line to enter the terrace had started forming hours before the 2 P.M. start of the draft and was teeming almost exclusively with adults. This was an unexpected development, seeing as this was somewhere near high noon on a Tuesday, midday during a typical workweek in a typically industrious American city. Weren't these people, more often than not wearing grown-up clothes—ties and suits and panty hose and dresses—supposed to be somewhere else, conferring and negotiating and constructing and manufacturing, paying the bills, building a better country, changing the world?

Kelly kept at it, handing out the trinkets and tally sheets, but the throng only kept swelling. Scott Brubaker, Kelly's boss and the vice president in charge of sales and marketing, passed by, impressed by the scene. He said the team had sent invitations to all the season-ticket holders (or, more specifically, since no one had yet to sit in an Arizona Diamondback seat, those who'd already mailed in big dollars to hold those seats *just for them, forever*), and had expected perhaps some two or three thousand to show up. The DBs were singularly adept at anticipating trends and demands, but this day's demand had apparently caught everyone by surprise, including Scott. Of course, this was not an unpleasant surprise. Just the opposite, in fact, for, as Scott was the first of many to comment that day, this was one more proof of how excited the good citizens of Arizona were by the entire baseball experience.

The event on the Symphony Hall Terrace was for the public, both outdoors and tented, readily accessible, and replete with food and games, country music, and cheerleaders. But that was the sideshow. The real action—the real business—was being conducted a couple of blocks away, in the massive ballroom inside the Arizona Civic Plaza.

This was draft headquarters, and contingents from all twenty-eight established major league teams were assembled to pay the piper. They had happily pocketed the $130-million entrance fee required of each of the supplicants from Phoenix and Tampa Bay, and now they had to fulfill their part of the bargain and let the Diamondbacks and the Devil Rays pluck some of the regulars from their ranks and begin to fashion squads of their own.

Most of the DBs' heavy hitters had convened in their war room off the ballroom. That's what they called it—"the war room"—without a trace of humor. Though the Diamondback organization publicly championed many admirable qualities, humor—which counts among its prime ingredients unequal doses of spontaneity, some ironic detachment, a feel for the absurd, and an appropriate self-deprecating sense of proportion—was not one of them. But then, this was no laughing matter, this was high finance, and God knows high finance has surely led to war often enough in the past.

Manager Buck Showalter was the commander in chief, surrounded by his general staff: general manager Joe Garagiola Jr., team president Richard Dozer, director of player development Mel Didier, director of scouting Don Mitchell, director of field operations Tommy Jones, draft coordinator Ralph Nelson, and some dozen other medical, field, and scouting aides. Roland Hemond was the point man in the ballroom, working the floor for any last-minute information, and relaying the DB draft selections from the war room to the podium, where they were then announced.

Until now, Buck Showalter had been a general without an army. Now Buck and his cohorts, huddled around the tables that formed a square that filled the room, surrounded by their charts and lists and profiles and calculations, were about to get some soldiers.

But the draft still awaited, and the festivities back on the terrace were well under way. All the team sponsors and ballpark vendors had been offered the opportunity to present their logos and wares during the party. (*Offered* might not be the precise word; one vendor quietly mentioned, when no one was looking, that the offer from the DBs had been a bit stronger than a suggestion, along with the suggestion that food was to be proffered free to the hungry patrons.)

Blimpies was slicing up six-foot-long sandwiches of ham and tomatoes and cheese and lettuce. Little Caesar's was passing out little pizzas. Ben & Jerry's was dishing out ice cream. Tacos, popcorn, hot dogs, soda, beer—all there for the taking.

Aside from free food, games abounded, some more elaborate than others, all with prizes to be won. Tossing two out of three balls into rings at the America West Airlines booth yielded a plastic, inflatable hat with an America West airplane on top, suitable for young children. McDonald's had a speed-pitch competition. Pick up the ball and let it rip: a throw of up to thirty miles per hour won a coupon redeemable for a free ice cream cone at any Mickey D's, fifty mph snagged a small fries, and over fifty was the grand prize, if you'll excuse the expression—one McDonald's hamburger.

Pepsi-Cola had a celebrity of sorts handling its action. The actress who served as the live-action model for the animated film *Anastasia* enthusiastically urged her contestants onto the basketball court. "You shoot, big boy," Anna Braga called out to one fellow, his tie flapping and his white dress shirt hanging over his sizable stomach, as he futilely chucked the ball up at the basket. "Show me how it's done!"

He failed to oblige, but enough did so that Pepsi ran out of their baseball caps in no time, with the Mountain Dew T-shirts soon to follow.

Miller Lite, in addition to being the overall sponsor of the affair, had a stall with the time-honored spin-the-wheel game, overseen by Miller Lite girls in tight shorts and Diamondback T-shirts. Spin the wheel and win whatever the needle pointed to when it stopped, though it was obvious that most of the men who lined up to play the game (if you can call spinning a wheel a game) weren't so much interested in the cup holders and other knickknacks as in the girls.

Fast food and games, free stuff and pretty girls—all a prelude to the real fun. For though the DB hierarchy was, as a collective, missing the humor gene, the organization was supremely skilled in creating and directing fun.

Gina Giallonardo, marketing manager, strode into view, clad as most of the other Diamondbacks in an official sports shirt, with the purple and turquoise *A* stitched over the left breast. DB shirts were produced in a virtually endless variety, long sleeve and short, button-down and pullover, on and on, all with the purple and turquoise *A* stitched somewhere on the material. A team shop was located right on the terrace, selling not only shirts but also hats and jackets and jerseys and baseballs and pennants and a host of other products, all displaying the purple and turquoise *A*. Literally cashing in on the Diamondback spirit, the shop did brisk business all day.

Meanwhile, Gina was moving fast and chattering into a walkie-talkie.

As she neared, there was a brief opening to ask what she was doing with that walkie-talkie.

"Nothing," Gina replied, still walking and talking.

This did not make sense, and the issue was pressed, forcing another reply.

"Putting out fires," she said, not slowing her pace.

In politics, that sort of answer was called a nonresponsive response and unavoidably begged the next question, i.e., What fires?

Gina smiled, in a fashion, and when she spoke, her tone implied that even the least astute listener should know what she was about to say. "I'm not telling you!"

The inescapable observation was that Gina, notwithstanding her gender, highlighted by a cascade of blonde hair, was a Diamondback through and through.

"You're right," she said, and then she was gone.

The action was heating up on the stage. Thom Brennaman, the television point man for the DBs, both as future play-by-play man when the team took the field and current administrator of their TV operation, was about to address the audience, which had overflowed from the booths surrounding the main stage and now filled the seats before him.

Thom was the prototypical Arizona Diamondback front-office type, from style: young, male, conservative in dress and manner; to substance: a true believer, impossibly, unflappably enthused about all things Diamondback and baseball. Brennaman, like so many of his colleagues, gave the impression of being professionally aggressive and personally settled, a modern version of the 1950s American executive ideal, half investment banker, half golf pro. One of the more peculiar impressions one was left with upon engaging a group of young DB officials was that even the single men in the organization somehow seemed married.

Thom's job today was twofold: to lead the festivities on the terrace on behalf of the DBs, and to comment on the draft on television for Fox Sports. His heart clearly belonged with the first role as he began by introducing the tall man who stood quietly to the side, whose appearance on the stage incited a mumbling through the people and an instant smattering of applause.

"We are going to have a very busy day here today," announced Thom, "and a man obviously who's done so much for this city, not only in athletics, but I think more importantly what he's done to try and make this a better town for each of us to live in—"

Thom, a broadcast veteran at the age of thirty-two, was uncharacteristically nervous, and rambled on a bit before getting to the matter at hand.

"—and the many things that he's done to make people's lives who are underprivileged in this area, or maybe people who are a little down on their luck, and oftentimes it goes overlooked, but unquestionably the man who has brought baseball to the Valley of the Sun. Please welcome Mr. Jerry Colangelo."

Cheers and whoops greeted Jerry Colangelo. From a near vantage point, it appeared that the managing general partner of the Arizona Diamondbacks, tall and fit, his broad shoulders accentuated by the double-breasted suits he usually wore, took the moment, and the acclaim, in stride. Proud but controlled. Overtly happy and almost smiling.

Jerry took the microphone from Thom. His ordinary manner of speaking was direct and quick and unhurried. It was the manner of a person accustomed to being listened to, and who accordingly told his story as he saw fit, starting wherever he chose. Jerry did not veer from his usual mode on this occasion.

"You can't imagine what's going on next door in the war room," he declared, "as we call it affectionately. But it's going to be a big, big day. I can tell you, for those who have the opportunity to be here the rest of the day and watch the draft unfold, don't leave early because at the end of the draft the trades will be announced, and there's going to be some interesting things that happen that will affect this franchise for a long time."

That got a grumble going in the rows, for there had been much discussion in the media in the preceding weeks about the many star ballplayers rumored to be on the trading block, owing either to their extravagant salaries, advancing ages, bad knees, or bad attitudes. Signing expansion-draft players was one thing, all-stars another. Jerry Colangelo and the Diamondbacks had already demonstrated a willingness to spend the proverbial whatever-it-took to garner the horses necessary to be major league competitive.

Thom picked up on that hint, and the two talked eagerly and yet vaguely about rumors and trades for a minute.

Vagueness only carried the conversation so far, and Thom moved on to the sure crowd-pleasing topic of . . . the crowd. "Here we are, an hour or two before the draft starts, and it's hard to even turn around in this place. I think you've known, obviously from the basketball side, these are the greatest basketball fans in America, and it looks like they're ready to do the same thing for baseball."

"Tommy," Jerry said, "I'm a little older than you—"

"A lot older," interjected Brennaman, who had rapidly regained his customary easy-as-pie, glad-to-be-here TV élan.

The audience *ooowwed* in delight at Thom's audacity, but his boss played the good sport. "In fact, a lot older," he confirmed. "I can tell you when I first came here in 1968, I never would have dreamed that we would be sitting here today with all of the things that are about to unfold. We're blessed and fortunate to be living in a great place. It is the sports mecca of the country today. People recognize it as such. We are going to have the best venues in sports. I'm very proud to be associated and I want to thank our fans for making it all possible."

That was a cue if Thom ever heard one, and he ebulliently petitioned the assembly, "Give yourselves a round of applause! Absolutely!"

The men, women, and children burst into applause. It was obvious and corny, to be sure, but there was also a lot of truth in those words. Maybe—definitely, actually—Phoenix wasn't the "sports mecca" of the country. Not that one such place, one central sports shrine, definitively existed. A lot of cities had professional teams, with spanking new stadiums and television contracts and corporate sponsors. But Jerry Colangelo and Phoenix and the entire state of Arizona could not, would not, be denied. This was a great place to live. It was home to terrific sports venues. And it was a sports mecca, albeit one among many.

The boys of baseball had been gathering in Phoenix for almost a week in anticipation of the draft. Oh, a few women lurked in their ranks, and most of the men hadn't been boys in more than a few decades, but the atmosphere when any number of them gathered together was decidedly boyish, with a lot of handshaking and backslapping and laughing. Good old boys telling good old stories.

The Scottsdale Scorpions and the Grand Canyon Rafters of the Arizona Fall League had a game the night before the draft. The Fall League played a short season on the heels of the conclusion of the summer leagues, allowing each major league club to place a handful of their most promising Triple A prospects on one of six teams for some additional playing time and game experience.

The Fall League was the reason Phoenix was selected to host the expansion draft. The general managers from the different major league clubs picked Phoenix so they could take in some games and watch the players while conducting the draft, killing two birds with one stone.

Though these minor league athletes were on the cusp of becoming major leaguers, and some would surely constitute the next generation of stars—the Dodger MVP, catcher Mike Piazza, was just one recent graduate of the Fall League—their games were played before practically empty houses. On occasion, the ever-present handful of scouts, with their radar guns to determine how fast a pitcher threw, were the only spectators.

But tonight was different. Scottsdale Stadium, just off downtown Scottsdale, held some three thousand bleachers and theater-type seats, all close to the field and the players. Behind the outfield walls were not rows of raised benches but a rounded lawn, where patrons could spread out blankets and have a picnic while watching the game. It was a terrific park, a sparkling patch of well-tended green and reddish brown dirt and white chalk lines. On a typical afternoon, maybe fifty, maybe one hundred people, would be scattered through the stands. Night games attracted larger crowds, perhaps twice as many or more—still not a lot.

But on this day, people began passing through the turnstiles early, long before the 7 P.M. start, and these early arrivals weren't the usual grandparents and grandkids, groups of teenagers, and executives fresh from the office. These were mainly older men, anywhere between fifty and seventy years of age, their faces creased by the sun, broad-shouldered men, with large, powerful hands. They resembled farmers—or former baseball players.

Without exception, every baseball man who entered the stadium wore at least one article of clothing emblazoned with a team logo. A bunch appeared garbed in green jackets and green hats. The logo was unfamiliar—at a glance, a swirl of fluorescent green. Closer inspection revealed the swirls to be some species of bird, no, fish, in midstride. Ah! That was it! Devilfish, aka devil rays, more formally know as *Manta birostris*, commonly found in the Gulf of Mexico and along the sountern coast of the United States. According to Webster's unabridged dictionary, a devil ray "may be fifteen to twenty feet wide and several feet thick with a weight considerably in excess of one ton [with] a pair of movable cephalic lobes used in guiding small

16

fishes into the nearly toothless mouth." This was the image evidently judged just right for a professional baseball franchise by the other new expansion outfit, the Tampa Bay Devil Rays. And here were Tampa Bay's officials proudly displaying the colors.

The other clubs were present as well, as revealed by the Seattle Mariners hats and Atlanta Braves shirts, on and on. They carried radar guns and stat sheets and lineup cards and baseball magazines and happily greeted their fellow fraternity members. They stood in the walkways and talked about golf scores and swings, and children and grandchildren, and, of course, jobs and job openings.

Soon forty baseball men were blocking the aisles, jabbering away. Buck was there, too. He and the other Diamondback muckety-mucks were always popping up at minor league games around town. On one hand, this wasn't too startling, given that baseball was their business, but on the other, considering they were working a minimum of ten hours a day, seven days a week, preparing for the draft, a trip straight home after office hours wouldn't have been out of the question.

But that wasn't the DB way. Buck set the tone for the organization, and he was already famous, from his tenure with the Yankees, for sleeping on a cot in his office so he could study more film, read more scouting reports, work harder and longer than any other manager in baseball.

In fact, Buck, who took pride in maintaining a stiff upper lip in the face of life's adversity, was so exhausted that one week before the draft, he took time out to visit a doctor for a checkup.

A few months later, Showalter made light of the incident: "I think it was the fifteen cups of coffee I had that morning."

Buck took a seat behind and overlooking home plate. This was the preferred seating for professional baseball types, and soon almost all the scouts and coaches and baseball-operations personnel were hunkered down behind the plate.

Roland Hemond also showed up at the game. Roland signed on with the Diamondbacks to act as a senior adviser, providing the benefit of his thirty-plus years in the front offices of various major league clubs. As such, he was always available to give a ready explanation for any baseball phenomenon, historical or current. And so his official reason why all these fellows wore all those logo clothes: not because they got them for free, but because they'd identify themselves to the young players, who would accordingly play harder to show their stuff and then come over and talk after the game.

Roland knew baseball backward and forward, and he was undoubtedly right, but free stuff still made an awful lot of sense.

The next morning, the morning of the draft, constituted sports-talk-radio heaven, as hosts and guests chewed over every possibility and angle. "Look what's baseball's come to," said one commentator, after the discussion had run through different players and how much they would cost the Diamondbacks. "We used to talk about a third baseman who hits thirty home runs, a shortstop who's a Gold Glover, a second baseman who can hit a solid .280, a first baseman who can hit for power and average. . . . Instead, we're talking about a third baseman who gets seven and a half million dollars, a shortstop who signed for six and a half million, a second baseman who gets five million, a first baseman who got a ten-million-dollars signing bonus."

The Diamondbacks had already made a splash with some high-profile, high-dollar signings of young prospects—thus the radio reference to the first baseman with the 10-million-buck bonus. Deals like those had prompted one unidentified general manager to grumble to ESPN about the "NBA-type mentality" already evident in Phoenix. This comment was an allusion to the obscene sums professional basketball teams were throwing at high schoolers with an aptitude for leaping. Fifty million dollars was regarded as small change, eighty was more like it, and one hundred and more was not out of the question—reading and writing skills optional. None of the other professional leagues were paying their players basketball wages, but all were edging, and sometimes leaping, higher up the ladder of financial excess. Times were changing fast in the sporting world. In 1966, the first year of the Chicago Bulls, the total payroll for all twelve players was $180,000. Thirty years later, Michael Jordan collected over $30 million from the very same Bulls, and that sum was nothing more than a secondary part of his annual earnings from his many business ventures.

Many in major league baseball were increasingly nervous about money.

Jay Bell only made them more nervous.

The DBs had signed Mr. Bell the day before the draft. The deal was for five years and $34 million. At the shortstop's insistence, it included a no-trade clause.

"I don't want to leave," Jay explained, only days away from his thirty-second birthday. "More than likely, it will take a while to be competitive. I want to be here when we're ready to win."

While everyone in the Diamondback organization was ready to win today—make that yesterday—Bell's point was well taken, given that no expansion team in any sport had ever finished at .500 its first season.

On the other hand, when you've spent $130 million just to get a chance to spend hundreds of millions more on a stadium, a staff, and a team, finishing at least even for the year didn't seem completely unreasonable, if still unlikely.

In ten seasons, Jay Bell had averaged .268, totaling 104 home runs and 553 RBIs. He had spent the 1997 season with the Kansas City Royals, hitting .291 while establishing career bests with 21 home runs and 92 runs batted in. He was the Kansas City Player of the Year, quite an accomplishment in his first year as a Royal. He had been a Pittsburgh Pirate the previous six seasons and had won the Rawlings Gold Glove in 1993, denoting him as that year's premier player at his position. He was also named for the first and only time to the National League All-Star team that same year.

Jay Bell was a fine player, an excellent fielder and a solid hitter. However, despite his excellent 1997 season, it would have been something of a stretch to claim that he was a top player. His statistics simply didn't support any such assertion, as anonymous people on other baseball clubs, stunned by the generosity of the contract, were quick to note to the media. The implication was that Jerry Colangelo and the DBs didn't exactly know what they were doing, and so, without the constraints of a player roster to support (not to mention scores of other employees and expenses), they were giddy with cash, giddy to spend, spend, spend. Jerry and his pals were upsetting the baseball applecart, and, according to other, often less prosperous baseball people, threatening the stability of the sport, which hadn't actually been very stable at all in the past few years.

In truth, it was all a matter of degree. The average baseball player's salary was already over a million dollars per year, so the debate was simply when did rich athletes become embarrassingly or ruinously rich athletes. Were millionaire pitchers somehow more athletically productive and publicly palatable than multimillionaire pitchers?

Did forking over three million dollars to a left fielder achieve the proper balance between providing him with a respectable lifestyle and keeping his competitive fires burning, whereas might another million or two suck out his unrelenting interest in the game? It was one thing to do well, to have sufficient funds in the bank to buy a nice house and a fast car—it's quite another to have more money than you could waste in three lifetimes by the age of twenty-three.

And that didn't even take into account the shoe contracts.

At the same time, much of the irritation expressed by some of the boys at the other clubs—or, more precisely, some of the other boys *in* the club—had nothing to do with philosophical visions of the future of baseball, but rather extremely practical concerns that they would be left behind in the scramble to sign up the best players and would be permanently stuck in the second rank of teams.

In the old days, expansion teams were supposed to be bad. When the Mets joined the game in 1962, they were lovable because they were laughable. They lost 120 games their first year, 120 out of 162. Now that was properly, respectfully bad.

But now the stakes were higher, as proved by the $130-million entry fee, and the new teams weren't about to be satisfied with bottom-of-the-barrel castoffs from the other clubs. For their money, they wanted some decent players. They weren't content to wander in the wilderness for lo so many years. They wanted to play ball, and with the best of them—or at least with the better of them.

Some of the other clubs didn't appreciate this attitude and the draft deal that would give Arizona and Tampa Bay each thirty-five picks. "Their payrolls the first year will be among the top six or eight in baseball," Houston Astros general manager Gerry Hunsicker told *Sports Illustrated.* "We don't have near the money that they have, and yet we're giving them players. It's Robin Hood in reverse."

The legendary Robin Hood stole from the rich and gave to the poor. Hence, GM Hunsicker's literary allusion, employed on behalf of the baseball owners, was false on its face, because it lacked one essential ingredient—the poor.

Additionally, Hunsicker's facts were also wrong, as the Diamondbacks' payroll would end up ranking twenty-third out of the thirty major league teams.

In any event, one would think that the Astros and the other established teams had to have at least "near" the two new teams' combined resources, because they had already extracted $260 million of it as the admission fee to MLB.

For his part, Jerry Colangelo made no excuses for his plans to ensure that his team would be competitive in a hurry. By draft day, he had already been quoted far and wide on the subject. "As in most professional sports," he told *Sports Illustrated,* "there is a disparity between the haves and have-nots. We hope to be one of the former. We have more debt than any expansion team in history, but we will spend if the opportunity is right, because we also expect to be a large revenue producer."

Colangelo was being modest; DB merchandise—hats, shirts, balls, etc.—was already the fourteenth-highest grossing amongst all thirty teams. And that was without winning a World Series, a division, or even a single game.

"We're going to try to do this the appropriate way," Jerry told the *Arizona Republic.* "I find it interesting when I see the payrolls out there, and people are worrying about what we're going to do. We'll decide how we spend and how much we spend. We'll go about our business and we won't question what they do."

In short, mind your own business, my fellow owners, because I'm certainly going to mind mine.

Jerry's toughest comment appeared in the *New York Times:* "Everyone ought to look in the mirror before anyone casts stones. We have a game plan and we plan to stick to it. And whatever we do is not going to be something that has to be torn down and sold."

That was a straight shot at Wayne Huizenga, the billionaire owner of the Florida Marlins, who, after only five years in the business, decided to cut to the chase and bought the players necessary to win a world championship. Upon winning the Series, Huizenga decided the prize wasn't worth the investment and immediately began dismantling the Marlins, cutting his overhead by trading away his most expensive players to other teams, and then casting about for somebody to offer him a nice profit and take the club off his hands. Huizenga's actions had embarrassed baseball, left his team in ruins, and made the Marlins' World Series victory a hollow triumph.

Jerry Colangelo had begun his sports career by helping start the Chicago Bulls in 1966. He moved to Phoenix two years later and started the Phoenix Suns. Now he was only months away from the start of the Arizona Diamondbacks' first season in their very own new baseball stadium.

Jerry Colangelo had spent his sports career as a builder of permanent identities and teams. He wasn't in this for the quick hit or the fast buck.

And that attitude led to another important component in the Diamondback calculation in how and on whom they intended to spend their money. For while the other clubs looked at Jay Bell and were not exactly overwhelmed with his career statistics, the DBs added in one more factor—the man himself.

By all reckoning, Bell was a good family man, a fine citizen, an outstanding American. The press release that accompanied Jay's signing noted, "Not only has Bell shined on the field during his career, he has been involved in a variety of charitable endeavors. He was the 1993 recipient of the Pittsburgh Points of Light Foundation Award, given annually for community service. He was also named the '93 Dapper Dan Man-of-the-Year, an award given annually to a Pittsburgh sports figure in recognition of outstanding achievement on a national level."

Thin and somewhat pale, with round, wire-rim glasses and short, neatly combed brown hair, Jay Bell could have passed for an accountant—and a forthright, polite accountant at that.

He was perfect, particularly for the Diamondbacks, because the Diamondbacks only wanted good men (with family or not), fine citizens, and outstanding Americans, as well as outstanding Mexicans, Dominicans, or Australians.

Jay Bell made no bones about how he viewed himself and his civic responsibility as a professional athlete. "I live to be an example," he said at the press conference announcing his signing, standing at the podium, wearing his brand-new Arizona Diamondback jersey over his shirt and tie. "I heard Charles Barkley say a few years ago he was not a role model. I disagree with that. We all impact someone. You may only impact one person, or some might impact the masses. I happen to be in a position where I can impact many."

There was a bit of an irony in the Barkley reference, as the DB podium was located in the media room in the America West Arena, just off the basketball court where Sir Charles had played and fought and talked, and talked and talked and talked, and became a controversial superstar while making himself and the Phoenix Suns and Jerry Colangelo an awful lot of money.

Barkley was many things, but the traditional portrayal of the good citizen—which had to include courteous, modest, conciliatory—he definitely was not.

And Bell wasn't quite finished: "As a Christian ballplayer, my objective is to make a spiritual impact. But that's as far as I'll go with that. I don't want to shove that down anyone's throat."

Direct but courteous and conciliatory—that was a role model.

Colangelo was still up on the stage when Brennaman introduced Jay Bell at the Miller Lite Expansion Draft Party. It wasn't even twenty-four hours after that press conference, but by now Bell was an integral part of the organization, nodding his head to the cheering crowd, advising Buck and the others on what he knew about the players available in the draft.

"Say hello, Arizona, to Jay Bell!" Thom urged, and the Arizona audience, which by now included hordes of ordinary fans as the gates had been flung open to one and all, roared their approval again. "Jay, I think there are more people here today than maybe saw you play any single game the last couple of years in Pittsburgh or Kansas City."

"It's probably true, Thom," Bell replied over the Arizona-first chuckles. "I tell you what, it's great to be here. The response has been wonderful. To see the enthusiasm, and what the city has turned out to be, it's truly amazing. Like Thom said just a second ago, you have to give yourselves a hand 'cause this is truly a great place."

And so the crowd did applaud itself, for if the inhabitants of New York City and Phoenix had one thing in common, aside from the Gap and Loehmann's, it was a frequently expressed pride in place, a feeling of we-happy-natives-of-our-exemplary-homeland. Naturally, the populace of each community took satisfaction in different virtues: the chance to sweat in hot weather almost twelve months a year versus the opportunity to order hot pizza almost twenty-four hours a day.

Thom wanted to know what made Jay choose to join the DBs. Aside from the money, of course.

When it came down to it, explained Jay, his relationship with Buck, and his trust in the manager's judgment, was paramount. And when Buck told him all about Jerry Colangelo . . . well, he was sold. (Or bought, as the case might be.)

"When we had a conversation on the phone," Jay said, "Buck told me about Mr. Colangelo, told me the type of person he was, told me the type of character that he had. And when you're involved with

23

people like that, you have a real good situation. So the city of Phoenix should be real proud, the state of Arizona should be real proud, of not only manager Buck Showalter, but the owner that we have here in Phoenix."

Jerry Colangelo, still on the podium, accepted his share of the acclaim with more than a modicum of cool. "Thank you, Jay," he said, and then was off with an anecdote about how Danny Ainge, former All-Star guard, current coach of the Suns, and onetime major league baseball prospect, could never hit a curve ball.

Colangelo wrapped that up upon spotting a familiar face in the back of the place and quickly made a nod to protocol. "There is a person I just recognized who's back standing in the corner here, one of our great supporters in terms of major league baseball and the efforts to make it possible. Sen. John McCain. John, would you wave?"

John waved. Though immensely popular in Arizona, this wasn't the senator's venue, not his day, and the people responded with polite but controlled applause. Neither Colangelo nor McCain pushed it—the former not inviting the senator onstage and the latter remaining in the background and not for too long, shaking hands and departing.

Back in the late eighties, McCain joined the Senate Task Force on the Expansion of Major League Baseball, a group with a long name and no formal congressional authority. Set up by Sen. Tim Wirth, its goal was to push Major League Baseball to expand. When Major League Baseball displayed an insulting lack of interest in the senatorial appeal, pushing led to prodding, which led to a threat of revoking baseball's antitrust status. Though it might have proved a hollow threat for a couple of reasons—first and foremost, ending antitrust severed any link to Congress and thus any influence the representatives might have had over MLB and where baseball would locate its new teams—it nonetheless helped concentrate the baseball owners' attention. The task force, composed of senators from different states, many eager for their own teams, including future vice presidents Dan Quayle from Indiana and Al Gore from Tennessee respectively promoting long shots Indianapolis and Memphis, as well as both John McCain and Dennis DeConcini from Arizona, had hoped for six new franchises. Six teams wouldn't satisfy all the longings of all their constituents for a franchise—the original group was made up of fourteen senators and the representative from the District of Columbia, and would soon grow—but it would go a long way, that was for sure.

Eventually, Major League Baseball settled on expanding to Miami and Denver—the latter the capital of Senator Wirth's Colorado, not incidentally—and the task force accepted the victory and went away.

At the time, it was generally believed that the Florida Marlins and the Colorado Rockies would be the last teams to join Major League Baseball in the twentieth century. That contention would prove incorrect, though not because of any further congressional pressure.

In truth, McCain hadn't done much of anything for the Diamondbacks, but that was all right because there had never been anything the distinguished senator from Arizona could do for the DBs that the DBs hadn't taken care of themselves quite adequately.

Regardless, baseball meant business and business meant politics, and one hand washed another in the power structure, so McCain was accorded his moment in the expansion-draft sun.

Before Bell and Colangelo left the party and returned to the war room back at the Civic Plaza, Thom had a final good bit of cheer to share with the crowd, and he began by addressing Jerry:

"Before you guys get out of here, I know you are very busy—you heard Jay refer to you a moment ago as 'Mr. Colangelo.' Obviously, this guy's upbringing was something special. His parents made sure that he said 'Yes, sir' and 'No, ma'am,' all that nice stuff. . . . We discussed yesterday [at the press conference] what an upstanding citizen Jay Bell is, and I know that is something that is of great concern to you not only in the Suns but in building the Diamondbacks. We don't want a lot of bad apples around this place."

"No, we don't," Jerry replied, seizing the baton and running with it. "And in fact in my first conversation with Jay, he said I feel as a professional—I am paraphrasing—that I have a responsibility to be a role model. Now how's that? Is that refreshing?"

The men and women of Phoenix, and the children, too, applauded their agreement.

This idea, aggressively promoted whenever the occasion arose, that the Diamondbacks were going to be a collection of not simply decent, law-abiding individuals, but assertively positive examples for the rest of America, was nothing short of revolutionary. For decades, apart from a few superstars, the Babe Ruths and Joe DiMaggios (as though there could ever be more than one Babe Ruth or one Joe DiMaggio), most professional athletes were poorly paid and relatively anonymous, enjoying short careers that frequently left them injured, broke, and adrift.

Times had changed. Athletes have joined actors, rock stars, models, television interviewers, and the other denizens of the celebrity world in that overprivileged and overpublicized tiny slice of America. Athletes have also adopted celebrity values, and that means they operate outside the morals and ethics and rules by which the rest of the populace lives.

There was a time when celebrities, meaning the wealthiest, most famous, most privileged individuals in the land, were not athletes or actors or any of the others. They were people like the Founding Fathers, who were the wealthiest, most famous, and most privileged men of their day, who used their wealth and fame and privilege to stand up for what they believed, who pledged their lives and their sacred honor to create a new nation.

Such men embodied the best of their people's convictions and hopes. They consciously aspired to live in such a manner so as to serve as examples for the rest of society.

Celebrities are no longer statesmen, nor scientists, soldiers, or explorers. We have forsaken our traditional heroes and replaced them with actors and athletes. This shift from, say, the winner of the Congressional Medal of Honor to the winner of the Academy Award for Best Acting means that where we once admired people who do great things, now we admire people who *play* people who do great things.

Nor are these modern celebrities role models. They don't have to follow the rules, and with surprising frequency they do not, in both small ways and large, from Dennis Rodman strutting about in a wedding dress through Manhattan streets to his book signing to Latrell Sprewell attacking his coach and gathering his fellow basketball players together to protest his firing.

And that's only the beginning of the bad news. From the National Football League alone, thirty-seven current or recently retired players have been arrested for or accused of crimes of family violence, from assault to kidnapping, in the past five years.

It often seems that the whole point of being a celebrity is so you don't have to wait on line at airports or pay for meals or get married to have children or be courteous or educated or honest or honorable.

The Diamondbacks were going to act differently. The Diamondbacks were going to be different. The manager, Buck Showalter, was different. The owner, Jerry Colangelo, was different. The team would be built in their images.

But were they serious, really serious? Would they pass up signing great players in the name of what . . . decency? Integrity? Good behavior? Al Davis, the man in charge of one of the most successful franchises in professional sports, had led his Oakland Raiders to glory under his slogan "Just win, baby." And wasn't that what sports was all about—winning? Did anything else matter? What would the DBs really do, when push came to shove, when they were one pitcher or outfielder away from a division title?

Perhaps a clue was offered a couple of summers ago, when the DBs were not much more than a name. It happened during the 1995 All-Star game and concerned an encounter that Jerry Colangelo did not hesitate to relate.

Jerry's flight from Phoenix happened to land in Dallas about the same time as the flight from San Francisco carrying Barry Bonds and his entourage. Depending on which expert was speaking, Bonds ranked anywhere between one and five among all baseball players. Along with his talent, he also had a reputation as difficult, imperious, and self-consumed.

Baseball had dispatched a bus to the airport to pick up arriving players. This did not please Barry Bonds, who expected a limousine, and made his displeasure clear to those around him by refusing to get on the bus.

Colangelo was right there to witness Bonds's behavior.

Not too much later, the Diamondback owner was at the hotel, waiting for the elevator, when who but Barry Bonds approached. Bonds recognized Colangelo and told him with a broad smile that he was interested in playing baseball in the desert.

"When you get your team together," Bonds said, "I'll be ready for you."

Jerry Colangelo looked over at the perennial All-Star and, to quote the man himself, replied, "I won't be ready for you."

And then Colangelo got on the elevator as Bonds, speechless, watched him depart.

So the Diamondbacks shunned Barry Bonds and signed Jay Bell.

And now the draft was about to get under way, so the DBs could find some more men who were capable and unsullied and deserving of wearing the purple and turquoise.

Chapter 2

Deep in the Draft

The expansion draft procedure was fairly simple and certainly direct: every major league team was allowed to protect fifteen players before the first round, meaning the fifteen best players from each team were taken off the table right at the start. Then Arizona and Tampa Bay would each choose fourteen players from the unprotected lists.

At the completion of the first round, each major league club would get to protect an additional three players. The expansion teams would then select another twenty-eight players between them.

Before the third round, another three players would be safeguarded by their teams, and then Arizona and Tampa Bay would each draft seven more players, for a total of thirty-five per club.

Arizona won the coin toss to determine which of the expansion teams would pick first and fourth, or second and third, in the first round. The Diamondbacks chose second and third, believing those middle spots presented them with the best chance at the players they wanted.

Thus, the Devil Rays stepped up to the plate first and chose pitcher Tony Saunders from the Florida Marlins. Saunders wasn't penciled in as the Diamondbacks' first choice anyway, so that left the field clear for their opening moves.

ESPN was covering the draft from gavel to gavel, as they say at the political conventions, from inside the ballroom, with Peter Gammons of the *Boston Globe* providing the expert analysis. Gammons noted that Showalter "had a managerial job unlike any other," in his ability to fashion the team as he saw fit.

"The Diamondbacks," Gammons said, "are all about Buck Showalter's vision of baseball."

A couple of months before, sitting in his office, leaning back in his chair, Buck had offered a somewhat pessimistic view of the approaching draft: "The most desirable player is a young man with a high ceiling as a player but with a low salary. And those are the first guys they'll protect. Most teams don't have fifteen good players to protect. They can protect twelve and do fine. And if there are three or four clubs with a lot of players, instead of letting us have them for free, they'll trade them."

Not much hope there, one might assume. Gloomy indeed. What was the point? Regardless, Buck must have thought there was some potential light at the end of this tunnel, considering how hard he drove himself and everyone else in the organization to prepare for this day. Most likely, his unhappy critique was his instinctive attempt to downplay expectations and reveal nothing that could prove of any value to any potential opponents. Loose lips sink ships, the World War II poster had warned gabby Americans, and the Diamondbacks were embroiled in their own form of combat, conducted with balls and bats instead of guns and bullets—a distinctly gentler combat, to say the least, as befitted a game, albeit one in mortal danger from a variety of economic and social pressures.

Now Jerry Colangelo mounted the podium to announce the Diamondbacks' first draft choice, which the fans outside on the terrace witnessed on giant television screens. As they leaned forward, many fans mumbled the names of players high on the list of prospects.

A photographer for an Arizona magazine readied his camera and whispered through the silence, "This is history."

Well, of a kind, it was. It really was.

Colangelo announced Brian Anderson and the terrace erupted in excitement. Anderson was a pitcher with the Cleveland Indians, a twenty-five-year-old left-hander, who had already pitched in the World Series and pitched well in a losing effort. His name had been tossed around for a while in the media as a likely draft selection. But it seemed evident that the cheering was less for Anderson than for the team itself.

Anderson didn't appear to be the obvious Diamondback. Oh, it wasn't his athletic ability, but his "free spirit," as the old folks used to say and the local newspaper still did, exemplified by his six tattoos, which didn't necessarily conform to the Diamondbacks' dress code. The code was Buck's dictum and included no long hair, no beards, the sorts of prohibitions that had gone out of style during the Johnson administration.

This was not to impugn Brian Anderson's character. In fact, his character was not in question, only his taste. On any other team, none of this would have been an issue. In fact, it really wasn't an issue with the DBs, which should have been obvious since they drafted him number one. But the club had been so vocal about crafting role models that it deserved and was accorded a mention in the media.

Just to show that his heart was in the right place, Anderson proclaimed that he was heading to Bob's Tattoo to get a big *A* carved or pricked or whatever into the middle of his back.

The Diamondbacks' second selection was Jeff Suppan, a twenty-two-year-old, right-handed pitcher from the Boston Red Sox. The enthusiasm on the terrace for this pick was visibly subdued, which was less of a baseball commentary and more a reflection of the realization that history can only be made once.

The Diamondbacks and baseball were getting to the heart of the matter now. Three young men in Diamondback caps and jerseys tried to get into the ballroom to watch the draft up close but were stopped by a contingent of security personnel and Phoenix police.

"I thought this was supposed to be for fans," one of the men complained.

Sorry, a cop explained. You need one of those badges to get in, and he nodded at the different-colored badges that people wore around their necks, denoting whether they were media or owners or baseball pros or guests or so on.

This didn't satisfy the fans or quite explain the situation to them, especially after several Miller Lites.

"Millionaires and all that shit," a security guy added.

That they understood. The trio grumbled and walked away.

The draft continued, and Tampa Bay and Arizona began filling up their rosters, like thirsty men falling upon a well in the desert. It didn't take long before the proceedings became quite mundane, conducted, after the initial thrill, with all the entertainment value of an old Soviet Politburo meeting. The players who were about to uproot their lives were generally not well known, or known at all, not only to the public but to many of the reporters as well. To put an extra damper on the whole shebang, the draft was scheduled to last some eight hours.

However, in some ways, the thrust of the baseball action was shifting from the ballroom and to the back rooms, where the wheeling and dealing was in full stride. For example, the Tigers had promised to send third baseman Travis Fryman to the Diamondbacks if the DBs drafted, and then traded, San Diego's Gabe Alvarez and the Pittsburgh Pirates' Joe Randa. The DBs wanted Fryman, though they wanted the Cleveland Indians' Matt Williams even more. The Indians were willing to bargain away the All-Star, but the price was high. In the meanwhile, Fryman was in the bag, if the DBs got Alvarez and Randa for the Tigers. The question then became, did they tap the two players at the top, thereby risking losing some more valuable players to Tampa Bay or the protected list, or did they bide their time while stockpiling other players and risk losing the trade bait?

The DBs ended up doing a little of both; they picked Alvarez in the first round and took Randa in the final round five hours later. The trade was effected, and Fryman became a Diamondback. However, his tenure with the team would be brief, as he would soon become trade bait himself, involved in a blockbuster deal that would be noteworthy not just because of what it meant in baseball terms, but what it meant to some of the people in baseball.

In order not to unnecessarily aggravate any of the players, the protected lists—and more to the point, the unprotected lists—were supposed to be strictly guarded secrets, to be kept from the players, the media, and the fans. It was thought that if a player discovered that his team had been willing to let him go and had stayed with the team only because nobody had drafted him, this knowledge could have a detrimental effect on his disposition and performance.

That meant surprises were to be the order of the day.

Cory and Melanie Lidle were passing through Phoenix on their way home to California, stopping off to watch some friends play in the Fall League. Cory's agent, Jordan Flager, was also in town, because Cory was a pitcher with the New York Mets and he and his agent had a little baseball business to attend to. Nothing special, just player-union matters. Pro forma stuff.

Cory and Melanie were supposed to fly home that morning, but they decided, on a whim, to hang around and watch some of the draft. So Cory, Melanie, and Jordan found themselves on the terrace with the other fans, drinking beer and sitting on the concrete ground because there was nowhere else to sit. They were having a fine old time, drinking and speculating about which of his fellow Mets would be gone with the wind when the draft was done. Cory himself had no such worries, having been assured by someone in the Mets organization that he would be protected.

So it came as a great shock to all three when they heard Cory's name called over the loudspeakers. The DBs' seventh pick, Cory Lidle was headed to Arizona.

Cory was not famous. In addition, not being particularly tall or lean or muscular, Cory did not look like the archetypal professional athlete. Nonetheless, he was an accomplished pro, and so he rose and looked around for somebody to tell that he was now a home-town player, one of their very own Diamondbacks.

Cory didn't have to worry about his Phoenix reception because the DB organization was Johnny-on-the-spot and Lidle was soon whisked onstage for Thom Brennaman to interview and the crowd to appreciate. Ah, from relaxing among the litter on the ground to basking in the spotlight on the dais in one leap—only in America.

It took the pitcher a little while to get his bearing. "I don't know what to feel right now," he told Thom. "I was told I wasn't going to be taken."

Thom took advantage of his proximity to a real live player to ask his opinion of the Milwaukee Brewers' Joel Adamson, the next player chosen by the DBs, yet another pitcher and Lidle's new teammate, at least until one or both of them were traded.

"Never heard of him," Cory said, earning a laugh from the crowd.

Cory might have imagined that his stint on the podium completed his public responsibilities for the afternoon. If that had been his not unreasonable assumption, he would have been mightily wrong. He was escorted off the stage and delivered straight into the arms of ESPN, which did its own thirty-second version of Thom's interview, which necessarily wondered how he felt and was he surprised and how did he see his role with the Diamondbacks?

The crowd around him had already adopted Cory as a true-blue (or true purple and turquoise) DB. Kids asked for his autograph, and adults shouted out encouragement to the pitcher.

"Welcome to Arizona, Cory!"

"You're in the right place now, Cory!"

A young man, exhibiting an especially kind of annoying self-importance that marked him as a member of the entertainment industry, tried to shoo away the children gathered for Cory's signature so Lidle could do a radio interview with his station.

DBs officials regained control and ushered Cory off the terrace and toward the ballroom, with a beaming Melanie and an equally pleased agent Flager in tow.

Bob Crawford, Diamondback media relations manager, took charge here. Cory went this way and that, into the war room for a hello to his bosses, then back for a press conference with the local media. Cory had his answers more in order now. When asked "How do you see your role? As a starter or reliever or whatever the club wants?" Cory answered, "Whatever the club wants."

Smiles all around, from the press to the DB officials. That was the Diamondback way.

The *Arizona Republic* reported the following day that Cory "was attending a draft party outside the draft room when he saw his name called. He quickly picked up a Diamondbacks cap and stepped inside."

Not for the first time, the *Republic* had gotten it wrong, just as it had Cory Lidle as the seventh pick in one article and number six in another—with both assertions on the same page. In any event, Cory's trip from draft party to draft room was a journey unto itself, with many an autograph and interview stop along the way. Nor had he instantly grabbed a Diamondbacks hat and placed it on his balding head, not until a writer—and not even a sportswriter—had suggested it just before Cory met the local press outside the ballroom.

Sadly, same as with so many newspapers across the country, the sports section was among the *Arizona Republic*'s most comprehensive, covering a medley of sporting events that occurred inside Arizona, high school to professional, and also the major contests outside the state and around the globe.

Unfortunately, that was a far better record than the news department of the *Republic* could boast.

One expected that the local TV stations would be sensationalist,

alternately fawning and outrageous, generally foolish and mislead-
ing, more intent on promoting their always likable anchors (even if
they couldn't pronounce the names of foreign leaders) than in
presenting actual news beyond car crashes and diet secrets and funny
weather, because that was the norm for local TV stations across the
country.

The following is a true story. The lead item (presumably meaning
that event judged most important and intriguing by the news authorities) on a recent Phoenix news program concerned a dog named
Scooter. Scooter had been abandoned by his owner, but not before
the lout had painted him, humiliating the dog, assuming a dog feels
humiliation. A Good Samaritan had rescued the dog, taking it to a
shelter, where it was recovering in fine form.

Okay. Horrifying and heartwarming, a two-for-one TV winner.

The second story that evening was about a baby who had been
abandoned. True, the baby didn't have a cute name like Scooter, and
he hadn't been painted, and an ugly orange to boot . . . but he was
human! A child versus an animal—and the child came in last place.

Of course, babies are abandoned all the time, and who knows how
often dogs are painted, so the big-city journalists went with the
obvious—at least to television—choice.

But even if TV was the modern equivalent of the Roman circus,
distracting the masses from the trials and tribulations of real life,
newspapers were supposed to be smarter, and in many cities they
were. The *San Francisco Examiner,* the *Philadelphia Inquirer,* the
Washington Post—good papers all. Even some smaller cities, such
as Austin, Texas, had good papers. Sure, a town might have a rag or
two, but it was often balanced by something better. New York had
the *Post* and the *Daily News,* but there was also the *Times,* still the
best of the lot.

Phoenix had no such luck. The *Republic* didn't look for trouble,
being quite snug with a virtually unrestrained business community
and an Arizona government that had seen more than its share of
corruption scandals, including the 1997 conviction of the governor.
As for the rest of the world—well, who cared? Certainly not the
Republic. Check the front page of the *New York Times* any morning;
it was more than a good bet that a couple of days later a story or two,
purchased from the *Times,* would appear on the *Republic's* front
page, edited to ensure brevity, naturally—even late news couldn't be
allowed to take up too much room.

And, by the by, wasn't it an overt problem, a stunning conflict of interest, when Phoenix Newspapers, Inc., became a limited partner in the Arizona Diamondbacks? Even if reporters weren't intimidated by working for one of the franchise's investors, shouldn't the obvious appearance of a conflict of interest by the leading Arizona representative of the fourth estate have been sufficient to stop the media corporation from investing in this singularly public and consequential Arizona business venture?

The *Republic* wasn't the first media company to buy into the hometown team. The Tribune Company owned the Chicago Cubs, the *Rocky Mountain News* had purchased a piece of the Colorado Rockies, CBS had owned the New York Yankees, and Ted Turner controlled the Atlanta Braves, Turner Broadcasting System, and then started CNN. Rupert Murdoch, who ruled over a global media conglomerate, was attempting to buy the Los Angeles Dodgers. Each of these situations was different, some more successful than others (CBS's ownership of the Yankees ranking as a disaster, while Turner had turned the Braves into a team with national appeal through his cable superstation system). Murdoch could, if he gained command of the Dodgers, deploy his newspapers and TV networks to forcefully thrust professional baseball into the international arena, forever upsetting the power structure of Major League Baseball, remaking the industry and the sport from top to bottom.

Though Murdoch held that kind of power, this shift, determined by the media, did not rely on him. Other media giants and corporations possessed similar capabilities to push baseball in that same direction.

This evolution, this next step in the marriage between the media and sports, was perhaps inevitable. For a media monarch such as Murdoch, sports could have existed simply to provide guaranteed programming for his television stations and print outlets. Aside from the spectacle of the games, sports allowed the media to create instant and disposable heroes and villains, artificial, easily comprehensible morality plays, and a variety of other usable and forgettable images and stories to fill their pages and airtime.

In other words, sports was a terrific moneymaker, for all corporate interests involved.

The effect this would have on culture and on society was another issue, as priorities and values and beliefs were changed and turned and transformed. The final reckoning of this effect was not necessarily a happy one.

In many ways, a small part of that large, overarching topic was there for examination in Arizona, if anyone cared to look. One example: the propriety of the state's foremost newspaper owning a part of the newest local franchise was not publically examined. One had to wonder how inclined the *Republic* would be to walk that fine line between offering legitimate support of the local club and covering up if and when the franchise committed the sort of mistakes that abused the public trust, or if players acted in a way that was irresponsible, criminally or otherwise, and deserved exposure.

It surely made the reader wonder why, every day for literally hundreds upon hundreds of days, the upper left-hand corner of the first page of the *Republic*'s sports section ran one of the Diamond-back logos, in full color, and beneath that, the number heralding how many "days till Opening Day." Was that supposed to be, however tiresome, a community service, or was it simply a minor stab at promoting the paper's investment?

When one considered that classic political thought decreed that a healthy democracy required the twin pillars of a vigorous, free press and a responsive, ethical government, the sustained vigor of the Arizona polity was nothing short of extraordinary. Quite a tribute to the lure of dry heat, wide-open spaces, low taxes, and cowboy mystique.

The weakness of both the press and the government played significant roles in the fate of the Diamondbacks, especially with regard to financing and building the stadium. In many ways, the impotence of these institutions had allowed the DBs to have things pretty much their own way. Nevertheless, the issue was not so cut-and-dry; stronger, more capable public institutions might actually have been a boon to the Diamondbacks and their plans by representing the people's interest so that much of the citizenry would not have felt run over in the rush to secure major league baseball.

Anger at how Diamondback issues were handled, which led to a long-running and eventually thwarted petition drive, spilled over into an instance of insanity, and the near assassination of a local politician.

Devon White was a thirty-four-year-old Gold Glove center fielder with the Florida Marlins, who lived in Paradise Valley, the most exclusive suburb of Phoenix, with his family in the off-season. Hence, White was in town during the draft, though not in attendance.

Instead, he was just across the street from the proceedings, seated inside the America West Arena beside his young son, watching a basketball game between the Suns and the Minnesota Timberwolves.

Devon's entertainment was interrupted when an Arizona official stepped up, bearing a DB cap and a DB jersey. "White" was sewn on the shirt's back.

"Are you teasing me?" Devon asked.

The Marlins were in no joking frame of mind as they continued to try to rid themselves of their more expensive athletes. Garagiola, well aware of Florida's fire sale, suggested a trade and the Marlins bit. The Marlins wanted pitcher Jesus Martinez, and the Diamondbacks obliged by drafting him away from the Los Angeles Dodgers. Martinez was sent to Florida, which dispatched White to the DBs. To complete the trade, the Marlins agreed to pay a substantial part of Devon's 1998 $3.4-million salary.

Back at the basketball game, White's change of job site was announced over the loudspeakers, and Devon was staring at his face up on the video board overhead in an authentic candid-camera moment. The crowd gave him a standing ovation. White waved, grabbed his son, and headed out of the arena and to the ballroom to join the whirlwind.

An event this big needed its own celebrity appearance—in contemporary America, that almost seems like a legal requirement—and actor Billy Crystal filled the gap. In this case, the celeb actually had an authentic reason to be here; his love of the game had led him to become one of many investors in the Diamondbacks. His relatively small stake, said to be $500,000, had brought him to Phoenix and a stop in the DB war room. Declaring himself a "forty-nine-year-old Jewish second baseman who can only go to his left," he announced he was ready to suit up and play.

Though his offer was not accepted, Buck did give Crystal the chance to comment on any of the available New York Yankee players. Crystal checked the list and replied, in mock dismay, "Hey, there's not one guy named Goldberg there!"

The media were definitely glad to see Billy Crystal, glad to have anything to break up the monotony of chronicling obscure name after obscure name, all day long. Crystal stated that he was prepared to help the Diamondbacks in one key area: "I can advise on a good caterer. There should be knishes at the ballpark. We can talk about that."

Perhaps the only actual fans who had made it inside the ballroom were a group from Tampa, whose members had won a radio contest and received an all-expenses-paid trip for the big event. The Tampa fans had entered the ballroom with great enthusiasm, but came straggling out after a few hours, ready for something—anything—more interesting. John Anderson, one Phoenix reporter who didn't mind admitting on camera that he was more than a little bored, was waiting for thcm. He cornered a middle-aged couple, wondering if they had enjoyed the draft. The couple diplomatically replied that they had enjoyed Phoenix, but the draft was like watching paint dry.

Anderson concluded his story with a nod toward Frank Robinson, Hall of Fame outfielder on temporary duty for MLB as the commissioner of the Arizona Fall League. "Frank Robinson's down there," he said. "Pick him. He's old, but at least we know him."

Several reporters from Tampa caught Don Smiley leaving the draft. Don Smiley was president of the Florida Marlins and not a happy man. After Wayne Huizenga had decided baseball wasn't for him, Smiley had resolved to put together an investment group to purchase the team. Unfortunately, he knew up front that he could never raise enough cash to carry the huge debt Huizenga had accumulated as his payroll rose to $55 million; that realization made the bargain-basement sale of the Marlins' stars unavoidable. Even slashing the payroll didn't render Smiley's task a foregone success—with the bad taste of Huizenga's legacy lingering in everyone's mouth, big-money people weren't exactly jumping up to toss their dollars into the hat.

As Don Smiley explained the situation to the cameras outside the Arizona Civic Plaza, "No one is beating down the door to buy the team."

And if nobody bought the team, there could very well not be a Florida Marlins team one day soon.

"It's a matter of survival," Don Smiley said. "It's a matter of trying to keep the team in south Florida."

Smiley was green with envy as he stood in the shadow of the great stadium rising in downtown Phoenix. "Look at this ballpark," he said. "You know they're going to be here a long time. Look at that roof."

The roof promised to be one of the new ballpark's innovations. That is, when the ballpark was finished, which was supposed to be just in time for opening day, 1998. This was a construction schedule on the "fast track," to use a professional term—"cutting it close" was how an amateur might have put it. But that was the way it had to be, because the clock was running and the ballpark had to be built. Time didn't stand still for any man—not even for a Diamondback.

Don Smiley excused himself and walked away from the reporters and back to the major league maelstrom that was his life.

A local TV station had set up its anchor desk right on the Phoenix Symphony Hall Terrace for its early-evening news broadcast. In case any of the viewers didn't get the point, the desk was adorned with a pair of Diamondback baseball caps, two Diamondback jerseys, and a baseball, National League regulation model. While it wasn't hard to figure out why the station had set up on the terrace—this was a big Phoenix story—decorating the desk was definitely overkill. How can an anchor sit there, reporting on a massacre in Bosnia, for example, when his desk looks as if it's been dressed up for a twelve-year-old's birthday party?

Of course, this was a station that had billboards all over town promoting its anchors with what might generously be called a "retro" campaign. They were typical of anchor sets, as stations everywhere sought to hit as many demographics as they could with only two people: a white male of older years and avuncular mien, matched with a much younger, attractive Asian woman, with long, black hair and a ready smile. So what would be an appropriate ad campaign to highlight their journalistic skills? How about a billboard with a picture of the older anchor as a young boy, with a young boy's hat, and the caption underneath: "Now he can stay up past 10," presumably implying that since he was now old enough to stay awake for the ten-o'clock newscast, so should the audience. For the female anchor, they had gotten hold of a similar youthful photo and written, "You've seen her at five. Now see her at 6." One can only wonder whether it had been a marketing or an editorial decision to spell out her age and to use the numeral for the time of the early-evening broadcast.

Any notion of dignity had clearly been usurped by the prerogatives of saccharine sentiment. Informative had been thrown out years ago. Intellectual never had a chance. Cute ruled.

Not that this station was alone in its approach. Another station was running commercials that had its anchor blabbering on, and on, about how her cat was a precious member of her family. The audience got to watch the cat climb along its carpeted, indoor treehouse, while the severely bleached-blond anchor watched approvingly.

The audience wasn't asked to respect her; the audience was encouraged to love her.

All good things must end, and so it was with the expansion draft. At the close of business, the Diamondbacks pronounced themselves satisfied. "Buck took on the responsibility of running the expansion draft for us," Colangelo stated, "and he did an incredible job."

The Diamondbacks' last selection was pitcher Marty Janzen from the Toronto Blue Jays. Back in the ballroom, Roland relayed the name to the proper baseball authorities, and that was that. Everyone in the war room applauded, and Showalter hugged Garagiola.

"It was an emotional day for all of us," Buck said. "So many things came together. We were fortunate that we were able to do some of the things that we wanted."

At this stage, the Diamondbacks' projected payroll was about $21 million, not even close to an extravagant amount, according to baseball standards.

"All our fans were expecting great things from this," Buck said, "and we took that responsibility very seriously."

Team president Rich Dozer had his own extra incentive to be content. The franchise had made a concerted effort to start to build a fan base in Mexico, particularly northern Mexico. Slowly, tentatively, baseball was expanding its audience. So many industries had gone global—why not sports? This wasn't merely a matter of peddling a few hats to the Japanese or selling TV rights to the Brazilians for extra pocket cash. Major League Baseball had to compete not only with the other monoliths of professional football, basketball, and hockey, and other professional sports, such as tennis and golf, and college and other amateur sports, as well as people actually going out and having fun themselves, but also with a world driven by competing entertainment media, from $100-million movies to interactive computers, rock shows to virtual-reality arcades, TV game shows to performance art, museum exhibitions to porn flicks, documentaries, CDs, DVDs, laser discs, network television, cable television, satellite television, and, yes, even a few books.

In response, the DB organization had staked out Mexico as its territory. It had huge potential, with tens of millions of sports-loving men and women, boys and girls, just to the south. The Diamondbacks had made several opening moves to appeal to this constituency and had made some progress. But Dozer knew that nothing the club did in the way of publicity or promotion could come close to comparing with one simple, unadorned move: signing a Mexican player.

The DBs had their eyes on one such player. Karim Garcia was the son of Francisco "Pancho" Garcia, one of the Mexican League's best players for fifteen years. Karim had been born in Ciudad Obregón, in the state of Sonora, which rubs up against the state of Arizona.

By the age of seventeen, Karim was with the Los Angeles Dodgers organization and the youngest player in the California League, finishing second in the league in triples. Two years later, in 1995, he was named Minor League Player of the Year by the *Sporting News* and was selected to the Triple-A All-Star team by *Baseball America*. Garcia was a prospect.

However, the Dodgers had too many players ahead of Garcia and couldn't afford to protect the young outfielder. Dozer really wanted him, but was nervous about having his business focus override the DBs' baseball interests. He needn't have worried, not with Jerry and Buck's club.

Karim was still available when it was time for the Diamondbacks' fifth pick.

"Don't do it because of me," Dozer said. "Take the best player."

Garcia was the best player.

"This is a guy the Dodgers thought would be a franchise player," said Peter Gammons of ESPN. "He is a very athletic player and is a guy who could really blossom if given the chance to play."

The Diamondbacks took him.

The DBs stunned the Milwaukee Brewers, so related *Sports Illustrated*, when they took Danny Klassen as their seventeenth selection. The scouting report on the twenty-two-year-old shortstop tagged him as an excellent hitter but a poor infielder, as demonstrated by his fifty errors at El Paso in Double A ball. Only the peripatetic habits of the Diamondbacks told them a different tale. Buck and Mel Didier were in El Paso, watching one more game, and found themselves seated near an injured El Paso pitcher. The pitcher told them that the field was in terrible shape, and after the game,

Buck and Mel took a stroll around the bases, verified his contention, and decided, on the spot, that maybe Klassen wasn't such a bad fielder. They also decided to draft him.

"After sitting in the room with those guys and seeing how they operate and what they stand for," Jay Bell told the *Republic,* "I feel great about my decision to come here. We're going to have a good club to put on the field every day."

Of course, simply because the draft was done didn't mean the same was true for the Diamondbacks. "The process was terrific," said Jerry Colangelo. ". . . We got a lot of good, young, excellent talent that will develop for us next year and in the future. But the process is just beginning."

The team's roster would hardly remain static, for the trading had only just begun.

It had been a good day for the Diamondbacks, and for baseball.

Chapter 3

The Aftermath

The Diamondbacks held a press conference the next day to introduce the new DBs who were in town. The media were invited once again to the pressroom of the America West Arena, and they all came: TV crews, radio reporters, newspaper writers, all the usual suspects. In Phoenix, when the Arizona Diamondbacks called, everybody answered.

When the media were assembled, a host of Diamondback officials entered, accompanying the six newest DBs who had been in town for the draft, either by happenstance or by plan. The six filed in, looking more like the youngest CPAs at the accounting firm's picnic than rough-and-tumble athletes. Three wore sports coats over their polo shirts, another just had on the polo shirt, one was garbed in a fancy half-warm-up, half-leisure suit, and the last was attired in a sweater of many conflicting colors and designs that was shockingly expensive and ordinarily spied, when it was spied, on wealthy, older men. Not one of them had hair long enough to even creep over the top of his ears, though Devon White did have a mustache and the stubbly outline of a beard, in that *Miami Vice,* 1980s way, and Chris Jones, a free agent from the San Diego Padres, needed a shave. However, his head was shaved, which sort of balanced out the five-o'clock shadow.

As a final bonus, they were even ethnically representative: three were white, two were black, and one was Hispanic.

Now these were Diamondbacks.

Thom Brennaman stood on the podium and opened the festivities by introducing Jerry Colangelo, "the man who is largely responsible for making all of this possible."

Jerry commended the work of his staff and added a word of praise for the people who had come out to the expansion-draft party. "Baseball was really impressed by the enthusiasm shown by the fans."

With that, Colangelo was finished, and Thom began calling the players to the podium, one by one. He commenced with the number one draft pick, Brian Anderson. Thom conducted a brief interview with each man, a quick clip for the cameras and a handful of quotes for the writers. Thom was good at this, able to keep the questions and answers easily flowing, setting a relaxed tone and placing the interviewee in the most favorable light.

Several of the players had been given a tour of the ballpark that morning, stepping carefully between the steel beams and concrete blocks and dirt pits, seeing where they were going to play once the roof was humming and the grass was laid and the seats installed— once the ballpark was completed and the season started.

Brian Anderson was mightily impressed. Back in Cleveland, he had heard the Diamondback stadium was going to be great and it was true.

"Outstanding," he said. "Outstanding facility." Anderson was especially taken with the swimming pool, or more specifically, the hole in the outfield where the swimming pool was going to be.

"It's like an amusement park," he said.

Jeff Suppan was next at bat. "I was sitting at home," he recalled, "waiting to see what would happen." Well, it happened; his name went up on the board.

"It was a great feeling," he said.

Suppan also loved the ballpark, though all the dust in the air was bothering his allergies.

Jorge Fabregas had been the starting catcher for the Chicago White Sox, and most baseball analysts were surprised that he had been left unprotected. Jorge was also surprised, but was ready to make the change. In one important way, Fabregas was already a Diamondback, telling the media that he intended to be "one of the Hispanic community leaders here."

He addressed the Anglo media in English and the Hispanic media in Spanish and said that he would answer to Jorge or George, depending on whatever worked at the time. Most people in baseball, he said, knew him as George.

Cory Lidle got to retell the story about how he and Melanie had casually decided to check out the expansion draft and were sitting on the ground, pushing away peanut shells, drinking beer, and then . . . One had the feeling that Cory, whether he liked it or not, was not through sharing this story.

By now, the shock had worn off and Lidle was thrilled to be a DB: "To get a fresh start here with a new team, it's an unbelievable feeling. I couldn't be happier."

Devon White also got to repeat his story. "All of a sudden," he said, "the Suns game didn't matter anymore."

Though still a young man, Devon's studious manner and three World Series rings made him seem like a grizzled veteran compared to the grown-up kids beside him.

White recounted how he had called his wife with the news of his trade, but she had refused to believe him until he had put his son on the phone for confirmation. White himself had paid scant attention to the draft, assuming his job with the Marlins was secure. However, now that he had been dealt to the Diamondbacks, he was excited to be playing for his hometown team.

And Devon saw one special benefit to the situation; he wouldn't get nixed out of his Suns season tickets if he was late with his payment.

From the far side of the room, Jerry called out that Devon probably didn't have to worry about being late with his check. "Now that he's on the team, we might have a payroll deduction."

"I'm actually looking for an upgrade," White added.

Chris Jones was last, and he was "thrilled" with the change in his fortunes. In seven season, Jones had already played with the Mets, Rockies, Astros, Reds, and Padres. Bouncing from team to team had evidently not been a delightful development for Jones, who declared his readiness to compete for a position with the DBs, and not only because he made his home in the Valley. "I figured out a long time ago that nobody was going to give me anything," he said, "and I'm happy to fight for it."

45

The program was over, and Thom loosed the media upon the players, to ask whatever they wanted. However, between yesterday's events and this press conference, it was hard to think of anything left unasked, and the questions devolved into the usual sports clichés, highlighted by a local radio station's query to Devon White: "Is this a dream come true?"

But the Diamondbacks were relentless, and the show rolled on. Another day, another press release faxed to all concerned, and now it was Karim Garcia's moment in the sun. The press was getting a little punchy by now, continually being summoned to the same window-less room in the America West Arena.

A cameraman setting up his equipment claimed he couldn't remember who they were meeting today. "Is Jerry Garcia here?"

"They moving the franchise?" a reporter loudly wondered, giving voice to the most taboo of all subjects, earning chuckles from his colleagues. "I'm trying to get banned from baseball."

No fewer than nine camera crews had made it for the press conference, the usual media augmented by additional representatives from the Spanish-speaking press.

Karim Garcia was accompanied by a small entourage, including his parents. All were ushered to the podium.

A smiling Rich Dozer led off the proceedings: "This franchise is all about the whole state of Arizona, the whole Southwest, and Mexico, particularly the state of Sonora."

The demographic lines weren't so clearly drawn between the Anglo and Hispanic worlds as were the national borders. Dozer noted that 50 percent of children in Arizona were of Hispanic descent. The Diamondback interest in appealing to both these communities was only the most recent ramification of the commingling of the two nations and two cultures.

Grinding poverty forced millions of Mexicans to migrate back and forth across the border in search of work. An inflexible and ineffi-cient Mexican government, pervasive corruption in both the public and private sector, only made worse by the growing narcotics industry, dangerous environmental conditions in urban and rural areas, increasing internal unrest and external problems with their southern neighbors, acted to further rob the people of hope.

Working in opposition to these factors, NAFTA, the North Ameri-can Free Trade Agreement, caused many U.S. corporations to relocate in Mexico in pursuit of cheap labor. Many communities on both sides of the border were experiencing tremendous growth.

Even more influential in blurring the distinctions between the two societies was the role of the media and popular culture. Effortlessly crossing boundaries of time, distance, and government, the countless arms of the media were re-creating the imperatives and values of the global audience.

More of that later. The issue at hand remained the Diamondbacks' effort to engage the interest and loyalty of legions of Mexican sports fans starved for a team from Major League Baseball to support. American culture, at least American mass culture, was ever more dominant on the world scene, and sports were part of that equation.

Every so often a couple of American pro teams would journey south to play a game and test the waters. These forays inevitably hinted at the enticing potential of the market.

Only a few weeks after the expansion draft, the Houston Rockets and the Dallas Mavericks traveled to Mexico City for the NBA's first regular-season contest in that country. They played before a sellout crowd of over twenty thousand at the Sports Palace. The AP reported that "scalpers were selling $11 tickets for $37.50—11 days' work at minimum wage."

The crowd was with the Rockets, who had played three exhibition games in the arena. Houston did not disappoint, as Charles Barkley, traded from the Suns to the Rockets, led the team to a 108–106 victory. "Fans stood and cheered every time Houston scored. They whistled every time Dallas attempted a free throw."

The news only got better for those considering the future of U.S. sports overseas.

"'I'm here to see Barkley,' said Fabiola Rivera, a 23-year-old elementary schoolteacher. 'I've been a fan of his for 10 years. Seeing him here today is a dream come true.'"

"A dream come true": sweeter words could not be imagined by Diamondback officials looking for a sign that their work would not be in vain.

And so it was Karim Garcia, Diamondback prospect, rather than the late Jerry Garcia, Grateful Dead icon, whom the DBs looked to for inspiration.

Though Karim spoke English and Spanish, his family did not, and so Dozer introduced Miguel Quintana, who would act as host and translator for the occasion. Rich said that Quintana, sporting a Diamondback tie, was "the Spanish voice for the team." Quintana had also been born in Sonora, like Garcia. He had worked as a sports broadcaster in Phoenix and Los Angeles and had recently been hired to do the play-by-play for thirty home games during the 1998 season on Phoenix's Telemundo affiliate.

"I want to be a window for the team to the Hispanic market and vice versa," Quintana stated in the press release announcing his hiring. "I think it will be an exciting time for everyone."

Miguel explained in that same press release that in his community baseball is a game of passion.

"Sometimes, if you listen or watch a game in English and then turn to the same game in Spanish, you might think you have two separate games," he said. "We are more dramatic, but that's what gets people's attention."

Quintana seemed nervous in his inaugural appearance as a DB representative, easily switching from English to Spanish and back again. However, like all Diamondback broadcasters, he spoke a lot and he spoke cheerfully.

Quintana asked Karim's mother what she thought of her son playing in Arizona. In typical mom fashion, she said she was happy because Karim would be close to home.

Quintana moved on to Karim's father, Mexican baseball great Pancho Garcia. Dad was also happy to have Karim just next door, so to speak. Miguel asked what advice Pancho had given his son, and Pancho's reply was brief and to the point: "First thing is discipline. Follow the rules and obey the manager and the coaches."

Damn—even the father was a Diamondback.

Karim, wearing a white shirt and blue blazer, looked something like an old Mexican movie star, with his slicked-back, dark hair, long sideburns, and goatee and mustache. The facial hair would have to go to comply with the DBs' dress code, and Garcia averred that he had no problem with that.

Karim had bigger concerns on his mind, and his face was flushed with excitement and some anxiety. He had had an operation on his throwing shoulder in July and, obviously a bit overweight, was intent on getting back in shape.

Additionally, like so many other ballplayers in his position, Garcia was stunned and disappointed that the Dodgers hadn't protected him in the draft. He felt he had something to prove to baseball and to baseball fans and, though he didn't say so, maybe even something to himself.

"I know a lot of people from Arizona and Mexico will want to come and see me," he said, "and I'm going to work hard to show them I am a good player."

The formal press conference ended, and the Hispanic media surged forward. To the Anglo press, Garcia was just another new ballplayer in town. The Hispanic press, from the United States and from Mexico, recognized him as someone considerably more significant.

Eventually, Karim's moment was over, and the Diamondbacks prepared to unveil their next player, their next star, their next announcement, their next surprise. And the DBs surely had a lot more to spring on the world about trades and promotions and ballparks and schedules.

But all that can wait a few moments. Now let's take a brief glance back to the past, because the past determined that the Arizona Diamondbacks would have a future. A little background will help fill in the crucial gaps and show how the Diamondbacks went from an idea to an entity, and a juggernaut of an entity at that. For the Diamondbacks were the product of not only Jerry Colangelo and Buck Showalter and the other DB executives and directors, but many people with many interests. And that story is not a story just of baseball, but also, as has been said before, of politics and business and the media. In other words, it is a story of our modern America.

PART II | The Players,
off the Field

Chapter 4

The Legislature Strikes First

B oyd Orth has lived his entire life in Arizona, aside from the three years he spent aboard U.S. Navy submarines during the Second World War. At age seventy-one, he is still a handsome man, with silver hair, a rugged, sun-creased face, and a ready smile. He is also a successful man, having built an insurance agency from nothing into a sizable company, which was then bought by Acordia, one of the largest insurance agencies in the country.

When Boyd was born in 1926, Arizona had been a state for only fourteen years, the last of the forty-eight contiguous states to join the Union. The entire state of Arizona contained just 140 miles of paved roads.

Phoenix was a big town more than it was a city. A population of some three hundred in 1870 had grown to about three thousand twenty years later, and perhaps ten times that in thirty more years.

This meant that Boyd grew up in a city with no home team for which to root. And in that pre-TV age, the Yankees and Red Sox and Cubs and all the other teams that visited Phoenix only through the crackling radio were as far away as the moon. As far as sports were concerned, Boyd and his friends were on their own, which, come to think of it, befitted the ethos, or at least the image, of the rugged individualism of the West.

"We didn't have any organized events," Boyd said, leaning back in his chair inside the bustling insurance agency. "When I was growing up, everything was centered around the neighborhood. School functions were held there, and on Sunday, Congregational Church services."

Phoenix wasn't an easy place to live in during those earlier days, especially before the invention of air-conditioning. In summer, when the temperature zoomed into the hundreds, even at night, people moved their mattresses onto their porches and slept outside. Many even wrapped themselves in wet sheets, attempting to get some relief.

As a youngster, Boyd enjoyed some singularly Arizonan activities, such as hiking the Superstition Mountains searching for a fabled, lost gold mine, and hunting rattlesnakes for their skins, which he would sell to craftsmen who would turn them into belts and hatbands. The secret, Boyd explained, was to track them at night, when the light of a flashlight would reflect off their eyes and make them easy to spot.

Not all of his activities were quite so Western. When he reached grammar school, his dad would take Boyd and his sister and his mom to the Phoenix Union High School every Friday night during football season to watch the game.

Later on, a baseball team came to town to play in the city-owned stadium in downtown Phoenix. Now and then, the family would head over to watch the Phoenix Senators play against teams that were either regionally based or touring the West. "I would say that the Senators were a professional team," averred Boyd, "if you could call anybody getting paid two hundred dollars a month a professional."

Once the Harlem Globetrotters passed through Phoenix and played a semipro basketball team sponsored by Del Webb, a real estate developer who later gained fame by developing the concept of the retirement community, and also purchased a piece of the New York Yankees.

"That was great," recalled Boyd. "We had never seen anything like the Globetrotters."

The radio provided the most powerful link to the world. "We listened to *The Jack Benny Show* and *The Shadow*," remembered Boyd. Sometimes he'd switch on a baseball game and listen to the faraway sounds of the excited announcer and the bat smacking the ball and the roaring crowd, but the action was too distant and the players too indistinct to grab his imagination and hold it.

More than any other sport, baseball is a participatory experience, a sharing of stories, a swapping of statistics, a feast of memories to be passed from one generation to the next. Why this is so is not exactly certain, but one would suppose that it has a great deal to do with the nature of the game, the pacing of the innings, and the time between innings. Baseball isn't ruled by the clock, unlike football, basketball, and hockey. Its playing fields are not chopped into geometric rigidity, but spread in singular patterns, different from park to park. It is a contest of skill and concentration, patience and determination, stamina and spontaneity, individual daring and team discipline.

Its stories can be told as a poet's moment, full of hesitation and grace, or as a statistician's dream, replete with numbers and facts and comparisons. A game can last a lifetime, replayed forever in the mind, and a season can be a blur, a part of an endless continuum, a piece of the American puzzle, a taste of the American dream.

Boyd missed out on all that growing up in pre–World War II Phoenix. And there was one more thing he missed.

"We didn't have any merchandise to buy," Boyd said.

No official major league baseball hats. No logo-laden shirts. No team-authorized socks and watches and leather jackets.

No air-conditioning in the desert is harsh; a world without imprints and emblems and trademarks is unimaginable.

Boyd hadn't done business in Phoenix for five decades without learning how the town operated. In fact, postwar Phoenix wasn't that different from a lot of other cities around the country: dominated by a relatively small, rich clique of businessmen, who were tied in directly, personally and professionally, to every public and private institution of consequence, from the banks to the statehouse to the newspaper to the judiciary. These men (and usually just men, women having only recently gained invitations into the clubs and board-rooms that constitute the inner sanctums of power and influence) worked with one another, supporting each other's projects and ideas, bringing the full force of their money and hegemony to bear to construct a city as they saw fit.

"The business community gets to do what it wants," Boyd said. "The government is run by the business community. If you don't do what they say, you don't get reelected."

This was and remains how the world works, particularly in small and midsized communities, where the power structure is contained and organized and overlapping. Phoenix has been like that since 1870, when Jack Swilling—soldier, adventurer, Confederate officer, and Union scout, the first person since the demise of the great Hohokam civilization centuries before to irrigate the parched land— optimistically named the humble collection of adobe homes Phoenix, for this was the place where a great society had once thrived and would rise to thrive again.

"The Roosevelts tried to bring in another newspaper," Boyd said. "This was years ago. There was only one newspaper in town, the *Republic,* and they wanted to compete with them. Now the story goes, the *Republic*'s sales staff went out to all these advertisers and said, 'We can't refuse you an ad in the paper'—they had contracts— 'but if we see your ad in the other paper, we'll put you so far back in the *Republic* that nobody will be able to find you with a flashlight!' " Boyd couldn't help but chuckle at that.

"And the law firm that represented the Roosevelt group," he continued, "they told them, 'You will never, ever see the name of your law firm in print again.' And then they called the bank, Valley National Bank, so the story goes: 'If you extend them any credit, don't ever look to us for any business.' "

When a city reaches a certain size, a critical mass, it's not so easy to maintain absolute market control with a handful of well-placed phone calls. Phoenix (more accurately, Greater Phoenix, including Scottsdale, Tempe, Buckeye, Mesa, Glendale, and many more, all together known as the Valley of the Sun) was growing so fast—an acre an hour, so said the media—it was quickly reaching that point. In addition, it was perhaps the only major city in America where the people moving into the city—many of whom hailed from Chicago, Los Angeles, and New York—were more sophisticated, more demanding, more urban, than the people already living there.

Phoenix was changing, slowly at first but with increasing speed, despite the resistance of many of the old guard. Still, for the time being, the old rules remained in effect, and the inbreeding spawned corruption and secrecy and cowardice.

That was why real estate developers ruled the roost and built shopping mall next to shopping mall, and miles of cookie-cutter tract homes over the horizon, with a cursory, public-relations nod to prudent urban planning, despite intensifying problems with air pollution and traffic congestion and neighborhood disintegration and community dislocation. Phoenix could have planned for mass transit, Phoenix could have had neighborhoods with schools and shops and movie theaters within walking distance, Phoenix could have had cleaner air—but it did not. It did not because the immediate, primary economic interest of the power structure was to extract as much profit as possible from the city's growth and to let future generations figure out how to fix the messes left behind.

We must not become another Los Angeles, the Phoenix mantra went, overgrown, overpopulated, overpaved, overpriced, over-strained, overwhelmed, over and out. We must not become another Los Angeles, and everyone chanted it, from the politicians to the press, the capitalists to the clergy, all down the line to the proverbial man in the street. We must not . . . but somehow, some way, it kept happening.

Fife Symington promoted his career as a successful real estate developer as the proper training ground for the office of governor of Arizona. The voters agreed, and Symington was elected. Unfortunately, it was later discovered that Fife Symington was not only *not* a successful real estate developer, but he was also a crook. At the end of the summer of 1997, in the middle of his second term, the governor was convicted of seven counts of bank fraud and removed from office.

In the small, centralized world of state power politics, sympathy for Symington was high. Jane Hull, the Arizona secretary of state who had acceded to the governorship upon Symington's forced resignation, told the press that she hoped Fife would receive a lenient sentence, declaring removal from office and conviction punishment enough. In an unusual show of bipartisanship, Eddie Basha, supermarket-chain owner, former Democratic nominee for governor, and then-leading contender for the same spot at the top of the state ticket, offered just about the same sentiments.

The lack of urban planning had resulted in the demise of down-town Phoenix. "Years ago," Boyd said, "downtown was the center of everything. Then stores started moving north. Goldwater's [the Phoenix flagship of a chain of department stores founded by Sen. Barry Goldwater's great-grandfather and his brothers] moved to the new Park Central Mall in the 1950s, and that started everybody else leaving. And pretty soon we had nothing downtown. Nobody lived there, nobody went there unless they had to."

In pursuit of greener pastures, the business community had

effectively abandoned the downtown area, leaving behind a flop-house hotel, some small shops, many empty buildings and vacant lots. But it wasn't the responsibility of storeowners to commit their resources to save and revitalize a community—that was the government's job. But the city and state representatives were not up to the task, not strong or smart enough to buck the trend and draw a line and plan for the future.

This abandonment would lead to a singular opportunity for the Arizona Diamondbacks when it came time to find a site for their stadium.

So this was the Arizona that Boyd Orth knew, an Arizona accelerating into explosive change, sometimes for the better and sometimes for the worse, an Arizona doing just fine without professional baseball. But others felt differently, and forces were at work determined to give aid and comfort to the sports deprived. So we'll leave Boyd for a spell and sally forth with those committed, for love or money—or both—to bringing Major League Baseball to Arizona.

In the late eighties, the air was filled with talk of MLB expanding to new cities. Phoenix was frequently mentioned as a leading contender. In 1989, the good citizens of Phoenix had the chance to fund the construction of a news sports stadium. They declined, in an unambiguous vote.

On the other hand, Scottsdale voters had approved a property-tax bond issue to overhaul Scottsdale Stadium, spring-training home of the San Francisco Giants. Thus, perhaps the issue wasn't quite so cut-and-dry.

The matter would not rest there. Rep. Chris Herstam, the Republican majority whip, rose to address his colleagues in the Arizona House of Representatives, offering an amendment to Senate Bill 1344. Herstam was a baseball fan of the first order. He wanted a team in Arizona, a major league team. Herstam knew that no such team would ever be forthcoming unless a stadium, or at least a stadium-funding mechanism, was already in existence, so he had submitted a bill triggering such a mechanism.

However, Herstam's bill was languishing. The measure, which relied upon some rather complicated language, couldn't get out of committee, and that meant that its chance of ever reaching the floor for a vote of the full legislature was nil.

Time was running out for Herstam. The legislative session was approaching its close, and Herstam was retiring from elective office. He needed to find a new way to get his bill through.

Senate Bill 1344 was the way.

The bill, which had already passed the Senate, addressed a technical adjustment in the groundwater code—something about the city of Phoenix purchasing a parcel of land to accommodate a water acquisition—but Herstam was not interested in groundwater. His amendment quite simply eliminated all the words in the bill that related to water, wiped the slate clean, and started fresh. The bill now authorized the Board of Supervisors of Maricopa County to constitute themselves into a county stadium district. This new body (which was actually exactly the same as the old body, just with a new title and new responsibilities), this stadium district, would have the power to levy a quarter-cent sales tax to raise funds for the building of a stadium.

Herstam purposely included two provisions: (1) the stadium would have to be new, not an old stadium renovated, and (2) the stadium would not be a multi-use facility, a combination baseball-football arena, but would be dedicated solely to baseball. As a fan, Herstam recognized that enlarging and upgrading a local ballpark would not be adequate for a big league club. He also knew that in the giant multi-use stadiums—popular in the seventies and an idea still promoted by Bill Bidwell, eager for a new home for his NFL Arizona Cardinals—the configuration of the field was unsuitable for baseball, leaving thousands of seats unusable, and the entire stadium a cold and distant venue.

Herstam was ready with his bill. The legislative rules have since been changed, but the "striker" bill, as it was called, was a potent, albeit peculiar, common contrivance. Herstam's bill was not subjected to examination by legislators in committee, nor by the taxpayers in a public hearing.

This striker tactic had not rendered the bill magically invisible. Herstam introduced the bill at a Republican caucus. Despite being a leader of the majority party, Herstam realized that he would have to rely upon Democrats, not quite so instinctively antitax as his own Republicans, to pass the measure. That brought Gov. Rose Mofford into the fray. Mofford was not only a Democrat, she was also a fellow baseball fan. Herstam concentrated on the House, while Mofford's efforts were centered on the Senate.

"Nobody asked me to introduce the legislation," stated Herstam in an interview in the *New Times,* a weekly, self-styled "alternative" paper, four years after the fact. "I just determined that there would be no chance at all for an expansion team without the funding mechanism for a stadium. I just thought I would go ahead and give it a try."

Phoenix's weak city government ran a poor second in influence and authority to the Maricopa County government, which was run by the elected Board of Supervisors. Phoenix was really big, but it was only part of Maricopa County, which was the size of New Jersey. If the Board of Supervisors pushed for a stadium, the city would not stand in the way.

Though the people of Phoenix had resoundingly rejected financing a stadium, Herstam's bill left it up to the board to choose whether a tax would be levied.

At the same time, Herstam's bill intentionally did not preclude the board from bringing the matter before the people for a vote. However, it was clear that neither Herstam nor the board expected the issue to be left up to the public.

"You elect five individuals to represent the entire county," he affirmed to the *New Times,* "and it is their job to make the difficult decisions."

As any secondary-school student should know, that presents the classic question of representative government: Is it the mandate of that government's elected officials to always and slavishly do whatever their constituents want, or is their basic responsibility to rely on their intellects and principles and do what they judge best?

Of course, it is not absolutely one way or the other. The answer, as with most matters political, is a little bit of this and a little bit of that. At the time of the American Revolution, as all those same secondary-school students should also be well aware, the people of the thirteen colonies were one-third in favor of independence, one-third against, and one-third unsure. If the men who gathered together in Philadelphia in 1776 had blindly followed the lead of the seriously divided American people, July 4 would just be another hot summer day in Arizona—or whatever French or Spanish or English appellation the owners would have selected instead of the name derived from the native Papago.

Nonetheless, as the political pendulum swings and choices must be made, it would seem that this case leaned nearer to the side of enforcing the people's will. The people had already voted, and more than once, and the results were decidedly mixed. Herstam's bill was potentially an end run around those uncertain findings.

Herstam's introduction of the striker bill near the end of the legislative session emboldened some representatives, attempting to get on the right side of public opinion, to subsequently claim that the bill thus escaped notice. This begged credulity, for the media certainly knew about it, as demonstrated by a not atypical article in the *Phoenix Gazette*, which began, "A key legislative leader has introduced a bill that would allow the Maricopa County Board of Supervisors to levy a tax that would help finance a baseball stadium in the Valley. . . . 'This is my field of dreams,' Herstam said. 'Build it and they will come.'" An editorial a month later in that same paper urged passage of the bill, stating, "The bill, if approved, would allow Phoenix to compete for major league expansion."

The allegation of ignorance, thus disproved outside the legislature, begged credulity inside its hallowed walls as well: as the measure came up for the vote, some legislators sang "Take Me Out to the Ballgame."

Still, only one politician rose to speak in opposition. Lela Steffey, who not only claimed to love baseball but also had a nephew playing for the San Diego Padres, submitted her own amendment to the bill, requiring a vote by the people before a sales tax could be enacted. She also stated she would support such a tax, because she believed in baseball and the money the sport would bring to the city and the county.

"I think that we should be able to trust our electorate," Steffey said. "If they want a sports stadium built with their money, then I think they should have a choice in the vote."

For his part, Herstam was willing to place his trust in the Board of Supervisors: "If they have the political courage to do what they think is a smart investment for Maricopa County, we ought to allow them to do that. They stand for reelection based on that record."

In rapid order, Steffey's amendment was defeated in the House and Herstam's passed, thirty-five to twenty. On the last day of the session, the striker bill returned to the Senate and was approved, eighteen to ten.

On the day Governor Mofford signed Bill 1344 into law, legislators surprised Herstam by presenting him with two baseballs, one autographed by every member of the House who had supported the measure, the other inscribed by every member of the Senate who had voted yes.

*　　*　　*

Bill 1344 meant that the Maricopa County Board of Supervisors had suddenly become a key actor in whether Arizona would be awarded a Major League Baseball franchise. Five local representatives, most of whom were unaccustomed to battling beyond the local stage about local issues, were about to have to deal with some eminent, tough players.

This did not include the major players on the Arizona political scene, because the only major political player in Arizona was Sen. John McCain, and his leading areas of interest and expertise—campaign finance reform and foreign policy—were national and international rather than local. A remarkably high percentage of the entire remaining political cast was stunningly second-rate, lacking the intellectual daring and political courage to make hard choices and search for innovative solutions, lacking the vision and the stomach to—in a word—lead.

How bad could it really be? Governor Symington wasn't the first Arizona politician to leave the top post in disgrace. Just nine years earlier, Gov. Evan Mecham had been impeached and removed from office for his own financial misdoings. Just after that, a federal investigation code-named Azscam nailed a bunch of state legislators taking bribes right on hidden video camera. While charges of influence-peddling concerning the savings-and-loan crook Charles Keating and five U.S. senators did not result in any charges being filed, the Keating Five scandal certainly did not help the reputations of those involved, including both Arizona U.S. senators.

Then, of course, there were those who were not corrupt, but merely invisible or incompetent—or bizarre. Starting with the last category, Frances Barwood, former vice mayor of Phoenix, former city councilwoman, declared her candidacy for Arizona secretary of state in early 1998 running on the UFO platform, pledging to force the government to reveal the truth about aliens. "I unfortunately have never seen anything," she said at her press conference. "What can I say? I don't know what is out there. . . . Whatever it is, I want to know, and I want a reenactment."

Moving along, Mayor Sam Campana of Scottsdale started her first term by getting lost within the borders of her own town and using her car phone to call 911 for directions, causing a public uproar and a lecture from the police on the proper uses of the emergency number.

The mayor of Phoenix, Skip Rimsza, had to be the least visible mayor of any city of any size in the country. It was no exaggeration to state that on the rare occasion he appeared on the nightly news, it was more often because of his young triplets—their feeding schedule, their sleeping schedule, *his* sleeping schedule, etc.—than for anything having to do with city business. Even more amazing, Mayor Rimsza most frequently appeared on TV not even on the news with his kids, but on a commercial for the *Arizona Republic,* walking outside a supermarket, smiling and waving to the camera, pushing you know who—and who and who—in a stroller.

Finally, amongst the Arizona congressional delegation, Rep. J. D. Hayworth was voted one of the ten dumbest members of Congress by a national magazine for an assortment of acts and statements, including, for instance, declaring that logging was a particularly beneficial activity because forests were a fire hazard.

A pretty pathetic state of affairs from a state that in the not-so-distant past produced statesmen on both sides of the aisle such as Barry Goldwater, John Rhodes, Morris Udall, and Stewart Udall.

Instead, Arizona is suffused with elected officials primarily concerned with keeping their jobs and salaries and perks, as well as ensuring a smooth, profitable entry, or reentry, into the private sector upon leaving office. It's the same in local governments across America, and also at the highest levels of the federal government. The damage done to U.S. interests by cabinet and White House and congressional officials who trade in their positions of public trust for well-paid jobs as lobbyists and influence peddlers and fixers with foreign governments and corporations is enormous and ongoing.

So back in Arizona, most of the politicians were pygmies, small obstacles to be dispensed with in the pursuit of objectives.

Nonetheless, one politician, state representative Chris Herstam, had started the process toward garnering a baseball franchise for Arizona with his striker bill. The bill would lie silent, undisturbed, unused, for a couple of years. Eventually, another politician would take that bill and wave it high as his standard in his quest to bring professional baseball home.

And though the real powers in Phoenix and Arizona remained business executives and entrepreneurs, the real estate developers and factory owners and attorneys and bankers and all the others who invested or built or controlled or speculated, this local politician, Jim Bruner of the Maricopa County Board of Supervisors, would play a key role in both promoting the idea of going after a Major League

Baseball club, and negotiating on behalf of Maricopa County with the private investors over the ballpark.

The process that followed must be seen as a mosaic, as different people with different agendas strive and work, sometimes in unison and sometimes at cross-purposes, to arrive at the same goal. Each of the prime players' recollections added up to a whole, or really more than the whole, because the final story was surely greater, and more consequential, than the sum of its parts.

Of course, when push came to shove and the money had to be raised and the deals cut, the real powers—and in particular a handful of the major players in town—would take Bill 1344 and run with it. And that is where to go next in our narrative—to the money, as usual. In running with the new law, the money people and deal makers would, depending on one's point of view, run right by a lot of people or seize the initiative and the moment, carrying an often reluctant community to glory.

Chapter 5

First Batter Up:
Swinging for the Fences

E ddie Lynch is a general partner of Westcor, a huge real estate firm he helped found, which builds and manages shopping malls, hotels, and other sizable projects throughout America. Westcor's headquarters in Phoenix occupies a large web of offices and conference rooms, with enlarged photographic maps hanging from the walls of ventures under development.

Eddie Lynch is another very successful man.

Lynch's office is at the end of a long walk from the reception area. The walls are paneled in dark wood, the rug is Persian, and sports memorabilia take up much of the counter space on the cabinets. An autographed football commemorating the Arizona State victory in the 1983 Fiesta Bowl—"ASU 32, Oklahoma 12" is inscribed on the ball—is arrayed beside two basketballs signed by members of the Phoenix Suns. Across the room a gigantic, bronzed basketball sneaker dominates the top of a bureau. A plaque under the oversize shoe reads "Edwin C. Lynch, M.V.P."

The award is a bit startling, since Eddie Lynch is a man too long in years and too short in stature to make a plausible professional basketball player. Still, if tenacity and desire alone could have won the award, then Lynch would have had a shot.

His grandfather arrived in Arizona in 1913, one year after the state entered the Union. Eddie was born a native, and, unlike Boyd Orth, a

65

native who missed having pro sports teams in town. Alas, the professional leagues shunned the desert town, a situation not rectified until a group of Los Angeles investors decided to start a National Basketball Association franchise in Phoenix. A young man was hired away from the Chicago Bulls to move to Arizona and direct the fortunes of the new team.

The year was 1968. Eddie Lynch met Jerry Colangelo, the transplanted Chicagoan, for the first time.

Singer Andy Williams owned 25 percent of the Suns, anteing up $500,000 of the total $2-million franchise fee. Tony Curtis, Bobbie Gentry, and Henry Mancini—actor, singer, and composer—were also owners. A small group of wealthy Tucson businessmen—Richard Bloch, Donald Pitt, and Donald Diamond—in conjunction with Andy Williams's attorneys (who grabbed a fat chunk of the franchise for themselves as payment), would act as the managing general partners.

Only one Phoenician had any financial interest in the team. Eddie Lynch had laid out $20,000 and purchased exactly 1 percent of the Phoenix Suns.

The Suns were not good that first year, not good at all. Even more distressing, the public did not rush to embrace the team and stayed away from Veterans Memorial Coliseum in droves. The arena was often an empty cave that first campaign, when the Suns won just sixteen games and lost sixty-six.

The Suns rapidly improved as the years passed, eventually reaching the NBA finals in 1976 and losing to the Boston Celtics in a memorable series. Though no one knew it at the time, this would be the high-water mark of the Suns for their first quarter century. For what goes up quite often comes down, especially in sports, and the Suns hit a rocky patch during the 1986–87 season, only made that much worse by a drug scandal involving the team.

And that would change everything.

Years before then, Eddie had gotten significantly more involved in the local sports scene, such as it was. He had become the head of the Phoenix Metropolitan Sports Foundation, an arm of the Chamber of Commerce, in the late 1970s. The goal of the foundation was to find major league franchises to set up shop in town.

It was not easy going. The United States Football League, an upstart group trying to compete with the NFL monolith, had a team in Phoenix for a while, but the USFL ran out of money and folded before long, and the Wranglers, who changed their name to the Outlaws after a merger with the L.A. franchise, went with them.

Eddie chased after a few football teams, coming close a couple of times. Then-governor Bruce Babbitt asked Lynch to pursue the Baltimore Colts "on the sly," to quote Eddie. Lynch traveled to and fro, but in the end lost out to Indianapolis, because of the vacant and waiting Hoosier Dome. Eddie had the Philadelphia Eagles in hand, ready to sign on the bottom line, emotionally packed up and ready to move, the whole deal on the hush-hush. It had to be that way; a city suddenly facing the loss of a team ordinarily reacted like a wounded and trapped beast, with dangerous desperation. Unfortunately, a Phoenix reporter got wind of the story, published it, and within a day or so the mayor of Philadelphia flew down to Atlanta, where the Eagles were playing the Falcons. Begging and pleading, he convinced Leonard Tose, the Philadelphia owner, not to leave poor Philly behind, and Phoenix was left out in the football cold again.

Pro football wasn't Lynch's only concern. He and Jerry and more than a dozen others had bought the Phoenix Giants, a Triple A baseball team, in the seventies from the club's Chicago-based owner. Lynch and Colangelo, as the only two Phoenicians involved with the Suns, had grown rather close, brought together by their love of sports and business. They were both ambitious men, brimming with ambitious ideas, neither content with the status quo with the Suns or with the Arizona sports scene.

The Giants cost their group $250,000. They later sold 75 percent of the team to Morton Stone, getting their investment back and retaining 25 percent of the ownership. They would eventually sell that percentage as well, and the team would change its name to the Firebirds. Though the Firebirds attracted a loyal cadre of fans, the wilting summer heat deterred the club from ever obtaining a wider following, and the team often played before meager audiences.

In a small irony, the advent of the Diamondbacks, Jerry Colangelo's new team, would cause his old team, the Firebirds, to depart Arizona for California after the 1997 season.

Of course, that summer heat was the greatest obstacle to Phoenix ever winning a Major League Baseball franchise. It was just too damn hot to chase baseballs in July, August, and September, too. More to the point, it was just too damn hot to sit in the broiling stands and watch other people chase baseballs in July, August, and September, too.

The only solution was a domed stadium. Eddie went to the state and municipal governments, requesting an evaluation of the feasibility of constructing an indoor facility. Combining contributions from several local governments, $100,000 was pledged to such a study, which determined that an indoor arena could be built, given generous suite licenses and commercial arrangements. The reality was that no baseball franchise would be coming to Phoenix without a stadium deal in place, and it would be hard to imagine a stadium deal without the promise of a franchise.

Lynch and others originally thought the stadium should be multipurpose, a suitable venue for both professional football and baseball. It seemed to make sense economically, getting the biggest bang for the sports buck, filling that facility as many days and nights as possible.

Events would alter that perception. The failure of multipurpose stadiums to satisfy the needs of both football and baseball, the intercession of the Arizona legislature, the respective ebb and flow of the fortunes of the Arizona baseball and football franchises, would end the notion of two teams under one roof.

Before that shift, Eddie was intent on chasing down any leads on dissatisfied professional football franchises to match up with a baseball team in an indoor facility. He heard that the St. Louis Cardinals of the NFL were unhappy in Busch Stadium, where they viewed themselves as second-class tenants to the St. Louis Cardinals of MLB. The baseball Cards were owned by the Busch family of Anheuser-Busch beer wealth, who also, obviously, owned the stadium. (Incidentally, Busch Stadium was the only ballpark in the land where the music played during the seventh-inning stretch was not "Take Me Out to the Ballgame" but, in deference to the local alcoholic pedigree, the "King of Beers" theme song.)

Eddie called Bill Bidwell and the talks began, waxing and waning for two years. A deal was eventually worked out for the Cardinals to use Arizona State University's Sun Devil Stadium, a 77,000-seat amphitheater situated between the mountains. It was a magnificent setting, even if the venue itself was a bit older and not quite up to modern NFL standards. That was okay, for the time being, because the Cardinals believed that the Arizona power structure had promised to build the team a new stadium.

The Cardinals of Missouri became the Cardinals of Arizona in

1989—but if the Cardinals believed their problems had ended with their migration to the Valley of the Sun, they were seriously mistaken. To the contrary, they were just beginning, and the Diamondbacks' fate would affect their own aspirations.

Back to the Suns, whose fourth straight losing campaign was almost reduced to a depressing grace note to the 1986–87 season, courtesy of the indictment of five current or former players on drug charges. Though the case never went to trial, the scandal rocked the franchise. The Los Angeles ownership quickly lost its taste for the team mockingly referred to as Phoenix House and wanted to cash out its investment. The owners offered Colangelo the opportunity to buy them out—if he could raise the money: $44.5 million. Not a bad return on a wounded team worth $2 million just nineteen years before.

"I thought they were crazier than hell," Eddie said, but Jerry quickly got down to business. Colangelo had to move fast; the NBA was talking about moving the team out of Arizona and starting fresh somewhere else. Besides, he didn't have the money, and it was far from certain he would be able to find it.

But Jerry Colangelo, with some help from allies like Eddie Lynch, did put the financing together and kept the club in Arizona. And then Colangelo did convince the city to build the franchise a new arena and sold sponsorships to corporations throughout the state. And he made some good deals with both the private and public sectors, good enough to cause *Financial World* magazine in September 1997 to rank the Phoenix Suns the second-wealthiest professional basketball franchise, trailing only the New York Knicks, who, by the by, reside in the largest, richest market in the world. One step better: *Financial World* ranked the Suns number nine among all sports franchises, with a value of $220 million.

So Eddie Lynch was doing okay, an integral part of the resurgent Suns, and still in search of a Major League Baseball franchise. Despite his best efforts, he knew that Arizona wasn't ready to bid against Colorado and Florida when baseball expanded in 1991. The Rockies and the Marlins came into existence at an entry price of $95 million per. It sounded like a lot at the time to Eddie—well, probably to everybody—but it would turn out to be a bargain, relatively speaking, when Arizona was ready to step up to the plate.

And all that—the tangled journey of the Phoenix Giants/Firebirds and the St. Louis Cardinals and the Phoenix Suns, not to mention the Phoenix Wranglers/Outlaws, Baltimore Colts, and the Philadelphia Eagles, as well as the Colorado Rockies and the Florida Marlins—would carve a crooked path to the Arizona Diamondbacks.

And also explain that gigantic, bronzed basketball sneaker spread over the top of Eddie Lynch's bureau.

Chapter 6

Second Batter Up: The Sacrifice Fly

I t is clear that Jim Bruner still doesn't quite get it. Sure, he understands that people were—and are—angry about the tax. Sure, he recognizes that people are angry about the process that brought them the tax. Sure, he realizes that was why he was retired from elective office by popular demand. Bruner knows all the facts.

Still, seated in his office at the bank's headquarters, Bruner refuses to acknowledge, or admit, that there may have been another way of handling this entire business. A better way. A smarter way.

No. Sorry. Absolutely not.

Jim Bruner is a lawyer and a banker, currently an executive vice president of the National Bank of Arizona. He is tall, with silver hair and glasses, and conservative in dress and manner.

It must be a comfortable existence, being the executive VP of a big bank, though perhaps lacking in the sort of spontaneity and excitement found in politics. Nevertheless, that's where Bruner finds himself, in the aftermath of what he must have thought was a promising political career.

It all began, and ended, in 1989.

After eight years on the Scottsdale City Council, Bruner was elected to the Maricopa County Board of Supervisors in the fall of

71

1988, taking office the next year. By his own account, his first order of business was to deal with the Cactus League, which had encountered some serious problems.

The Cactus League was the name given to spring training in Arizona, the short season from February through March when major league teams prepared for the rigors of the long season ahead.

In 1947, Horace Stoneham decided he wanted to spend the winter at his home in Paradise Valley. He spoke to Bill Veeck, who owned a ranch near Tucson, and the two men agreed that Stoneham had a pretty good idea. That was how Stoneham's New York Giants and Veeck's Cleveland Indians came to train for the upcoming season in Phoenix.

Stoneham and Veeck divided the state in two; the Giants took Phoenix and the north, and the Indians claimed Tucson and the south.

Dwight Patterson, known today as the "father of the Cactus League," convinced the Chicago Cubs, who had been training on Catalina Island off southern California, to migrate to Mesa.

Another spur to the development of the Cactus League was the integration of baseball, beginning in 1946, when Branch Rickey invited Jackie Robinson to join the Dodgers' Triple-A Montreal team, promoting him to the major league club the following year. As the process accelerated and baseball finally started hiring black players, the racism that was so rampant and vicious in Florida caused several teams to move to the West, to both Arizona and California, where race relations were considerably easier.

Eight teams made up the league in 1988, based not only in the Valley of the Sun, but also south to Tucson. The other eighteen teams of MLB at the time trained in Florida, in the Grapefruit League. The Cactus League might have been substantially smaller than the Grapefruit, but it remained a vital part of the baseball universe, bringing some major league excitement for the tourists, the media, and the entire state of Arizona, as well as, most importantly, more than $150 million in revenue—and in just thirty days.

And that didn't include the Yakult Swallows from Japan—not part of the Cactus League, but a revenue producer nonetheless—who trained in Yuma's Ray Kroc Baseball Complex.

The problem was that the Cactus League teams were no longer satisfied with their old, small parks. They wanted bantam versions of their major league venues, with well-tended practice fields and modern exercise facilities and spacious locker rooms. And if they couldn't get what they wanted in Arizona, they were ready to find it in Florida, where the offers from cities and corporations to move were just as lush as the foliage.

The Cleveland Indians skipped Tucson for Florida after the 1992 season. After forty years in Arizona, the shock of the Indians' departure was only exacerbated by the realization that it could be the first of many to go. According to Bruner, both the Chicago Cubs and the San Francisco Giants had pledged to leave unless new stadiums were constructed for their use. That would bring the league down to too few teams to bother having a Cactus League at all.

Concerned Arizonans, including Senator McCain and Bruner, met with MLB commissioner Fay Vincent. Vincent commiserated with Arizona's plight and declared his fondness for the Cactus League. However, Vincent also said he wouldn't stand in the way of any club that found a better deal elsewhere.

It was up to Arizona to save itself.

Fortuitously—most fortuitously—for Arizona baseball's future, the state had the right governor in office to take on the job. Rose Mofford, who had succeeded to the gubernatorial chair after the Evan Mecham debacle, was the sort who naturally brought people together and could convince battling interests to work toward a common purpose. In this complicated case, with so many competing municipalities and interests involved, this was a crucial gift.

However, even more significant was Mofford's previous career on the diamond, for the governor had been an all-star first baseman in the 1940s, when women's softball teams, sponsored by companies, were big attractions. In Phoenix, a game could draw six or seven thousand fans.

The leagues lost much of their popularity in the fifties, with competition from other sports and that new entertainment medium, television, distracting their fan base. But Rose Mofford, who was so handy with bat and glove that today she is in the Arizona Softball Hall of Fame, was ready to hit the field one more time when a fellow governor, Florida's Bob Martinez, openly solicited major league teams to abandon the Cactus League for the Grapefruit.

Mofford organized the Governor's Cactus League Task Force, appointing Joe Garagiola Jr., Dwight Patterson, and a score of other political and business leaders to serve.

With teams spread far and wide—the San Diego Padres were in

Yuma and the California Angels across the border in Palm Springs, California—the task force arrived at a twenty-eight-point program to strengthen the league. The key elements were devising taxes for new training facilities, tapping state funds for promotional efforts by the Department of Tourism and the Commerce and Economic Development Commission, and going after some Florida-based teams to transfer west.

"The governor's recommendations put the Cactus League in scoring position," said Geoffrey Gonsher, Mofford's special assistant, and the author of the report. "It's now up to the legislature to bring it home."

And so the legislature did, voting to create stadium districts in Maricopa County and Pima County (the latter, Tucson's home), giving the counties the power to levy rental-car taxes to pay for new stadiums. Taxing rental cars and hotels was becoming increasingly popular across the country, because those services were primarily used by out-of-towners—nonconstituents, in other words. It was thus a means for politicians to raise money for their pet projects while still maintaining their stirring antitax stance for the voters back in their own districts.

Together, Maricopa County and the city of Peoria, located in the northwest quadrant of that same county, invested $32 million in a glorious stadium and compound for the Seattle Mariners and San Diego Padres. New or renovated stadiums were or would be constructed in Scottsdale, Mesa, Phoenix, and Tucson, the last the new facility to be shared by the Diamondbacks and the Chicago White Sox beginning in 1998. Together, these ballparks cost in the vicinity of $200 million.

Those were public dollars, naturally, taxpayer dollars, and hardly anyone objected. Perhaps it was because the money was spread out among several stadiums in several communities. Perhaps the individual outlays weren't large enough for the media or pressure groups to sit up and notice. Whatever the reasons, this lack of widespread outrage might have lulled some politicians into a false sense of voter support—or voter apathy—with regard to funding sports facilities.

If so, that warm, cozy feeling would be shattered soon enough.

Meanwhile, in the spring of 1990, talk was in the air that Major League Baseball was prepared to expand again. State representative Herstam phoned Bruner, who was not only on the Board of Supervisors but was its chairman, wondering how the supervisors would feel about being handed taxing authority sufficient to build a stadium.

Chairman Jim Bruner thought it was a swell idea.

In fact, Bruner was so impressed that he lobbied the legislature to pass the bill.

Bruner called Joe Garagiola Jr., who was not only the son and namesake of the famed catcher, but also an attorney who had worked as general counsel and assistant to the president for the New York Yankees. Garagiola had kept his hand in sports after moving to Phoenix in 1982, concentrating on sports law and serving as chairman of the Phoenix Metropolitan Sports Foundation for a couple of years, the same foundation Eddie Lynch had also headed. He quickly tallied up more local sports credits, aside from the Governor's Cactus League Task Force: the Mayor's Professional Baseball Committee on Phoenix, the Arizona Baseball Commission, the Board of the Maricopa County Sports Authority.

Bruner wanted to approach the baseball powers about Phoenix, and he wanted Garagiola along for the ride. Of course, the two of them did not constitute a complete package. Another person in the game was Martin Stone, the owner of the Triple-A Firebirds, who wanted to step up to a major league franchise. Stone was busy attempting to raise the $90 million MLB required to buy into baseball, but he wasn't all that close.

That couldn't have been much of a surprise to anyone vaguely familiar with the Arizona economy. Nineteen ninety was not the best time to be hustling cash. Arizona lived and died by the real estate market—high-flying in the seventies, it had crashed in the eighties. That meant hard, cold cash was in short supply, and nobody, from the banks to the corporations to wealthy individuals, was rushing to lend money for speculative ventures like baseball teams.

It seemed that whatever money was actually around had already been appropriated by the Phoenix Suns and was earmarked for construction of America West Arena. Of course, the Suns and the new arena consumed Jerry Colangelo's attention and resources, leaving not a whit for anything as grand as professional baseball.

So that left Martin Stone as the leading financial type interested in the deal, and so that was who led the Arizonans into battle.

Governor Mofford also accompanied the group, demonstrating the official state interest in baseball.

The presentation was made to MLB's executive committee, but the commitment wasn't strong, the money wasn't in place, the whole effort just wasn't good enough.

Instead, Colorado and Florida got their teams.

Those Arizonans pushed back down the baseball mount determined to climb back up and plant the standard of the Grand Canyon State. When the San Francisco Giants were up for sale, Bruner and others thought the club might consider a new home. It was a long shot, to put it charitably, and the Giants stayed where they were. Nonetheless, no stone was left unturned—and no team hurried on down to Phoenix.

In the early summer of 1993, the media began reporting that MLB was interested in expanding again, and perhaps to Phoenix and Tampa–St. Petersburg. Bruner had already been at this for three years, and he had serious doubts that he was ever going to get anywhere.

But Bruner truly believed professional baseball was important, and particularly important to Phoenix, and he wasn't willing to get off that merry-go-round just yet.

Bruner called Garagiola and asked him to check with his sources inside Major League Baseball and find out if Phoenix was really in the running for an expansion club. Joe returned with a positive response. Phoenix had a chance, a good chance, but only if everything was properly organized, and that meant the right ownership group, with a fat check in hand.

Back into the fray, Bruner and Garagiola looked around the state for a new champion to lead the Arizona group, somebody with a proven track record in sports, somebody who could tap into the institutions and individuals who could provide the enormous sums that it would take to get into baseball.

Those prerequisites narrowed the field in a hurry, starting and ending with one man: Jerry Colangelo. By this time, the Suns were playing great, and America West Arena was selling out, so the factors that had ostensibly stopped Colangelo from getting involved before were, theoretically, no longer hindrances.

So Bruner and Garagiola made an appointment and went to see Jerry Colangelo.

Colangelo listened for over an hour as his two supplicants explained the sad history of baseball in Arizona. Bruner recollected that Colangelo was noncommittal, unsure as to what he wanted to do. The most Colangelo would say was that he would make some phone calls over the summer and get a feel for the lay of the land.

Jerry Colangelo promised to phone Bruner and Garagiola after Labor Day and tell them what he thought of the whole business.

That was that.

The two men left Colangelo's spacious office overlooking downtown Phoenix in America West Arena not really knowing when or if they would hear from Colangelo.

They would not be kept in suspense long. True to his word, Jerry Colangelo called Jim Bruner the day after Labor Day. Colangelo said he had spoken to people in and out of Major League Baseball and was convinced that the time was right and a team could be won for Arizona. Colangelo was ready to head the ownership group and do what it took to emerge victorious at the end of the day.

So Jerry Colangelo set himself to raising the immense fortune that would constitute his baseball war chest. Simultaneously, he began negotiating with the Board of Supervisors about building a stadium for the new team. After all, without the promise of a state-of-the-art stadium, Major League Baseball would never award any city a franchise.

Here was a certain irony. Bruner had been instrumental in getting Colangelo and his allies committed to bringing baseball to Arizona. After years of effort, he had accomplished his goal. But having succeeded, his job was now to turn around and negotiate, along with the rest of the board, to ensure that Maricopa County got the best deal possible for its taxpayer-supported stadium. That placed him in an adversarial position with Colangelo, who, as the prospective baseball owner, had a specific view of what was fair and reasonable.

If Bruner and the rest of the Board of Supervisors couldn't strike an arrangement with Jerry Colangelo, then there would be no stadium, and there would be no team. Bruner was in a position to kill the very plan he had worked so hard to realize.

The state legislature had given the county the power to levy a sales tax to pay for a stadium. To Bruner, it didn't seem like a radical approach to funding. After all, stadiums had been built all across the county and beyond in Arizona as well, using public money. While those were much smaller facilities, the operating principle was the same.

Bruner said he asked a lot of investment bankers and other

business types if they wanted to build a stadium without using tax dollars. No way, was the answer. Too rich for the investment community's blood, with too uncertain a return.

Colangelo wasn't about to bear the brunt of the stadium tab. According to his calculations, the economics just weren't there. Beside, the team, all by its lonesome, was more than expensive enough, thank you.

The five members of the board were split. Citing a conflict because of land she owned close to the prospective stadium site, Betsy Bayless recused herself from the entire issue. Tom Rawles early and forcefully proclaimed himself against the tax. Ed King and Mary Rose Wilcox favored the stadium.

The price tag for the stadium was $288 million. The proposal was to enact a quarter-cent sales tax until $238 million was in the kitty, leaving the Diamondbacks with a manageable $50-million contribution

Food and medicine were specifically excluded from the tax, so those essential items would not increase in cost. The plan was to raise the money within four years.

Lawyers for both sides handled the bargaining, until lawyers did what they often do—talked themselves into a dead end. It was up to Bruner and Colangelo, the two men closest to the entire endeavor, to sit down and talk, face-to-face.

Bruner had a few nonnegotiable items on his agenda. He insisted on a cap on the tax, even if the construction had setbacks and overruns. He wanted the county to get a share in the stadium naming rights, a percentage of the skybox rentals, a percentage of nonbaseball revenues, and a guaranteed lease payment. Finally, he wanted all stadium operating expenses borne by the team.

Several years later, Bruner remembered the one-on-one negotiations as tense, with both men pressing their points, giving no ground. He said he was prepared to walk away.

In January 1994, Tom Rawles publicly announced that he would oppose the stadium tax. Apart from his philosophical objections to using public funds for a private business project, Rawles said he had discovered that two other members of the board, Ed King and Mary Rose Wilcox, had secretly gone to Colangelo and worked out a stadium deal on their own, satisfying their concerns and priorities. Of course, going behind the backs of their own attorneys, and Bruner, too, did not exactly strengthen the county's negotiating position.

Three days later, King and Wilcox conducted their own press conference, stating their support for the tax.

The tally thus far was one supervisor abstaining, one against, and two in favor. That left Bruner with the deciding vote.

Bruner had something else on his mind as well. It was common knowledge he was planning to resign from the Board of Supervisors and run for Congress that same year. His political pals told him to walk away from the tax issue. Drop it and forget it, if he was serious about the election. Voting for a new tax, and a controversial one at that, was not the sure ticket to electoral victory.

The public outcry against the tax was only starting to build. Citizen taxpayer groups wanted information, they wanted a say in the matter, and neither was forthcoming. The politicians looked as if they were playing games, baldly unfair games at that, one after another. The year after Herstam's striker bill was enacted, the state legislature revisited the measure and chose to amend it, expanding to all fourteen counties in Arizona the power to levy a sales tax—but only if the voters approved it. To Maricopa County alone was reserved the capability to impose a sales tax without the affirming votes of the electorate.

Again, this was not to say that the politicians of Maricopa County couldn't put the tax to a vote.

The standard political line by those who later sought to disavow any responsibility for the Herstam bill, as unbelievable as it should have seemed to any reasonable observer, was that the bill had slipped by before hardly anyone noticed. But could anyone make the same case for the amended bill as well?

As the debate, or nondebate raged, the board scheduled a public hearing, after the negotiations had been completed, and as the board was ready to vote. In fact, the vote was just a ratification of a fait accompli. The supervisors were set in their positions. Nothing was going to change their minds, not after all the public statements. So what was the point of the public hearing?

Public relations. Damage control. Spin-doctoring. Business as usual for a bunch of politicians hoping to turn a troublesome situation to their advantage. Unfortunately, for them, this bunch of politicians, in pretending that this public forum wasn't a sop to an agitated electorate, demonstrated the PR agility of the tobacco industry pretending it had no idea cigarettes cause cancer.

The police were on hand to keep the peace. The questions and comments from the public were often filled with fury, a fury undoubtedly fueled by the obvious inability of anyone to affect a done deal.

The hearing ended, and it would be hard to imagine that anybody on either side judged the encounter a success.

Bruner's vote secured passage of the tax. In March 1994, just weeks later, he resigned from the Board of Supervisors. The primary was set for September, only six months off. That August 12, the baseball players went on strike against the owners, the two sides beating up each other in the quest for a bigger slice of the bloated money pie. The strike did not exactly endear the American people to either the players or the franchises, or to sales taxes to build for the players and the franchises very expensive stadiums, or to the politicians who had passed those sales taxes.

Four years after the fact, Jim Bruner recollected that a local newspaper columnist had anointed him the "eight-hundred-pound gorilla" in the upcoming congressional contest, the leading contender for the Republican nomination. But that was all before the stadium-tax issue exploded in his hands.

One week before the primary, Major League Baseball officially canceled the World Series.

Bruner and his wife had always agreed they would stay in politics as long as it was fun. Sometime during the summer of 1994, as they were lying in bed, Bruner's wife turned to him and said, "It's no longer fun."

Jim Bruner came in third in the primary. His political career was over.

Bruner returned to the thrust of his argument again and again. Argument: The Board of Supervisors routinely contended with a budget that was a couple of billion dollars, and nobody got especially upset when money was spent this way or that.

Answer: In the three years prior to sanctioning the stadium tax, the board had slashed the county budget by more than $50 million, cutting programs and freezing salaries in order not to raise property taxes. So even though the stadium tax was based on sales, not property, the distinction was lost on the electorate.

Argument: A city is more than streets and fire trucks and police cars and other essential services. A city is also parks and libraries and ballparks, those things that make life interesting and rewarding.

Answer: Parks and libraries benefit all the people, or at least all the people who choose to avail themselves of their services and advantages. In fact, not only do the people benefit, but so does the entire society, as libraries help educate the citizenry, and parks and other recreational venues humanize a place and create a friendlier, safer, more unified community. A major league stadium is a business proposition, and one with profits that accrue to a precious few, just like the team. (The lone exception is the Green Bay Packers and storied Lambeau Field, which is owned by the community, through a private nonprofit corporation.)

However, the second part of the answer goes deeper. Even if we accept that professional franchises and stadiums possess intangible value to society, as do libraries and parks, then we must ponder whether we wish to put those values on a very public par with education or community spirit or whatever. We must decide whether we wish to grant professional sports, and those who play the games and those who own the teams, such exalted positions of authority and significance in our country.

Just about all who are familiar with the story readily acknowledge that two people are primarily responsible for bringing Major League Baseball to Arizona: Jerry Colangelo and Jim Bruner.

Jim Bruner is proud of what he accomplished. The sales tax was so successful that it did not require four years to reach the $238-million mark, but only two and a half years. The sales tax was stopped after that. News reports showed that few noticed the difference, and with good reason, as demonstrated by just one example: the price of an iced tall latte at Starbucks in Scottsdale, according to local resident Betsy Sherman, dropped from $2.41 to $2.40.

Regardless, none of that mollified angry taxpayers. Bruner himself is not completely mollified by events. Though Bruner has a banker's restraint—or maybe it's a lawyer's restraint, or a politician's—but he can't stop the bitterness and regret from creeping into his voice here and there.

It is certainly there when he states in no uncertain terms that neither the current mayor nor the one before did anything to help the cause of Arizona baseball. It is also there when he talks about how close he was, how very close, to getting elected to the U.S. House of Representatives.

It is without emotion, either positive or negative, that he mentions that Jerry Colangelo and he were never friends, never developed any kind of personal relationship. He has never been in Colangelo's home, and Colangelo has never been in his. Now that Bruner is out of office and Major League Baseball has arrived, he hasn't spoken to Colangelo in months.

It was always about business and the future. It was always for Phoenix and for Arizona.

And no, Bruner has not personally benefited from helping bring the franchise to town. He has four season tickets, and he pays full price, no discounts. The team did invite him to come in and choose his seats—his one bonus—and so he'll be sitting eight rows behind third base and the Diamondbacks' dugout.

Good seats. Damn good seats. Though it is clear that Jim Bruner would happily, cheerfully, absolutely blissfully, trade those choice seats for a congressional seat in a heartbeat.

Chapter 7

Third Batter Up:
Going Down Swinging

The people were not happy. To be more specific, many of them were not happy, particularly many who lived and worked and paid taxes in Maricopa County.

Art Kaufman was so unhappy he decided to do something about it.

Kaufman had settled in Arizona after World War II, after his discharge from the army in 1945. He did well for himself in the vending-machine business and lives in a small house maybe fifteen minutes from downtown Phoenix and the new stadium.

Kaufman is an exuberant man who speaks so quickly that his words often tumble over one another. Dressed in a Ralph Lauren polo shirt and walking shorts, his face is both suntanned and pink, and the back of his hands are spotted from that same exposure. He squints a lot, even indoors, and is a constant whirl of activity, sorting through papers scattered over his kitchen table, answering a steadily ringing phone.

This was hardly Kaufman's first foray into the public arena. Plaques on his wall attested to his community involvement. An "Award of Appreciation" was dated October 31, 1981, from the Metro-Phoenix Citizens Council "for his Foresight and Persistence in the Organization" of that same group. Another tablet hailed—"For Service and Leadership"—his term as president of the Arizona

Automatic Merchandising Council, 1977–78. He has served as chairman for both the Maricopa County Red Cross and the Phoenix YMCA.

The other side to Kaufman's civic engagement was his fierce opposition to taxes. His own bio stated that he was "a key player in removing Arizona's tax on food, the Phoenix excise tax and a Phoenix one-cent sales tax."

Kachina dolls and carved heads and an assortment of plants filled up the living room and kitchen. More than any furnishing, Kaufman's documents and newspaper clippings and transcripts set the tone for the house, because this was a working house, the headquarters for Citizens Right to Vote and the antitax groundswell.

Some people were angry. Art Kaufman was very, very angry.

With a big smile, Kaufman handed his visitor a T-shirt emblazoned with an antitax stop sign and got right to brass tacks. "I came here when this town had sixty-five thousand people," he said. "I've been here most of my life. I've seen it grow. Last month alone, the state of Arizona created one hundred and thirty-eight thousand new jobs—without any sales tax. So what the hell are a few hundred new jobs with a ballpark? I'm not opposed to baseball. I'm opposed to this tax. The state is growing—we have good weather, we have good work. We have businesses coming in and making things happen."

Kaufman grew up in Pittsburgh in the 1930s. A real baseball fan, he claimed.

"Have you seen Motorola, the plants they have in town? They employ forty thousand people at six plants. Every one of those plants was built with their own money. All those people were hired and they produce revenue. We don't have to give them taxpayer money. What he's got over there is a building put up by the taxpayer."

Kaufman was a fan of Arizona sports, and he put his money, and his attention, where his mouth was. "Many years ago, I had an investment in a major league football team," he said, though that franchise never materialized. Kaufman was also a longtime supporter of another Colangelo venture. "My season-ticket-holder number for the Suns is three hundred eleven. I sit right behind the bench."

Art Kaufman wanted a baseball team for Arizona; he just didn't want to use public money to pay for any part of it. Nor did he appreciate the tactic of the striker bill, readily providing his own spin on why such a maneuver was employed: "A stadium district does not actually come under our constitution. Our constitution says that if you have any governmental entity that passes a bill, you can apply as citizens for a referendum to stop that until there's a vote. Or you can have an initiative against a government. But what they did was create a stadium district which would be made up of the Board of Supervisors of Maricopa County."

In other words, by creating a special stadium district, which was not subject to the rules of referenda and initiatives, the rules of voter participation in the legislative process, the politicians deliberately circumvented the electorate and its opportunity to vote.

Kaufman noted that Jane Hull was the Arizona legislature's influential Speaker of the House during the striker bill affair and supported its passage. Before Hull ascended to the gubernatorial spot upon the forced resignation of corrupt Fife Symington, she had left the legislature to become the Arizona secretary of state. The job had a fancy title but few serious responsibilities. The secretary was more a glorified clerk than anything else, charged with overseeing the paper apparatus of electioneering. Jane Hull's seemingly innocuous post would soon have grave significance for Kaufman.

Kaufman had swung into action, determined to rally the populace and stop the tax. His strategy was straightforward: collect enough signatures to get on the ballot and force the government to allow the people to vote, up or down, yea or nay, on the stadium tax. To vote again, actually, since the people had turned down the idea of providing tax money before, the action that had triggered the striker bill.

Kaufman understood something about the bureaucratic technicalities of electioneering. He wanted to keep the election a county matter, not a statewide issue, because sticking to the smaller venue would mean he would need to gather together fewer signatures on his petitions to compel a vote. Besides, it only seemed right, as only Maricopa County was going to have to pony up the bill for the tax and the stadium.

However, Kaufman ran into the first of many obstacles in the form of the county attorney, Rick Romley, when he went in search of an official number for a petition drive. In Kaufman's retelling, the county attorney's explanation sounds like the setup for an old comedy routine, minus the punch line. "And Romley said, 'I can't give it to you because there's nothing in the constitution that says you can get a number from a secretary of a special district. You can get a number from a secretary of a county, you can get a number from a secretary of a city clerk, you can get a number from the secretary of state, but you can't get anything from a special district.' So they formed a special district to circumvent the law!"

If Romley had sanctioned the county petition, Kaufman would have had to round up sixty-seven thousand of his fellow Arizonans to sign on the dotted line to accomplish his aim. But Romley's action put a finish to that. "Romley was part of the county philosophy," Kaufman said, "and the county wanted that stadium. He could have ruled the other way, he could have argued the bill was unconstitutional. But he didn't do that, in no uncertain terms."

A county vote was out and the state was in, and the bar had been raised to 112,961 signatures. "And so what they did," averred Kaufman, "they made it tough for us."

Tough and expensive, because petition drives were not cheap to organize and run. Nonetheless, Kaufman and his friends and allies managed to get 131,000 signatures. That might have been the end of the story, a victory for the army of populism, but of course it wasn't. "We had more than enough," Kaufman said, "but they managed, through the clerk of election of the county, to throw out enough of our signatures, as did the secretary of state, that we didn't get on the ballot."

Now it started getting really interesting, as Kaufman and his group tussled back and forth with the bureaucracy on the legitimacy of the signatures. According to Kaufman, county elections officials (employed by the Board of Supervisors), violated something called the "Arizona random check procedure" and also counted numerous invalidated signatures twice. Perhaps most damaging of all, a large bloc of signatures was tossed out because a circulator—the person delegated to manage some of the petitions—had changed his residence.

This seemed to be a flat-out incorrect interpretation of the law, and Kaufman had a legal precedent to back him up.

"In a case in Cochise County," Kaufman said, "this wasn't our case—the circulator moved, and the state supreme court ruled that the circulator can move, as long as he remains a registered voter."

This was important, this was key, because Kaufman and Citizens Right to Vote had lost eight thousand signatures because of a circulator problem. "So I took those eight thousand signatures back to Jane Hull, the secretary of state," Kaufman said. Hull might not have had a lot of power on a lot of state issues, but she was just about the final authority in this affair.

"She said, 'I'm sorry, Art, go to court.'" But Art and his group had run out of money, and they had run out of pro bono lawyers. In addition, as Hull was well aware, the clock was running out on filing the petition, and Kaufman might miss the deadline if he had to find a lawyer who would take his appeal to an Arizona court for relief.

Jane Hull wasn't always so strict about enforcing the exact letter of the law. Not at all.

"She's the one who got Skip Hayworth on the ballot when he was six days late in filing and the original filing was a forgery," said Kaufman.

Ah, J. D. "Skip" Hayworth. Sportscaster turned congressman. His bid for a second term hit a snag when he forgot to sign the papers required to get on the ballot and flew off to Washington. Two of his aides back in Arizona, realizing the dilemma at the last moment, took it upon themselves to forge Hayworth's signature and hand in the affidavit.

The forgery was discovered and Hayworth refiled. Both the state attorney general and the county attorney investigated, and the two aides confessed and were fired. Hayworth said he was shocked and outraged and had nothing to do with it; the court system whipped into gear and the aides were quickly fined and placed on probation by the court.

That was the end of the affair, at least from the standpoint of Arizona officialdom, who, from the county attorney to the state attorney general to the Arizona secretary of state, were, it must be noted, all members of the Republican Party, same as Hayworth. Thus, even though he had missed the deadline, his refiling was accepted. All this occurred not long after Kaufman and his constituency were blown out of the water, courtesy of the politicians.

"She put him on the ballot and said, 'Well, he's going to sue us and he's going to win.' How the hell did she know what he was going to do? Or that he would win? She could have said the same thing about our group. The end result was, she didn't put us on the ballot, and the people didn't get a chance to vote. Right now, the FBI has the case, but I don't think they're going to do anything about it. We thought it was election fraud."

The FBI, historically as political an outfit as a law enforcement agency can possibly be, apparently wasn't interested.

Kaufman made it to Maricopa County's superior court, armed with binders stuffed with exhibits and evidence and facts and figures, but the judge never considered any of them. Instead, she threw out Kaufman's case because he was ostensibly one day late in filing his suit. As with virtually every other move in this political game, that allegation was seriously in doubt. A complainant had ten days to file, and Kaufman had filed in eleven days—but only if the court included holidays and weekends. That manner of counting seemed patently unreasonable, given that Kaufman and his supporters had to use the county computers to check the numbers, and the county computers were not available on holidays and weekends. Thus, how could anyone reasonably count those off-days?

But then again, who knew if sweet reason was the controlling principle here. Kaufman battled on, winning some and losing more—and he never had a chance.

"One hundred thirty-one thousand signatures means maybe a million people would have voted for it," mused Art Kaufman. "That's a lot of people to disregard."

So that was Kaufman's experience with the Arizona political process. Obviously, Kaufman recognized that none of this was Jerry Colangelo's doing.

Which is not to say that Kaufman didn't have his problems with the sports magnate: "He's a first-class operator, and as far as a businessman, I respect him highly. I respect what he's done."

On the other hand . . .

"If Jerry Colangelo is the public-spirited citizen he says he is, he wouldn't allow this kind of tax. Because who are you taxing? You're taxing the average Maricopa County family. Well, for his tax, he says it's only twenty-five dollars a year per person. Well, that doesn't sound like much, but in the four years it will take to build this thing, that amounts to four hundred dollars per family."

Actually, since the tax was in force a year and half short of four years, perhaps the cost was only $250 per family—or perhaps the actual amount was something else again. No one really knew.

The point was, it did cost *something*, and that something, even the extra penny on that Starbucks latte, grated on Kaufman and many others. Kaufman's attitude toward Colangelo veered between the admiration already expressed, and a feeling that Colangelo couldn't be trusted. So many funny deals were in the works that it was rational not to trust *somebody*—the problem was that Colangelo wasn't necessarily the person who deserved that suspicion. What did Kaufman mean when he said Colangelo shouldn't have "allowed" the tax? Jerry Colangelo was neither an elected official nor a judge. When did he gain legislative power? Besides, it was no secret that Colangelo wasn't involved in baseball in any form when the legislature created the mechanism to fund the stadium, when the legislature made sure that the public would be shut out of the process.

That was hardly the end of the dubious deals. The twenty-two acres selected as the site for the stadium had been private property before the county took the area through condemnation. Three landowners subsequently sued, arguing that the stadium agreement was nothing less than a gift to the Diamondbacks, because the rental fee that the franchise was going to pay the county was less than market value. In other words, this was a sweetheart deal between Maricopa County and the DBs, and a sweetheart deal provided no legal justification to condemn the land, because it did not benefit the public interest. Article nine, section seven, of the Arizona Constitution did not mince words: "Neither the state, nor any county, city . . . [will] make any donation or grant, by subsidy or otherwise, to any individual, association, or corporation . . ." So on and so forth, the message being that any contribution or bequest of public money for private purposes was illegal.

That wasn't the only possible problem with the arrangement. The law that established the Maricopa County stadium district specifically prohibited, as per Chris Herstam's desire for a baseball-dedicated facility, the construction of a stadium that would be "used for football games of the National Football League." However, granting a corporation "any special or exclusive privileges, immunities, or franchises" also violated the Arizona Constitution.

Article nine demanded further consideration when it stated, "All taxes shall be uniform upon the same class of property within the territorial limits of the authority levying the tax, and shall be levied and collected for public purposes only." That, too, didn't necessarily sound as if the legislature or the county could keep the NFL from sending a team into the stadium and creating more revenue for the county treasury.

All in all, a lot of potential problems loomed, especially for a stadium in the midst of construction. The NFL exclusion was the lesser of the two constitutional questions; Herstam's reasoning was sound, both in baseball and economic terms, guaranteeing the most attractive and efficient venue. The condemnation issue was another matter, holding out the threat of a real problem. But then—poof!— the problem vanished when the Arizona Supreme Court declined, without comment, to review the two-to-one decision by the Arizona Court of Appeals that pronounced the condemnation constitutional.

Oh, well. Next.

The next was, as the saying goes, a doozy. The city of Phoenix decided, in the infinite wisdom of its leaders, that a new parking garage was needed downtown. Not only downtown, but right across from the stadium. Not an unreasonable idea at first sight; after all, the day would soon arrive when forty to fifty thousand people headed to the ballpark and, given the lack of public transportation, would all be coming in their cars. So why not a new garage?

This was why: Proposition 200, passed in 1989, required a public vote on any sports or entertainment-related projects that would cost $3 million or more.

The law really could be a nuisance.

Never mind, though—Arizona politicians were hardly the first in their profession to discover that when the law or the voters or the constitution got in the way, sometimes the easiest thing to do was to ignore them and go ahead anyway.

And that's what the city of Phoenix did. Officially, the mayor and the city council and the city bureaucracy suddenly realized that the Science Center and the Symphony Hall and the Civic Plaza were about to be overrun by visitors, and the only solution was—once again—to condemn a stretch of land. This time the victim was the Greyhound bus terminal. This held a definite irony, as a recent trip to the Science Center demonstrated. On this particular day, a typical morning in the middle of the school week, the center was filled with kids, hundreds of kids. This was good, because children were the reason for the center, all partaking in the terrific interactive learning experience that the facility offers. The irony was that all these students were brought to the center by—what else?—*bus,* and the city demolished a *bus* station to make more parking spaces.

Seven stories tall, the garage was budgeted at a whooping $43 million. With 2,700 spaces, the cost per space was some $15,930. A nearby garage with almost 1,500 spots had cost $5,260 per to build. Even better, a public-private partnership was putting up its own garage just around the corner for a measly $5 million for 1,097 spaces. Another one thousand spaces would be housed in a new structure just to the southeast of the stadium, for an even more miserly $3.5 million. (Incidentally, and not too surprisingly, Eddie Lynch had a hand in that last garage deal.)

Then again, not every garage had an overpass to the Science Center and landscaping and an expensive facade.

On the other hand, a study done in January 1995 by an outside firm and commissioned by the city concluded that the massive garage was not needed—unless it was built expressly for baseball. A second version appeared a month later, juggling the figures on traffic and population growth, but still arriving at the same verdict. A month after that, the firm tried again, but ended up with the judgment that it would be "difficult to justify" a parking lot of more than five to six hundred spaces—without baseball.

After three tries, the firm, or whoever rewrote the report this time, got it right and suddenly realized that the structure under construction was, at the very least, *three hundred spaces short* of the anticipated pressing demand.

This was too much. The entire affair was too much. Rich Dozer, the Diamondbacks' president, recalled a meeting with city officials in which he explained that the team, the team that was supposed to be the unspoken beneficiary of this edifice, didn't think the garage made sense. Dozer's opinion evidently didn't make much of an impact.

As might be expected, this was just one more situation that drove Art Kaufman crazy. In fact, he once took full advantage of an encounter with Mayor Rimsza to ask His Honor exactly why the city wanted the garage.

" 'Well,' he said, 'we're not going to turn away any business, and if we can make money, we will.' I said, 'Are you going to keep baseball out?' And he said, 'Hell no.' "

Maybe it happened exactly that way, maybe it didn't. What absolutely did happen was that the ground was leveled and the building began.

Members of the local media reported these stories, and in detail. It didn't make a difference. Perhaps the press didn't push hard enough; there was a difference between reporting and pursuing, pursuing until every rock was turned over, pursuing until the public and the leading institutions in town and even the government had to take notice.

Maybe it had nothing to do with the media. Maybe the garage was backed by too many of the right people, and that was that, and everybody recognized it and so nothing was done to try to stop it— really try to really stop it.

For better or worse, rightly or wrongly, Art Kaufman tried. He tried to stop everything, dead in its tracks. More than anything, he tried to stop the stadium tax. When that failed, he tried another tactic; if he couldn't stop the tax, then he would attempt to put a 20 percent surcharge on each Diamondback ticket and on other franchise revenues. The money would be used to repay Maricopa County for the original quarter-cent sales tax and to help maintain the stadium. After that, the remaining funds would be doled out among schools and charities. One of Kaufman's ideas was to build a shelter for the homeless the size of the right-field section of the ballpark.

By this time, however, Kaufman faced a fundamental problem. The stadium was racing to completion, and every day it looked bigger and more beautiful. As the stadium became a more tangible structure, gaining its retractable roof and swimming pool and picnic area and Cooperstown West, it also served to remind and further excite the people of Phoenix and Arizona that before long that fabulous ballpark would be filled with fans, with *them*, partaking in the Diamondbacks' inaugural season.

The tax was over and done, and it apparently hadn't hurt anyone, and certainly not anyone with any clout or visibility, and what was left behind was Major League Baseball and a downtown well along the path to rehabilitation and rejuvenation.

The people were happy. To be more specific, many of them were happy, including many who lived and worked and paid taxes in Maricopa County.

Boyd Orth was happy, too. He had grown up in a city with no home team to root for, and now Phoenix had one. It was good for business, good for the community, good for the future. Boyd still didn't like the machinations employed to put the tax in place, and the citizens who had been angry about the tax were, in the main, still angry. But that anger was frequently diffused, or perhaps overlaid, by, on one hand, the deep longing of deprived baseball fans waiting to cheer the action in person, and, on the other, by the ceaseless boosterism pushed upon the public by a relentless local media.

For his part, Boyd was more interested in the promise of Phoenix's tomorrow than in any problematic issues that were neither problems nor issues any longer. Boyd Orth was a realist, and he had settled on the reality that baseball would soon be here, and baseball looked as if it was going to be a tremendous success.

The Citizens Right to Vote committee was replaced by Have Our Money Returned, H.O.M.R., enunciated "homer." Whatever he called his group, Kaufman remained the chairman, and he needed another 112,961 signatures, starting from scratch.

Art Kaufman was raring to go.

Chapter 8

Batting Cleanup

Jerry Colangelo might be the most powerful man in Arizona. There's probably not—there's absolutely not—another owner of a sports team in any other city in any other state in the Union about whom that claim could be made.

But it might well be true in the case of Jerry Colangelo.

Now that's not because Arizona is some backward bog of a banana republic. Not at all. The Grand Canyon State is a bustling beehive of upward mobility and modernity, people and corporations rushing in to partake in the glorious economy and resplendent weather—or maybe that's the resplendent economy and glorious weather.

Of course, as has previously been noted, the local government has been something of a haven for the corrupt and incompetent, and the local media have been the house organ for the rich and powerful and, not incidentally, the banal.

More than anything, Arizona is a state where business gets done, which hardly distinguishes it from every other state. And sports is hardly the biggest business in Arizona, just as it's not the biggest business in New York or California or Texas.

But still, Jerry Colangelo has achieved what his fellow basketball and baseball and football owners have not achieved anywhere else. He has gained the foremost position in the whole desert state, number one, the citizen most likely to get his way, the Arizonan most likely to lead.

The Arizona Diamondbacks have a mission statement. Many teams and corporations have mission statements. They are invariably heartfelt, sincere, and good. And so is the Diamondbacks':

"The Arizona Diamondbacks' mission is to establish a winning tradition that embodies the genuine spirit of baseball; an organization to which all Arizonans will point with pride, which conducts its business with integrity and community responsibility; so that Arizona's children will grow up knowing the rich tradition that has made baseball America's national pastime."

Many teams and corporations have mission statements, with decent, even noble aims, probably not all that dissimilar from the DBs'. The difference between all those mission statements and the Diamondbacks' could be that the Diamondbacks—and the Diamondbacks, particularly in this instance, were truly a reflection of Jerry Colangelo's values—might just actually mean theirs.

Today, Jerry Colangelo occupies a handsome office on the fourth floor of the America West Arena, where he is surrounded by plaques and photos and autographed sports memorabilia. He looks out upon a fabulous view of downtown Phoenix from behind his walnut desk and leather chair. Everything is just so, even the various blinds participating to create the proper environment, independently and constantly shifting in automatic, regulating response to changes in the almost ever-present sun.

Today, it is hard to imagine that anything could ever be out of place or out of control—out of Jerry's control. Today, it is hard to imagine that there is not, that there was not, an inevitability to Colangelo's success and arrival at this place and moment.

It might be hard to imagine, seated in this office, surrounded by these trophies of triumph, but it would be an utterly mistaken impression.

Horatio Alger has nothing on Jerry Colangelo. During one of his innumerable speaking occasions, Colangelo offered a quick description of his origins: "I grew up on the south side of Chicago in the 1940s and '50s in an area called Chicago Heights. The people there labored in the steel mills and in the factories. They were honest, hardworking people who took pride in their work and in their heritage. My family lived in the Italian neighborhood everybody called Hungry Hill. When you talked about your family on 'the Hill,' you were talking about the whole neighborhood. People respected one another. They took care of their own."

Despite that rather benignly romanticized portrait of the old neighborhood, Colangelo declined, as was his prerogative, to mention that his family was so poor that Jerry went to work before the age of ten delivering newspapers twice a day, and his father was so abusive that Jerry, as a teenager, literally threw him out of the house to protect his mother.

Jerry was a good athlete, so good in fact that he was offered seven professional baseball contracts and sixty-six college basketball scholarships. The left-handed pitcher deferred in favor of the point guard, and Colangelo set off for the University of Kansas to join Wilt Chamberlain's team. However, when Chamberlain left school in 1958 to play with the Harlem Globetrotters, Colangelo returned home, transferring to the University of Illinois. He captained the basketball squad, made the all–Big Ten team, married his girlfriend, Joan, and hoped for a chance to play in the NBA.

That chance never materialized as Jerry went undrafted. Instead, Colangelo entered into business with a friend, opening a shop that rented and sold formal wear, later expanding into dry cleaning.

Colangelo's destiny was not to be in tuxedos, for the business was never much more than a break-even proposition. To supplement his meager income, an income that had to support his wife, mother, and first child, Colangelo played semipro basketball at night for $50 a game.

Three years after graduating from college, Jerry was going nowhere fast, and he knew it. At this auspicious moment, he found the business card of Dick Klein in his jacket pocket, given to him some time ago by his father-in-law.

Dick Klein owned an incentive merchandising firm, which assisted companies in putting together programs to help sell those companies' products. "I was making gift packages for big companies like Ford," Klein said, "and I needed a bright kid."

Klein hired Colangelo the day they met. Jerry's new salary instantly doubled his take-home pay, and that didn't include the prospect of potentially sizable commissions.

But what was good was about to get better. Jerry accompanied his new boss on a business trip to learn the ropes. The pair were driving somewhere along Route 41 in Indiana when Klein told his young employee about his dream of bringing a National Basketball Association franchise to Chicago.

Then and there, Jerry jumped into the mix, ready to assist in any way possible. So while he dove into the business, peddling those gift packages, Colangelo also attended meetings with bankers and prospective investors.

Before long, Klein had lined up an impressive list of investors for the team, including Lamar Hunt, the owner of the NFL's Kansas City Chiefs, Harold Meyer of the Oscar Meyer Company, and Elmer Rich, whose family owned Simoniz Wax.

"I never set my sights on making all this happen," Colangelo told one newspaper. "I just take the next thing that needs to be done."

He told another, "I had no grand illusion, no grand design. I'm just someone who's always looking forward."

The NBA had told Klein that the new franchise would cost $750,000. However, when Dick went to New York to close the deal, the price tag had suddenly escalated to $1.25 million. (Some three decades later, Colangelo would find history repeating itself, though in substantially exaggerated form, as he went down to the wire in his negotiations with Major League Baseball.)

In any event, Klein anted up, and the Windy City was the proud site of the NBA's tenth franchise. Klein and Colangelo worked together to pick a name and design a logo, and the Bulls were born.

Colangelo worked both the business and basketball sides of the team, functioning as head of marketing and chief scout. The year was 1966 and he was twenty-six years old.

Though it might seem hard for many to believe today, with the NBA so extraordinarily successful, the team was no sure thing. In fact, several franchises had already failed in Chicago.

Management had to be creative and conservative, exciting the city, attracting the consumer, selling those tickets with imagination and verve, while squeezing the most out of every nickel. The Bulls had just a handful of employees, which befitted a team, as previously noted, with a payroll of $180,000 for twelve players.

These days, that kind of money wouldn't pay the wages of the Chicago Bulls for *one game*. Never mind that—that kind of money would be exhausted, finished, gone, after paying for Michael Jordan's services for *one half of one game*.

The Bills grossed $400,000 the first year. One hundred thousand dollars of that total came from the club's television contract. On the court, the team won thirty-three games and lost forty-eight. Tickets cost two, three, or four dollars.

The league expanded again the very next year. Seattle and San Diego were the eleventh and twelfth franchises.

Colangelo received a call from the Seattle owner, offering him the number two position with the club. Jerry was flattered but not interested. He was happy with the Bulls and incredibly busy, traveling all over the country on his scouting forays. In that bygone era, the Bulls were one of the few teams who did their own scouting—most teams simply relied on basketball magazines for player evaluations.

The NBA expanded again the following year, adding Phoenix and Milwaukee. Colangelo was quite familiar with Milwaukee, but Phoenix was another story.

"Why," he wondered, "would anyone put a team in the middle of the desert?"

Colangelo's reputation had only gained more luster with another year in pro basketball under his belt, and Milwaukee offered him its general manager's job. Colangelo was enthused about the club's prospects, especially because Al McGuire, the successful head coach at Marquette University, had been tapped for the same position with the new team.

Colangelo was in Denver on a scouting trip, watching, in his words, "a seven-foot stiff stumble around the court," when he fielded a call from Dick Bloch. Bloch was a Tucson investment banker living in Beverly Hills and was heading up the group that owned the Phoenix franchise. The GM post was open, and Bloch wanted Colangelo.

Jerry was willing to fly to Beverly Hills to talk. Why not? It never hurt to talk. Talk was cheap. However, matters did not get off to a propitious start.

"The first thing I discovered was that they had already picked a coach," Colangelo recalled. "And the coach's wife was going to keep the club's books. I told Bloch that wouldn't work. More to the point, I wasn't interested and headed home to Chicago."

By the time Colangelo had landed at O'Hare Airport, the deal had changed. The coach and his wife were out, and Bloch asked Colangelo to fly to Phoenix and meet with the other investors.

Colangelo flew to Phoenix, far from convinced any of this made a whole lot of sense, at least for him.

"My skepticism changed a bit when I got off the plane in Arizona," Jerry remembered. "It was winter in Chicago and twenty degrees below zero when I left town. When I arrived in Phoenix, the sun was shining and it was seventy degrees."

Chalk up one for the desert.

Jerry and the investors didn't waste much time. Colangelo asked for a three-year contract starting at $20,000 the first year and rising to $25,000 for the third.

"At the time," Colangelo said, "I knew that GMs were earning ten to twelve thousand, so I was asking for a lot."

The owners countered with a two-year contract at $22,500 per year.

Colangelo replied that he wasn't sure, that he had to return to Chicago and think about.

He also wondered if he could use the phone for a moment.

"My wife answered," Colangelo said. "I told her to pack the bags and our three kids. I told her we were moving to Phoenix."

Once again, Colangelo hadn't planned this, hadn't even imagined that a nonexistent basketball team in the desert would prove the avenue to his next opportunity. But there it was, and Colangelo hadn't hesitated to grab hold.

"He came to Phoenix in 1968 with six suitcases, three kids, no car, no furniture and less than $1,000 in his pocket." That was from *USA Today,* January 22, 1996. It was one of those stories from the Colangelo chronicles that made all the newspaper profiles—and actually, the precise amount was $800. Regardless, Jerry Colangelo profiles were becoming all the more frequent as the man's fame spread near and far. His life had the sort of straightforwardly classic tempo—rags to riches, abrupt shifts of fortune, hard work and honesty overcoming adversity—that was tailor-made for the press.

Phoenix was Jerry's chance to run the whole show, his way. The absentee owners advanced Colangelo $10,000 to get the club started. The Suns opened their doors in 1968 with five employees, including Colangelo, operating out of a storage room converted into an office.

"My primary challenge was to field a team and get people to fill the 12,471 seats of the Veterans Memorial Coliseum," Colangelo said. "The citizens of Phoenix had not stormed city hall demanding their own professional basketball team. The investors had taken it upon themselves to bring the team to the Valley of the Sun. I had to go out and convince the public that the Suns were worth watching, were worth leaving home and driving downtown and spending good money on tickets."

Colangelo's mantra was simple and direct: "This city doesn't owe us anything. We have to earn its support."

"I knocked on every door in town," Colangelo said, "selling every company and firm and industry on the virtues of doing business courtside. I pulled every salesman's trick I knew to move those tickets."

From the beginning, Jerry showed his readiness to act and act fast for the good of his franchise. He had convinced his old friend John Kerr to leave Chicago and come down to Phoenix to coach the team. Midway through the club's second losing season, Colangelo decided that Kerr wasn't the right man for the job.

"I knew what I had to do. Regardless of our relationship, the franchise—meaning the investors' money, the jobs of my employees, the security of my family—was my responsibility, and I had to do my best to protect and promote the Phoenix Suns."

Colangelo fired Kerr and assumed the coaching duties for the rest of the season. The team posted a 24-20 record during his tenure and actually made the playoffs. Down 3–1 to a Los Angeles Lakers team that included Jerry West, Wilt Chamberlain, and Elgin Baylor, the Suns fought back to a 3–3 tie, finally going down in the seventh game.

"I never begrudged Jerry for what he did," John Kerr, now a TV commentator for the Bulls, told *Hearst* magazine. "My dad died when I was three, and I felt like we had a lot in common. We were survivors."

Jerry stepped in as coach one more time, during the 1972–73 season. He posted a 35-40 mark this time out; added together, his complete professional coaching record stood at 59-60.

The Phoenix Suns slowly became an accepted and integral part of the community. Over the next seventeen years, the team posted a .522 winning percentage.

Life was good for Jerry Colangelo. He was a successful entrepreneur, a respected civic leader, an NBA power, a happy family man.

Of course, the situation was not absolutely perfect. Even though Colangelo ran every aspect of the franchise, top to bottom, even though he essentially functioned as an owner, he was not an owner but an employee. He wanted more. He wanted to buy the team, but the Beverly Hills group wasn't interested.

But then arose a situation that changed everything for Jerry Colangelo yet again. However, this situation, this opportunity, was different from his previous opportunities in that it began disastrously for everyone associated with the Suns, including the team's general manager. Still, when the dust cleared, it ended up as the key to Colangelo's achieving his next goal.

At the end of the 1986–87 season, three current and two former Suns players were arrested on drug charges. The political and media fallout was astounding, as an excitable county attorney and overzealous Phoenix police chief pursued gambling and drug conspiracies that never materialized, though several players did enter drug rehab.

"It was a witch-hunt," Colangelo later told the *Contra Costa Times*.

More than a decade later, it is hard to imagine how quickly the franchise abruptly foundered, and how close the Phoenix Suns came to becoming the Columbus (Ohio) Suns, or some other city's NBA prize.

But it was close indeed.

The Phoenix Suns were publicly ridiculed with the nickname Phoenix House, a reference to the drug rehabilitation center. Colangelo was booed at Suns games. Rumors had him going to another team, in another city.

Regardless, all was not lost. The bluster slowly subsided, the furious rhetoric gave way to more prosaic facts, and because of miscues and missteps the case never went to trial.

Nonetheless, the bloom was off the rose for the team's owners. Bloch and his partners were ready to sell and gave their general manager first crack at raising the money required to buy them out.

Jerry Colangelo didn't have much time. Groups representing San Diego and Columbus were waiting in the wings, eager and ready, bids in hand—and the NBA was seriously considering relocating the club.

Colangelo gathered his friends and allies and went to work.

"This was it," Colangelo said. "This was my chance to step up and not only run the team but own it."

In six weeks, Colangelo called every person and business with a dollar in the cookie jar and raised $44.5 million.

"Of course," he said, "it wasn't as simple as that. I actually raised $20 million in equity and had to borrow the rest from banks in Phoenix. The team had no collateral to offer the lenders, and neither did I. Still, the banks gave me the money because, simply put, they trusted me and believed in my vision and my competence. I had earned their respect and trust through my hard work in the community. I had paid my dues in sweat, and sweat equity was my only collateral."

Actually, Colangelo's sweat equity specifically translated into 1 percent of the partnership—paid for with borrowed money—and that amount would rise only after his partners' investment was returned.

Cut it any which way, the result was the same—Jerry Colangelo had his team.

Now that he was in charge—really, completely, in charge—changes came fast and furious. Colangelo wanted a new basketball arena, and Terry Goddard, then the Phoenix mayor, wanted it downtown. Colangelo helped persuade the city council to pass a hotel and rental-car tax to pay for almost half the construction of a new $110-million basketball arena in downtown Phoenix, a downtown that was in dire need of rejuvenation.

America West Airlines bought the naming rights, and when the arena opened in 1992, its total sold signage was already second in the entire NBA. The place was beautiful, intimate, and still seated 19,023 unobstructed fans. The *Boston Globe*, noting that "many people feel [America West Arena] is the finest indoor sports facility in America," then briefly considered Boston's own basketball arena, the arena where the beloved Celtics played, deciding, "compared to this, the FleetCenter is almost an embarrassment."

The city owned the arena, but the Suns acted as both the landlords and tenants. Colangelo devised a formula to divide the profits between the public and private sectors, a formula, he claimed, that has served as a model for other professional franchises.

In short, concessions and parking were split 60 to 40 percent between the city and the Suns. The Suns received $26 million over thirty years from America West Airlines for the right to name the arena, as well as suite revenue. The city was to be paid an annual rent, beginning at $500,000 and increasing 3 percent each year. Ticket revenues from the Suns and other attractions were the sole property of the team.

It is important to understand how unusual this was: this was the first financing of an arena done "on the come," with promises of future revenue streams to pay for the building costs.

Colangelo insisted that the annual gross revenues be allocated in the following order: (1) ensuring that the arena is operating in the best manner possible; (2) servicing the club's debt; (3) rent to the city; (4) building refurbishing account; (5) marketing fee due to Suns.

The original deal stated the city's investment in the arena was to be paid back in seven years. America West Arena was extremely profitable from the start, and on Colangelo's initiative, he renegotiated with Phoenix to increase the payments to the city and ensure that its investment was repaid even more rapidly.

The marketing prowess of Colangelo and his organization maximized the arena's and the team's various revenue streams, generating tremendous profits. This accomplishment was rendered all the more notable when one recognized that, unlike New York City, for instance, which incorporated the communities of three states into its megalopolis, when one left the water-fed Valley of the Sun, one plunged into the water-starved, semiarid desert, where human beings gave way to Gila monsters, scorpions, and prairie dogs, none of whom watched, let alone owned, TVs. This meant that Phoenix had no suburbs, and no suburban TV sets, and thus the sixth-largest city plunged to only the seventeenth-largest television market.

Colangelo's original lone percentage point would rise to a much healthier 18 percent. His investors had also profited handsomely. An investment of $1 million in 1987 was returned in four years, after paying 8.5 percent interest annually, and that $1-million piece of the team was now worth an impressive $6 million.

Forbes magazine profiled Jerry Colangelo in its December 19, 1994, issue, under the headline, "It's All in the Packaging." The business periodical explored how Colangelo had succeeded far beyond anyone's reasonable expectations, ascribing much of the franchise's singular prosperity to the management of the arena:

"In a move catching on among other team owners, Colangelo set up arena soccer, tennis and football teams to generate revenue during Phoenix's sweltering off-season and tap a lower-brow audience. The Arizona Rattlers won the arena football championship last year and sold out every game."

Forbes was referring to the Arizona Rattlers—of the Arena Football League—which Colangelo not only showcased in his arena but also owned. Other teams that can now be included on the America West Arena playbill (post–*Forbes* article) are the Phoenix Mercury (another Colangelo property) of the Women's National Basketball Association, and the Phoenix Coyotes, of the National Hockey League, of which Colangelo was part-owner and helped bring to Arizona.

Back to *Forbes:* "The Suns may be most effective in packaging marketing tools to attract and retain sponsors. Corpus Christi, Tex.–based Whataburger, for example, has a ten-year deal that includes radio and TV ads, signs and exclusive burger concessions in the arena. The exposure has boosted local sales significantly. When Coca-Cola put former Suns' stars on six-pack cartons in Phoenix, it quickly sold all 400,000.

"Says Colangelo: 'We don't say, "We're your team. Support us." We say, "We'll put together packages to increase traffic in your stores, including team appearances, displays and schedules. It's our ability to market that's enabled us to take a small market and put ourselves at the top."

" 'If you take all the aspects of the Suns' operations together . . . they are in the 99th-plus percentile in diversification into sports,' says NBA Commissioner David Stern. 'Jerry Colangelo's lesson is that meticulous attention to every aspect of a franchise's operations, venue and place in the community yields success.' "

Events scheduled for January 14 through 24, 1998, demonstrated the typical, continual churning of varied activity at the arena: January 14, the Phoenix Coyotes faced off against the Florida Panthers; January 15, the Discover Stars on Ice production featured Olympic medalists; January 16, the Suns played the Orlando Magic; January 17, the Harlem Globetrotters performed their unique brand of basketball; January 18, the Suns took on the Miami Heat; January 19, the Martin Luther King Benefit Concert starred the Isley Brothers and the O'Jays; January 20, the arena was dark; January 21, the Suns played the Lakers; January 22, a show entitled Scotland the Brave highlighted authentic Scottish music as performed by a one-hundred-member ensemble, as well as the Regiment Band of the Scots Guards and the Pipes and Drums of the Black Watch; January 23, the Suns were on the court against the Denver Nuggets; January 24, the Coyotes skated against the Edmonton Oilers.

Add all those galas and games together, and close to 2 million people walk through the arena's doors to attend one or another event every year.

Colangelo also diversified off the court, with a health club, advertising firm, radio and TV production company, sports merchandise stores, not to mention rental cars and real estate, and undoubtedly other ventures as well.

As the Suns' fortunes rose, so did Colangelo's standing in the community. He has probably won every local award available, whether given by business or charity, been named Most Influential in the Valley five years in a row by the *Arizona Business Journal,* and has served on too many good-deed committees to count, including the Phoenix Art Museum, the Greater Phoenix Community Alliance, the Phoenix Suns Charities, the Valley Big Brothers, and the Christian Businessmen's Club.

That last mention is of special notice, because Colangelo, raised Roman Catholic, has been a born-again Christian since his mid-twenties. He was led to his newfound faith by Joan, even before he joined Dick Klein and commenced his sports career. Just as Colangelo's conversion predates his involvement in sports, so he proclaims his religious beliefs far more important to him than his business interests.

In fact, when asked, Jerry Colangelo rates his faith the paramount factor in his life, his family second, and his work third. And for a man who prides himself on his strong relationship with his wife and four children—and eight grandchildren—as well as his obvious commitment to his teams and venues and all the businesses that have sprung from them, that is saying quite a lot.

Not that these three components of Colangelo's life have always remained separate and distinct from one another. Just as he brought his son Bryan into the business and trained him for a leadership position, so his religious influence, plus his distressing experience with the Phoenix House Suns, led him to consciously rebuild his basketball team around some overtly upstanding citizens. These included Mormon Danny Ainge and born-again Christians Kevin Johnson, A.C. Greene, and coach Paul Westphal.

But back to business—good religious folk notwithstanding, Colangelo traded Greene and fired Westphal when he was unsatisfied with their performances.

And then there was forward Charles Barkley, a legitimate basketball superstar, and an opinionated, difficult, freethinking, fast-living superstar. Barkley might not have fit the new Suns' mold, but he was a great player, acquired in a blockbuster trade.

The Suns came close to the NBA championship more than once during the Barkley years, but never won it all. They lost in six games to the Chicago Bulls in 1993, after winning the third contest in a triple-overtime thriller.

Winning or losing, Colangelo would not tolerate bad behavior. In 1994, when new sex and drug scandals involving several Suns occurred, Colangelo traded away four players. One year later, when during a game Robert Horry threw a towel in the face of Danny Ainge, retired as a player and now the coach, the forward found himself dealt out of town four days later.

Finally, in 1996, after four frequently turbulent, contentious years, Barkley was as unhappy with the Suns as they were with him. A change was needed, and the Suns traded Barkley to Houston, with no love lost between the organization and its former star.

With Barkley gone, the rebuilding of the Suns would begin in earnest. Hand in hand with rebuilding, the Suns were, once and for all, committed to the good-guy approach.

When Danny Manning turned down a seven-year contract worth $35 million from the Atlanta Hawks to sign for $2 million for a one-year deal from the Suns in 1994, many wondered why, including *Forbes* magazine. "This is everything I wanted, except the money," Manning said, whose loyalty was later rewarded with a $40-million, six-year contract in 1995. "I've played around the league, and I've never heard one negative thing about Mr. Colangelo. That's pretty impressive in this cutthroat business."

In 1998, *Sports Illustrated* polled the NBA's executives and agents to rate the best and worst of the front-office bosses. Basketball legend Jerry West, now the vice president of the Los Angeles Lakers, received the most votes in the best category, commended for his "perfect blend of business sense and instincts of an ex-player." Jerry Colangelo tied for second, saluted with the following words: "His word is gold. One of the few."

The strength of Colangelo's personality set the tone for his operation and his corporation, a phenomenon quite familiar to organizations run by charismatic individuals. In politics, for instance, it is not uncommon for a campaign staff to take on the personality of its candidate, often resulting in an exaggerated group attitude and distorted mode of behavior. In former Senate majority leader Bob Dole's case, his presidential campaign staff adopted his sharp edge but missed his equally sharp-edged humor. The same goes for political administrations. Could anyone doubt that Richard Nixon's White House embraced his particular brand of ferocious insecurity, or that Bill Clinton's minions inculcated their boss's unequaled ability to spin shameless opportunism into self-righteous ruthlessness?

A similar sort of situation seemed to be true with Jerry Colangelo's staff. Working for a boss singularly confident and commanding, some of the staff tried to adopt a like manner and emerged as pale imitations of the original. Not as smart, as skillful, or as shrewd, some would be secretive when Colangelo would have been subtle, dismissive when he would have been inclusive, arrogant instead of appreciative.

Perhaps Colangelo's bold, blunt leadership style had permanently intimidated some members of his staff, even high-ranking members, causing the intimidated to sometimes cower and sometimes bully, in the hope of finding just the right mix to ensure their own success.

Maybe the most telling fact about the organization was that an astonishing number were quick to volunteer the fervent proclamation that this was not only the best job they had ever had, but also the last job they ever wanted. While such exemplary loyalty could be viewed as commendable, it could also be remarked that it was a bit strange that such an ambitious bunch would display such poor ambition.

Thus, the organization presented something of a familial feel to the outside world, albeit a family overseen by a dominating father whom no one dared contradict. With this in mind, it was not surprising that two of Colangelo's most aggressive and successful executives were authentic members of his family: son Bryan Colangelo, installed as general manager of the Suns, and son-in-law Scott Brubaker, who headed up the Diamondbacks' sales and marketing.

In the meanwhile, Major League Baseball was shuffling in its own peculiar way toward expansion, arguing and calculating and resisting. Phoenix was in the mix, thanks to a few baseball-loving individuals who were trying to raise the required funds, a legislature that had passed the stadium-tax bill, and the lure of Arizona's phenomenal growth. In the last go-round, when Colorado and Florida won their teams, Colangelo was too busy building his basketball arena to get involved with any other deals. Now, with America West Arena a perpetual juggernaut of events and happenings, and Bryan running the Suns, the old southpaw pitcher from Hungry Hill was ready to take on the world of baseball.

He tapped the Arizona power structure for the money, and the Arizona power structure responded. Viad Corporation, formerly known as Dial, became the largest single investor, with an $18-million stake. An investment group controlled by Phelps Dodge Corporation kicked in $6 million, as did Phoenix Newspapers, America West Airlines, Swift Transporation, Arizona Public Service, Circle K Stores, Five B Investment, Discount Tire, and Globe Corporation, a Scottsdale investment firm. The local banks contributed, too: Bank One was good for $6 million, through its investment corporation, as was Wells Fargo, Bank America, and the Finova Group, a commercial finance company.

The Phoenix Suns Limited Partnership invested in its corporate partner, to the tune of $9 million. Danny Manning, who had turned down that big offer from the Hawks to come to Arizona because of his faith in Colangelo, returned that faith, and some of his basketball salary, with a $6-million capitalization. Other celebrity investors, in addition to Manning and Billy Crystal, included actor Louis Gossett Jr. and singer Glen Campbell.

Eddie Lynch headed a group that chipped in $9.6 million. Sen. John McCain's father-in-law, Jim Hensley, who distributed Anheuser-Busch beer, was part of a group that invested $6 million.

Entrepreneurs and investors outside of Arizona wanted a share of the venture, too. Phil Knight, owner of Nike, invested $6 million. The second-largest investor was a group dominated by Nebraska businessman Dale Jensen, who personally pitched in almost all of his small band's $15.6 million.

Those were some of the limited partners. The general partnership, which ran the franchise's operations, only has a 1 percent share of the team for its $1.75-million investment. Following the formula Colangelo used with the Suns, the general partnership's share could rise to 25 percent once the limited partners' initial investment has been repaid.

Colangelo personally owned 53 percent of the general partnership, of which he operated as the managing general partner. His 18 percent ownership of the Suns meant that he had a nice chunk of the Phoenix Suns' $9-million investment. Between those two groups, Colangelo says he put $2.5 million of his own money into the baseball franchise, a figure that could rise in value to the tens of millions before long.

Before all those profits could come rolling in, Major League Baseball had to award Phoenix the franchise. Colangelo and his partners and lawyers flew to Palm Beach, Florida, in the first week of March 1995 to appear before the expansion committee, which consisted of some the toughest owners in baseball, including Jerry Reinsdorf of the Chicago White Sox and George Steinbrenner of the New York Yankees. It was imperative that Colangelo secure the deal pretty much then and there, because the state bill that promised to fund the stadium would expire if a franchise hadn't been secured by the end of that month.

Everything seemed to be proceeding just fine, right on schedule, for both Phoenix and the other leading contender, Tampa Bay, and some in Colangelo's party were ready to celebrate. The price for the franchise hadn't been exactly set, but it was presumed, as had been discussed during the past few days in Palm Beach, the bill would amount to $120–$125 million. It was a lot, a hell of a lot, and considerably more than the $95 million Colorado and Florida had put up as their entry fees only a few years before.

For months before this March meeting, the franchise fee bandied about had ranged from $115 million to $120 million. Wayne Huizenga, the billionaire owner of the Marlins, pushed to raise the price, asserting that the new clubs were going to have it so good, with their new stadiums and sweetheart leases, that they could well afford to pay more. The other owners weren't too hard to convince, especially since the disastrous strike-shortened 1994 season, resulting in the first cancellation of the World Series since 1904, had caused the teams to lose millions. The owners were more than happy to start making up their shortfall courtesy of their new partners from Phoenix and Tampa Bay.

So the price jumped up another $10 million or so, and the new franchises prepared to swallow hard and pay out. But then Colangelo received a late-night phone call from Jerry Reinsdorf, the owner of both the White Sox and the Chicago Bulls, and also an old friend.

109

Reinsdorf told Colangelo that the committee had decided to raise the expansion fee even higher.

Colangelo was perturbed. Very perturbed. Extremely perturbed. Unable to sleep, he waited until early the next morning to phone Vince Naimoli, Tampa Bay's principal. They met in the hotel coffee shop, and Colangelo filled him in on MLB's machinations. Naimoli was as angry as Colangelo, and both men were so angry that the whole deal was in doubt.

"I don't think I've ever seen Jerry get this upset," Eddie Lynch told reporters assembled that morning in the hotel lobby. "I think he's ready to burst."

Colangelo and Naimoli went their separate ways to plot and plan, and then Naimoli was summoned before the committee. After the owners were through with Tampa Bay, it was Phoenix's turn. The committee pronounced its unease that Colangelo had so many investors in his partnership. The members of the committee owned and controlled their teams by themselves, or with a few trusted, or at least silent, confidants.

Colangelo's response was perhaps uncomfortably appropriate, stating that as long as Major League Baseball kept charging these astonishing admission fees to the Show, the list of qualified individuals would only grow smaller, and the grouping of individual and corporate interested parties would necessarily increase.

When Colangelo left the conference room shortly thereafter, he left without a deal—and the owners were left without their expansion fee.

"I'm optimistic we'll get something done," Bud Selig, acting MLB commissioner and Milwaukee Brewers owner, blandly informed journalists.

Boston Red Sox owner John Harrington dropped the gloss in his comment to the press: "We're at a crossroads."

Rumors in news reports had the fees rising to $150 million, even $175 million.

While some in the Diamondback group despaired, Colangelo spent some time alone on his patio deck, staring out at the ocean. The expansion committee met during that day, then met with Colangelo and Naimoli, and the owners knew that both prospective franchises were too promising and their money too good for the owners to fiddle too long.

On March 9, 1995, the deal was done and announced to a waiting world. The expansion fee was settled at $130 million per new club, plus another $20 million the new franchises agreed to forgo in future television revenue.

Jerry Colangelo returned to Arizona in triumph. But that triumph was about to be tarred by the controversy brewing over the stadium tax.

A poll taken by O'Neill Associates in January 1994 queried valley residents on how they stood on the stadium tax. Fifty-nine percent of the respondents said, given the chance, they would vote against it, 30 percent were in favor, and the rest held the proverbial no opinion.

Of course, where they stood on the tax mattered not a whit, because Arizona's elected officials had seen fit to ensure that those sentiments remained of import solely to pollsters.

An intriguing side point: the results were the same whether the respondent was a Democrat, Republican, or independent.

Colangelo had faced criticism before. The uproar over the Suns' legal entanglements was surely a difficult time. In another instance, when the Suns took many of their games off free TV and moved to pay-per-view, the outcry from their loving fans was loud and sustained.

But none of that prepared Colangelo for the stadium tumult.

The sports magnate was attacked on all fronts. Protesters attended some of his public appearances. Art Kaufman was conducting his petition campaign to force a vote on the tax. One local politician called Colangelo "an egomaniac" to the media, while another declared, "He believes his initials give him a greater calling." Both outspoken public servants preferred to offer their comments anonymously.

Of course, the politicos knew better. They knew politicos had conjured up and passed both the stadium-funding mechanism in the Arizona legislature and the Board of Supervisor's taxing bill, not Jerry Colangelo. They knew politicos were responsible for unleashing this trouble and turmoil upon them all, not Jerry Colangelo.

Some of the media jumped in as well, and the criticism was in full bloom. Around Phoenix, the facts were frequently forgotten, and the offending tax was, and continues to be, more often than not laid on Colangelo's plate.

At the same time, this was not merely a case of mistaken identity.

The story was more complicated, for Phoenix, true to the business-first atmosphere fostered by the community leadership, was a web of overtly crossed loyalties.

Consider: The Maricopa County Sports Authority was organized by the Board of Supervisors to advocate and aid the cause of athletics in the valley. Mike Lawrence was the executive director of the taxpayer-funded group. He had also founded a group of his own, a privately funded group, the Coalition for Major League Baseball, which worked to promote Colangelo's baseball bid.

As detailed by Dennis Wagner in the *Phoenix Gazette*, "While Lawrence insists the public agency is not an advocate for Colangelo, it is coordinating a ticket lottery created to show public support for a stadium deal. Those selected in the lottery have dibs on season seats at a ballpark that hasn't been built for a franchise that doesn't exist."

Some people didn't think Lawrence should be operating in this dual capacity. Lawrence disagreed. "That's an easy rock to throw, but it's ill-advised. I don't feel it's a conflict, and my board doesn't."

Uh, which board might that be—the public or private one?

Nor was everyone entirely at ease with the idea of Joe Garagiola Jr., the Sports Authority's chairman, resigning to become Colangelo's chief stadium negotiator.

Putting that aside, other problems presented themselves. One problem was the clumsy manner in which some of Colangelo's enthusiasts displayed their support. When Supervisors Mary Rose Wilcox and Ed King decided to go behind the backs of Jim Bruner and the board's own negotiators to cut their own stadium deal with Colangelo, instantly and materially weakening the county's position, the evidence of either stupidity or impropriety—or both—was overwhelming.

While Wilcox and King surely thought up this dubious scheme on their own, the facts remained that Colangelo served as finance chairman for Wilcox's campaign, and that King, a charter member of the Maricopa County Sports Authority, received contributions from a slew of Colangelo allies.

The two supervisors worked out an agreement that guaranteed that the taxpayers would be dunned for no more than $280 million to pay for the stadium. They were quite proud of that. Furthermore, Wilcox stated at their surprise news conference announcing their coup, "We're all a team working together."

Jim Bruner was not so proud, and the negotiations continued. The final taxpayer bill would be capped at $238 million.

The truth was, Colangelo was doing what business types, as well as advocates of every industry and cause, always did, spreading money around to make friends and influence people, as well as hiring a task force of high-powered lawyers and lobbyists to labor on his behalf. That was the way things got done, and certainly not only in Arizona.

Of course, that didn't make it any more palatable for a sizable segment of the public.

Nor was Colangelo's public posture—his readiness to stare straight into that television camera and tell the audience what was what in a tone and manner that could be described as aggressively blunt—designed to soothe any citizen's nagging concern about one man possessing too much power over the political and business process.

"I've always been out front," he said. "There's nothing to hide. People want to hear me. They don't want to hear a spokesman."

Well, then, let the chips fall where they may, and now they were falling, here and there, on Colangelo's head.

One might imagine that a man who had worked his way to the top, a man who gave as good as he got, a man who was smart and tough and unafraid, would be unmoved by the slings and arrows of a sometimes ungrateful community, would be covered with a strong, thick hide.

Rather, Jerry Colangelo resembled Rudy Giuliani, mayor of New York City, another smart, tough, combative fellow of Italian ancestry who took opposition personally and with bad humor. Colangelo wasn't as thin-skinned as Giuliani—few in the public arena were— but he didn't appreciate negative comments. In fact, he almost seemed confused and hurt by any criticism and didn't hesitate to publicly vent his surprise and irritation.

"I put my soul into this community," Colangelo said in a memorable interview with Shaub Assael in *Hearst* magazine. "Because the legislature made a tax available, am I to blame? Because of my position? My critics think I don't have any connection with the little guy. Not letting that get to you is easier said than done."

Later in that same interview, Colangelo stated that "the antitax people are also the types who are against the American flag and apple pie."

113

That statement would be reprinted and distributed by stadium-tax foes.

Again and again, Colangelo would regard any criticism as personally motivated. An article or editorial that took issue with the stadium or the team or the owner's influence or power could provoke an irate and mystified phone call from the man himself, demanding an apology or explanation or retraction. Such phone calls could be confrontational affairs, and last an hour or more.

For such a sensitive soul, Colangelo did not hesitate to antagonize his opponents, and sometimes his presumptive allies, especially his fellow owners.

From the start of his baseball journey, Colangelo insisted that the Diamondbacks belonged in the National League. Given their proximity (if one understands that, in sports, rivalries are often, though surely not always, prompted by geographic location), the Colorado Rockies, Los Angeles Dodgers, San Diego Padres, and San Francisco Giants of the National League Western Division made the most sense as natural rivals to Colangelo, and to most baseball people. However, the issue was not resolved for a couple of years as MLB struggled with realignment, the attempt to shift teams into new divisions in order to create more regional rivalries and generate more fan interest. The whole notion had some serious flaws. Though about as far apart as two teams could be, the New York Yankees and the Seattle Mariners had developed one of the most unforgettable rivalries through the 1990s, because they were both top-ranking clubs that battled against each other again and again in memorable contests, memorable not only because they were hard fought but also consequential to their respective division races.

Regardless, realignment was the rage. While his fellow owners talked, Colangelo lobbied unendingly for inclusion in the NL West. He attended only National League meetings during the owners' talks held in Phoenix in March 1996, reportedly insulting and upsetting those from the American League. In fact, he employed the tactic for more than a couple of years, annoying the owners anew each time they met. As per his entry agreement, Colangelo had a veto over any division transfer once they were situated for two years. When the Diamondbacks were finally, inevitably, placed in the NL West, and Colangelo was asked what he would do if the other owners decided to move his team after that, Colangelo replied, "I would say let them try it."

The Tampa Bay Devil Rays, incidentally, were placed in the American League West, quite a stretch considering the only thing western about Tampa Bay was that it was on the western coast of Florida. Several of the owners wished to rectify this ludicrous situation by shifting Tampa Bay to the AL East, Detroit to the AL Central, Kansas City to the NL Central, Houston to the NL West, and—uh-oh—Arizona to the AL West.

It was never going to happen. "My response is that we were put in the National League West," Colangelo said, "and that's where we're staying."

After he had sat through one last, interminable, nine-hour discussion on the pros and cons of situating the Diamondbacks in the NL West—a discussion that he thought was only supposed to be a fast, affirming vote—Colangelo stood up to tell his fellow owners precisely what he thought of their behavior and modus operandi—and Colangelo wasn't handing out compliments.

"A lot of them liked the things I had to say," Colangelo told the *Arizona Republic*. "But one of them came up to me and said he'd never been so insulted in his life."

That particular owner's protest did nothing to soften Colangelo's stance: "I told him, 'Your problem is that the truth hurts.'"

Whether it was because of Colangelo's manner or money or moves—he was constantly telling the press that the Diamondbacks would be one of MLB's "haves" and not the "have-nots," and that the club would be a "payer" in the revenue-sharing plan, not a "payee"—it was no secret that some of his fellows owners privately held him in contempt, and some publicly so.

Peter Magowan of the Giants and Drayton McLane of the Astros and Peter Angelos of the Orioles had openly criticized and questioned one or another of Colangelo's actions. So had Wayne Huizenga, and in a dramatically confrontational way. Huizenga, whose free-spending ways first helped secure a World Series for his Marlins and then almost immediately led to the team's dismantling—setting back the cause of Major League Baseball in south Florida for years to come—rose at an owners' meeting to inquire how someone with Colangelo's small personal investment in his franchise could have the same voting rights as Huizenga, whose $80-million cash infusion in the Marlins constituted exactly thirty-two times Colangelo's individual stake. Colangelo attended that meeting, was actually seated in the room as Huizenga posed his obnoxious query.

115

Then there was George Steinbrenner, who had actually welcomed Colangelo into the fold and then fairly quickly changed his mind. Though he hadn't expressed any indignation or resentment at Colangelo's signing Buck and his Yankee coaches, it was hard for many to imagine that Steinbrenner was happy about it. And when Colangelo signed shortstop Jay Bell (not a Yankee but a Royal) to that amazing $34-million contract, Steinbrenner sounded off. He called Colangelo a "neophyte" and a "renegade." Steinbrenner's opinions were not exclusive to him; a general manager was quoted in *Sports Illustrated* calling the deal "absolutely insane," and another owner dubbed it "absolutely irresponsible." Both those two fellows remained anonymous.

Steinbrenner's ire overflowed when he couldn't settle with star center fielder Bernie Williams on a long-term agreement and got it into his head that the Diamondbacks were to blame. The DBs had just signed Andy Benes, giving over another overflowing basket of money. Both Bell and Benes were clients of agent Scott Boras, as was Williams. It was speculated that the Diamondbacks were overpaying those Boras clients to accrue goodwill with the agent to help them get the inside track if Williams didn't sign up for a long tour of duty in the Bronx and became a free agent the next year.

It was a ludicrous notion. When and if Williams entered the free market, his decisions would be determined by his market value, not by his or his agent's gratitude for Bell's or Benes's financial security. However, what could legitimately worry Steinbrenner was not any agent bribery, but rather Williams's excellent relationship with Buck Showalter, his former manager. But never mind that; stories noting the Boras connection had appeared in New York, and Steinbrenner had seemingly embraced the possibility to the extent that he had alerted the commissioner's office to the tampering charge.

"I don't know whether that's the case or not," Steinbrenner told the press. "I hope it isn't, because it would be tampering in the worst way if there's been any contact whatsoever. We'll just have to wait and see."

A reporter asked Steinbrenner if he thought Buck was involved in any tampering.

"I would hope not," Steinbrenner replied.

The *New York Times* said Steinbrenner "smiled slightly" during this conversation.

The Diamondbacks replied via a press release: "The Arizona

Diamondbacks have not been advised by Major League Baseball that any type of complaint has been filed with their office. Any inquiries to our office appear to be a backdoor reference to potential tampering charges which simply do not dignify a response. There will be no further comment from our organization unless we are notified that a complaint is filed."

And that was that. Perhaps the whole matter was just a poke in the eye from George Steinbrenner to Jerry Colangelo. Of course, Colangelo poked back when Bernie Williams, in the midst of all this commotion, found himself in Phoenix for his salary arbitration hearing. Williams really wanted to take in a Phoenix Suns game, and the Suns' front office generously provided him with a ticket. Colangelo elected to borrow his buddy Reinsdorf's private plane to fly up from spring training in Tucson to also attend the game. Lo and behold, the two ran into each other at the arena—in the pressroom, in fact—and the encounter somehow showed up in the press, with accounts of a Bernie Williams just thrilled to shake Jerry Colangelo's hand.

If that constituted a return poke, then Colangelo's next stroke—his masterstroke, perhaps—was a vicious body slam to every owner in the game.

Jorge Fabregas had been left unprotected in the expansion draft by the Chicago White Sox, and the Diamondbacks had selected him in the fourth round. Afterward, Chicago's general manager had ungraciously commented that Fabregas didn't handle pitchers well, and several of the White Sox had seconded that view.

In any case, Jorge wanted a raise from the Diamondbacks, offering his services for $1.5 million per season. The DBs countered with $875,000. The case went to arbitration and the team won.

Then came the twist. Jerry Colangelo set aside his victory and awarded Fabregas a two-year deal, valued at $2.9 million.

This had never been done before, never ever. The whole point of arbitration was winner-take-all, and every winner, whether the team or the player, had always accepted his triumph, and his money, with a grin.

"I think very little of the process," Colangelo declared. "The sooner it goes, the better. . . . What I wanted to do was do the right thing, and that's what this is."

Right or wrong, Colangelo achieved three things: (1) he made Fabregas eternally grateful; (2) he made all the prospective free agents out there tingle with excitement, hoping for the chance to come to Arizona to be properly appreciated by a franchise that loved its players; (3) he made all the other owners angrier than ever and sent them a message that he really didn't care and would continue to do business his way, like it or not.

Oh, and one addendum, of special interest to George Steinbrenner: Jorge Fabregas's agent was Scott Boras.

"Hc has no real investment and yet he's working fast and furiously to set the market," a "prominent major league owner" told the *Republic*'s Pedro Gomez, referring again to Colangelo's relatively small personal investment in his franchise. "He figures, 'What the hell?'"

As usual, Jerry Colangelo had a reply: "We've been aggressive in building a product. We're trying to create a new model in a positive sense, one that should be emulated by a lot of people rather than those who are taking shots at me. When they make it personal, it goes way out of bounds. That's something I won't participate in."

Gomez ended his article with a last word from the owner of the Diamondbacks, a couple of lines that had Colangelo's forceful imprint, but didn't necessarily ring totally true. "I don't care about what people think. I don't have time to worry about it."

Worried or not, Jerry Colangelo was busy designing and realizing every aspect of his model of a modern major league franchise. And he was doing it not just to create a winning team, but to create something much more valuable.

"Look out there and you see what can happen if you're willing to dream," Colangelo urged a reporter from the Knight-Ridder newspapers, staring out one of his office windows. "What we've been able to do, well . . . we were able to make dreams come true. . . .

"I've kind of taken downtown under my wing. . . . I want it to be vibrant, to be all of the things people may have dreamed of it becoming. All I know is this: between the arena, the ballpark, the civic center, the theater, and symphony hall, 10 million people a year will be walking the streets going to these venues.

"What's happened? We've had over forty new businesses pop up because of the [America West] arena. There will be close to one hundred new businesses open up because of the stadium. If that's not a private-public partnership, what is?"

It was Colangelo's idea to build the stadium downtown, just two blocks from the basketball arena. The city hadn't pushed him to choose downtown. Neither had the county. As usual, the government officials were happy if Colangelo was happy.

Colangelo could have saved millions by doing what so many franchises had done before—relocate out of the city and to the suburbs, where the land was less expensive and plentiful, where the parking and the living were easy.

A stretch of open, available land was waiting for the Diamondbacks, away from the problems and decay of downtown Phoenix. Rich Dozer, for one, claimed that Colangelo had paid millions of dollars in higher constructions costs and lost annual parking fees by choosing to build the stadium in the city.

"He is an example of how a relationship between a sports franchise and its community should exist," NBA commissioner David Stern said. "He understands as well as anybody the importance of being engaged with the area where you operate. He knows and embraces the idea of public-private partnership, works extraordinarily well with the corporate resources within his community and the local governments, but at the same time, has a strong understanding toward the feelings of the fans."

Seated in his office, overlooking Phoenix, Colangelo related a story he had recently heard. Not long ago, the chairman of the board of Westin Hotels was in town. For years, the luxury-hotel chain had resisted building a hotel in downtown Phoenix, and for good reason. The area was deserted not only at night but for most of the day as well, consisting of a few storefronts, bars, an SRO flophouse, and many boarded-up, crumbling edifices.

But this was a new day, and now the Westin chairman stood beside an associate of Colangelo's on the corner of Jefferson and Third. He looked at the America West Arena, Bank One Ballpark, the Arizona Science Center, Patriot Square, the new restaurants and cafés and other businesses and, most pertinently, at the block where a thirty-eight-story Westin Hotel was going to be constructed. He turned to Colangelo's associate and said, "This may very well be one of the great corners in America."

That transformation has benefited the entire community. And while it did not quite begin with the America West Arena and would continue after Bank One Ballpark was completed, it simply would not have happened without Jerry Colangelo.

Colangelo started with nothing. He has completed over $1 billion in deals. He oversees some four hundred full-time employees and

119

over two thousand part-timers. He has spent the past thirty-two years in professional sports, building his business not by virtue of some grand master plan, but by seizing his opportunities and making the most of them. The course of his career parallels the extraordinary growth of the sports industry. Present at the birth of the modern sports era, with a key role to play in its development, Colangelo will surely carve out an even greater role as the sports business continues to grow and change.

And how the business progresses—or regresses—will affect all of America, for better or worse.

After telling his story about the man from Westin, Colangelo left his office to walk over to the stadium, now in the latter stages of construction, less than one hundred days away from opening. He has picked out a new office in the stadium, one that overlooks not the green playing field but the entrance, where he can watch the people buy their tickets and walk through the turnstiles, making sure that the operation is running smoothly.

This isn't to suggest that Colangelo is abandoning his digs in the arena. He'll be using both offices, keeping track of his expanding empire, leading his contented troupe of subordinates from one victory to the next.

Besides, his office in the arena has one keepsake he can never leave behind. Nor would he want to. It is a black-and-white photograph of his home back on Hungry Hill, hanging in a corner behind his desk, a remembrance of where he came from and who he was, and whom he remains, beyond the power and prestige, a remembrance he quickly points out to visitors so there will be no misunderstanding.

Colangelo himself has never needed reminding, because many of the friends from the old days are still his friends, regardless of their different stations in life. The boy from Hungry Hill is now a man, and the street on which he grew up is now named after him.

"Would I have gotten into this knowing what I do now?" Colangelo asked in the February 27, 1998, issue of the team magazine, commemorating the Arizona Diamondbacks' first spring-training game. "I'm not sure. But when they play the national anthem with forty-nine thousand fans standing in the ballpark—fathers, mothers, kids, grandparents—I know it will all be worth it, and then some."

Ponder the question all he might for the benefit of the magazine, the issue was never in doubt. Of course he would have gotten involved, because it was worth the work and effort and aggravation. It was worth it and more. It was worth everything because it gave full expression to Jerry Colangelo's talents and dreams and allowed him to achieve all that he imagined.

There are Arizonans who have more money than Colangelo, and Arizonans who run larger, more important companies. But there is no one who has had a greater impact on Arizona, economically and culturally. Colangelo has done it on his own terms, while receiving the gratitude of his partners and employees, and the respect of most of the community. That's why Jerry Colangelo might not only be the most powerful man in the great state of Arizona, but could remain so for some time to come.

PART III | The Players, on the Field

Chapter 9

Opening Day: The First Time

I t was approaching dusk and it was almost cool, at least cool for Arizona in the early summer. The temperature was nearing one hundred degrees, which, hard though it was for many who had never been to the desert to believe, was remarkably comfortable because the heat really, honestly, was dry heat.

Scottsdale Stadium was filling up nicely. The people were streaming through the gate, the concessions were doing brisk business, and the air was filled with the sort of anticipation only found at live events.

This was a live event of the first order, for it was the Diamondbacks' inaugural opening day.

Of course, this inaugural opening day was the first of many firsts. Opening day for the Arizona Diamondbacks of the National League wouldn't arrive for almost two more years, but opening day for the Arizona Diamondbacks' franchise was here, now, June 25, 1996, in the form of the Phoenix Diamondbacks of the Arizona Rookie League.

Scottsdale Stadium is a charming venue, a scaled-down rendition of its major league counterparts, with graceful lines, a brick facade, terrific sight lines from every seat and stand, and a raised, sloping lawn in the outfield, perfect for family picnics and children chasing one another, to and fro.

A long line curled around the tunnel inside the stadium, snaking between the booths selling food and minor league souvenirs. The prices for all these items were far from minor league, however. A Scottsdale Scorpions cap sold for $16, hot dogs were $2.50, and bottled water was $2 even. Three bills got the hungry fan either an oversize, fresh-squeezed lemonade or something called Cheddar-wurst.

The line was made up mainly of fathers and young children. It was reasonable to say that the idea to queue up had originated with the fathers, because the adults were the ones who displayed most of the expectant excitement. Even at an early age, the kids were familiar with many members of the sporting world, owing to either their size or accomplishments or lifestyle. Regardless, they probably hadn't heard much about Buck Showalter, who didn't actually look much like an athlete and hadn't hit any home runs or thrown any touchdowns anyone could recall and didn't date a supermodel or get arrested for drunk driving or have a sneaker named after him. But the dads knew that Buck was the real deal, and so they waited, holding baseballs and programs and small hands, because they thought their children should meet this man, and because they wanted to meet him, too.

Buck sat at a card table by himself and shook hands and signed autographs and answered questions and made a few jokes. A boy of about eight in a white Diamondback cap way too big was next, his dad beside him. The father gave a slight prodding and the boy handed his cap to Buck.

"What's your name?" Buck asked.

"Bobby," the boy said shyly.

"Where do you want me to sign it, Bobby?"

Bobby shrugged his shoulders.

"The bill would be great," Bobby's dad quickly said.

"Sure." Buck signed the cap and returned it to Bobby. "There you go."

Bobby took the cap, looked at the signature, and then put it back on his head. "Thank you," he said, clearly uncertain how he felt about having the white brim of his new Diamondback cap scribbled on.

Buck got it and smiled.

"I was watching them warm up," the father said, referring to the rookies on the field running through their pregame routines. Don Mitchell roamed the sidelines, Tommy Jones threw batting practice, while, a few yards up the third-base line, the catcher rolled out a ball, picked it up, hurled it to the first baseman, who hurled it back, then repeated the procedure with the other infielders, one by one.

"They look pretty good," the dad said.

"They're young," Buck said. "Don't have to put much shaving cream out for them."

"Can I have one of these for my little brother?" Bobby suddenly chimed in, pointing to the stack of papers on the table, which detailed the lineups for both the Phoenix Diamondbacks and the Phoenix Athletics.

"Take two," Buck said. "They're cheap."

"Good luck, Buck," the dad said, and he and Buck shook hands.

"How about you?" Buck said, and extended his hand to Bobby. Bobby accepted and they shook, too.

In the stands, 6,124 citizens of Phoenix watched as the Diamondbacks—"the baby Diamondbacks," as they were widely called—finished their warm-ups. The crowd, which had almost achieved the realization of that sports cliché, the display of a proverbial sea of the home-team colors of purple and turquoise on their shirts and hats, offered a smattering of applause as the boys hustled off the field.

With some brief welcoming remarks, Jerry Colangelo opened the ceremonies commemorating this occasion. His eye, as usual, was firmly on the horizon and his ultimate destination.

"We have six hundred forty-five days to opening day," he announced, receiving a roar in response. Jerry then introduced Buck, who also got his fair share of cheers from the people.

The five-piece band that had serenaded the crowd during the America West Diamondback plane rollout was on the scene again, this time decked out in Diamondback attire, but playing the same baseball classics. A color guard carried out an enormous American flag, followed by a Little League team.

A six-year-old girl with long, blond hair, wearing a blue shirt adorned with white stars and a white, mini-stovepipe hat walked onto the field behind them. The music started and the little girl lit into "The Star-Spangled Banner," even hitting the high notes with some vibrato at the close. The audience gave her a huge, approving yell as she abruptly stopped and ran into the waiting arms of her mother, who had been recording the performance on video.

Jerry Colangelo threw out the first ball from the mound. Though the newspaper reported the pitch as low and outside, it appeared to most fans that the old pitcher had tossed a strike straight and hard, eliciting a distinctly audible "Ohhh" from the stands.

As the home team, the Diamondbacks took the field first. Roland Hemond, in the preferred pro's seat behind home plate, who surely couldn't count how many games he had attended over the years— how many big games, with titles on the line—found himself so distracted and nervous by this game that he'd left his glasses in his car in the parking lot. Refusing to leave the stadium now, even for a few minutes, he watched the start of the contest through his sunglasses.

Ben Norris, an eighteen-year-old Texan, was the starting pitcher for the DBs. Like many of these young players, he was tall and thin— six foot three and only 185 pounds. It was expected that he would only get stronger and better as he filled out.

But that was in the future. Now it was time to pitch.

With his father watching in the stands, Norris retired the side in order, three up, three down.

Norris and his mates dashed off the field to the audience's loud approval.

Juan Garcia, a young outfielder from the Dominican Republic, stepped up as the leadoff batter for the Diamondbacks. Most likely it was just happenstance, or perhaps the heavens granted a touch of magic; either way, Garcia smacked a home run, bringing his team-mates out of the dugout and the crowd to its feet. It was a gladdening, glorious moment.

The next batter walked, and then the third baseman nabbed a short bouncer and hurled the ball into center field trying to catch the runner going to second. The traditional rallying music, that series of chords rising in crescendo heard at every sporting event—*Da-da-da-da!—da-da! Charge!*—blared over the loudspeaker, courtesy of a recorded organ, and the crowd rose in a responsive yelp.

However, the excitement was cut short, for three batters in a row struck out.

On those last pitches, the umpire got a little carried away and started yelling out indiscernible sounds to denote strikes. A small boy turned to his dad and asked, "Why does that man say 'Aahhh!'"

"That means strike," his father said.

"Why doesn't he say *strike*?"

"That's how he says *strike*."

Of such conversations was the natural distrust of the ump born.

The fans settled into a rhythm familiar to anyone who has ever attended a baseball game. There was no clock counting down the periods or quarters, creating urgency. People strolled around the park, greeting friends. Others went searching for something to eat. Two women seated just behind and to the right of the visiting team's dugout planned a wedding.

The stadium provided diversions between innings, keeping the fun going. After the bottom of the second, two boys were pulled out of the stands and, starting at home plate, raced around the bases, heading in opposite directions, as the crowd shouted its encouragement. Both boys received Diamondback caps for their effort.

Garcia hit another dinger, a two-run smash, during his next at bat, and the Diamondbacks were ahead 3–0.

Roland, a storehouse of baseball knowledge, recalled that in 1951, rookie Bob Nieman of the St. Louis Browns had hit home runs in his first two appearances at the plate in his professional career, in a game against the Boston Red Sox.

A check in *Total Baseball: The Official Encyclopedia of Major League Baseball* revealed that Bob Nieman only hit two home runs his first year in the majors. On the other hand, he only appeared in twelve games, and his batting average was a gaudy .372. Nieman eventually played twelve seasons, winding up with 125 home runs and an exemplary .295 batting average.

Maybe those statistics boded well for Juan Garcia.

Ben Norris pitched well. His night ended in the top of the third, just as planned by the coaches, after he'd recorded five strikeouts and given up only one walk and one hit.

The lead he had garnered was not to last, however. The A's scored once, twice, and didn't stop there.

Buck grabbed a seat in the stands in the row just ahead of his wife and two kids. He paid close attention to both his children and the game, while conversing with adults stopping by to shake his hand, and with kids seeking autographs.

Nearby, a young man from the franchise clocked the pitcher's deliveries, stating the speed in miles per hour. "Eighty-nine," he told Buck, and then set for the following pitch. "Ninety."

"I'm more interested in his off-speed stuff," Buck said. "I got a million guys who can throw hard."

Angela Showalter was an attractive, petite blonde in a short teal suit. Beside her were two more cute blonds, nine-year-old Allie and four-year-old Nathan.

Nathan was chewing on some sort of blue candy, and Buck turned around and asked to see his tongue. Not surprisingly, Nathan's tongue was blue, and he proudly showed it to onc and all.

Josh McAffee, the Diamondback catcher, was at the plate. "Watch this kid," Buck said. "He's going to be a player. He's already an above average thrower."

McAffee had brought his own small cheering section—family members who gave him a singularly rousing reception when the starting lineups were introduced.

The catcher hit a shot hard and deep straight ahead, but the center fielder made a spectacular catch and disappointed the entire McAffee clan.

A boy of maybe ten years approached Buck with baseball outstretched.

"What's the score?" Buck asked quickly. The boy started to turn to the scoreboard.

"Don't look!" Buck ordered.

The boy froze and started to walk away.

"Wait!" Showalter took the boy's baseball and signed his name. "Here you go, son."

The boy, his universe beginning to make sense again, took the ball and walked away.

"I scarred him for life," Buck commented.

Jerry Proctor was up. "This kid gets some muscle," Showalter said, "he's going to play in the big leagues." At six four and 193 pounds, Proctor had the frame to pack on a great deal of muscle.

He had been the club's number two pick in the recently completed amateur draft, and the Diamondbacks thought he had a world of potential. Proctor showed some of that potential on this night by banging two hits.

"Watch him," Buck said.

Allie Showalter looked bored, as only a nine-year-old can look bored, and when she was asked why, she replied, "I'm not too big a fan."

"How come?"

"I've been to too many games," Allie said mournfully.

Contrary to what some might have expected, Buck was unperturbed by his daughter's indifference for the game. In fact, soccer was the sport of choice for his kids, as was increasingly true throughout the country. Buck recognized this was baseball's most pressing challenge, to regain the loyalty and love of America's youth.

Regardless, for his own family, Buck was quite relaxed about their interest or, more to the point, their lack of. "I could care less if they played or never played," he said. "It wouldn't faze me at all if they never picked up a ball. If Nathan never played a sport in his life, it would't bother me."

Besides, Buck was facing a more urgent issue. He stood up and accompanied Nathan to the bathroom.

Another inning over, and a crew appeared on the field to slingshot Diamondback T-shirts into the stands.

Bottom of the sixth, the Phoenix Athletics were ahead 10–3, but the Diamondbacks were threatening. With men on second and third and two out, and Juan Garcia up again, the DBs had a chance to make up some ground. But their opportunity was squandered when Josh McAffee, the runner on third, a bit too eager to score, got caught in a rundown, ending the inning.

"He's young," said Roland, who had sufficiently calmed down once the game began to go out to the parking lot and retrieve his glasses from his car. "He'll learn."

They were all young, they made a lot of mistakes, and that was why they were all here, to play, to try, to learn. That was why neither Roland nor Buck nor any of the other Diamondback luminaries got too upset when Jerry Proctor in the outfield and the shortstop got mixed up on a fly ball and let it drop between them. That was why they did not get upset when one of the A's punched a ground ball to first with two men on, and the first baseman threw the ball to the catcher to get the force-out. Unfortunately, with only two men on, there was no force at home, so the runners stayed on second and third. Realizing the problem, the catcher threw the ball back to first to nab the hitter streaking to the bag. However, his throw was off, allowing not only the hitter to reach first but also the other runners to advance, scoring one run.

"Maybe it's past their bedtime," Buck said.

With so many hits and errors and runs, the game was going long. By the seventh-inning stretch, the crowd had seriously thinned, and hardly anybody remaining had the energy or inclination to stand and dance when the five-piece band, still on duty, played a hopping "Bill Bailey."

It was 10:15 P.M. and the score was 15–5. It was time to call it a night.

"They won't have time to dwell on it," DB scouting director Don Mitchell said. "That's one thing that's good about baseball. There's always another game."

And there would be so many more games for the Diamondbacks.

Chapter 10

The Buck Stops Here

November 5, 1997. Another Arizona Fall League game, another sunny afternoon, another empty stadium.

William Nathaniel Showalter III enters the ballpark in the second inning. Attired in a warm-up suit, he walks slowly along the aisles heading toward the first-base dugout, to get a closer look at the action.

Not too tall, not exactly thin, with thinning blond hair and a pale complexion that tended to turn red more than tan in the Arizona sun, he isn't instantly identifiable as a former professional athlete. Nevertheless, his fame precedes him, especially in a ballpark, major league or otherwise.

So it is in Phoenix Municipal on this day. A middle-aged man clutching a scorecard and a pen recognizes the manager and stands in his seat. He's a big guy, and his T-shirt hangs over his stomach.

"Hey, Buck!" he yells. "I'm from New Jersey, and I'm a Yankee fan."

Buck smiles and keeps walking. He's heard it all before. "So am I."

"You got a raw deal, Buck," asserts the Yankee fan.

Buck's smile stays in place. "It worked out okay," he replies, still moving.

* * *

November 5, 1995. Buck Showalter is in Arizona for the first time in his life. He is seated beside Jerry Colangelo at the Phoenix Suns' home opener. Events are moving fast. Just days before, Buck was a New York Yankee. He had been a Yankee for nineteen years. Seven years in the organization as a minor league player led him in 1985, at the age of twenty-eight, to his first managerial job with the Class A team in Oneonta, New York.

Buck established fierce work patterns from the start, and they only grew more ferocious as his career advanced, surely in part because of his intense preparation.

"He was the kind of manager who scouted *umpires*," said *Sports Illustrated* in a 1996 profile, "and he would sometimes tweak his rotation to get the best possible matchup of his pitcher and the strike zone of the home plate ump. He knew which two American League managers didn't change their catcher's signs with runners on second base during a game. Showalter, of course, would routinely change signs during the same *inning*. He worked such long hours that during the '94 strike, when he went home to Pensacola, Fla., he found himself inside a grocery store for the first time in three years."

Buck is in America West Arena because of George Steinbrenner, the sometimes erratic, always egomaniacal, inevitably tyrannical Yankee owner. Despite being named Manager of the Year in 1994, despite taking the Bronx Bombers to the playoffs for the first time in fourteen years the following season, Steinbrenner was dissatisfied. The source of his dissatisfaction was neither exactly clear nor relevant; sports owners seem to have a special affinity for spoiled, childish behavior.

Steinbrenner exhibited his anger at Showalter, who was finishing a three-year contract, by insisting that if the manager wanted to keep his job, he had to fire several members of his coaching staff. Buck refused. Time and again he had preached to his players the importance of loyalty, loyalty to each other and to the team. How could he turn around now and abandon those who had been loyal to him and to the Yankees? It was a matter of principle.

Perhaps nothing proved Buck's fealty to those principles he believed the Yankees embodied as much as his leaving the franchise.

He was thirty-nine years old, and out of the organization and the job that he had always treasured, out of the organization and the job that he loved. In private, Buck cried.

* * *

His office was small and functional, up on the eleventh floor of the Arizona Center, the temporary nerve center of the Arizona Diamondbacks, pending completion of Bank One Ballpark and its suite of offices and conference rooms. A television set was perched high on the wall, like in a hospital room. The set was on, because there was a baseball game in Toronto.

"I respect the game so much," Buck was saying, one eye fixed on the TV and the game. "I have a passion for it. It's something I grew up with. It's something you think you can hold your own in, and then you learn something new. You're always trying to get a little better. I learn something every day about baseball, about people. I hope I'll still be in it and learning when I'm sixty. I know I will. This is a very humbling game. This game can humble you in a hurry. You're never as good as you think you are and never as bad either. You lose two or three games and you think, 'Oh, God, what am I doing?' And you win three and you think there's nothing you can do wrong. It's an emotional roller coaster, but you can't show that to your players. It's just not healthy. Now behind closed doors, in front of your peers, in front of your coaches, you ache a little."

But for now, the aching hadn't begun. It was all hearts and flowers; Arizona was in love with the idea of the Diamondbacks, and pretty much in love with the Diamondback manager, the renowned Yankee skipper come West to build the hometown team into a winner.

Buck was the first to know that it wasn't going to last, not if the losses started coming in bunches or if that division title didn't come quickly enough or if a popular player was traded away.

"We're going to be criticized," said Buck, referring to player moves and coaching hires and minor league games. "Anytime you do anything important, you're going to be criticized. And we're doing some things that are very important to some people here—fans of baseball—and they're going to be fans of ours. They're going to put close to fifty thousand people in that place every night for eighty-one games, not counting exhibitions."

Showalter paused as the announcer commented on the fog starting to roll into the Canadian stadium. "That's important," Buck continued, "and you can criticize me. Now what's great about this is that we're talking about baseball issues, and not the strike or labor unions and other things. There's not a game that's talked about more, in the off-season or during the season. People banter back and forth about baseball. In between innings, you can pick out people in the stands talking about should you have the pitcher out, should you have sent the runner. . . . I get a great thrill out of listening to people talk about that, instead of talking about the problems of baseball."

Showalter never bought a home in New York. Even when he was the Yankee manager, Pensacola, Florida, remained his family's permanent residence.

Buck and his family rather quickly bought and moved into their new home in Scottsdale, Arizona.

According to *Harnett's Arizona Sports,* a local magazine, a certain insight can be gained into Buck's character—as well as his idea of a good time—in his "odd fondness for *The Andy Griffith Show.* He has nearly every episode on tape."

Perhaps more understandable than Buck's own patronage of the series was his notion that the show was appropriate fare for his children.

" 'There's a moral to every story, and there's no vulgarity,' Showalter says. 'There is no sexual innuendo. It's something the kids can watch and I don't have to worry about it when I leave the room.' "

Buck didn't have much time to enjoy either his new digs or Andy's antics, as he was constantly on the road in search of Diamondback prospects. His travels didn't take him only to the usual major league haunts, but kept him bouncing from Japan to the Dominican Republic to Canada to Korea to Mexico and back again.

"I bring one suitcase home," he said, "I grab another, and my wife washes what's in the first one."

Not surprisingly, Buck didn't have much time for other sports. "I can take or leave a lot," he said, "but it's probably because of my lack of knowledge. I don't know a lot about them. I tried to watch Arizona State play basketball, but it bored me to tears. The NBA . . ." Buck pauses to shake his head disapprovingly. "I'm not into this trash. The look-at-me mentality that permeates pro basketball just sort of makes me sick."

Watching college football was all right, when he had the time. The same for professional football—when he had the time. Ditto for golf.

The discussion inevitably returned to baseball. "Satellite TV, digital TV, whatever," Buck said. "It's going to be the death of me. I was watching the Carolina League–California League All-Star game last night at one o'clock in the morning. We had some players in it."

Apart from checking on his players appearing on late-night television, Buck voluntarily assumed a wide range of other responsibilities.

Of course, without an actual ball club to skipper, he needed some tasks other than the usual managerial jobs to fill up his ordinarily very long day, which began at 4:30 A.M. and went until . . . until whenever.

Showalter was the ultimate arbiter on all baseball personnel, including directing and deciding all draft choices and trades, performing a job assigned to most general managers. And Buck did have a couple of minor league teams to check on, though they had their own managers and coaches to lead them.

But his duties don't end there. Oh, no. Not by a long shot.

There was Buck the amateur architect, one of many overseeing the construction of the Bank One Ballpark. While Buck didn't select the nuts and bolts most suitable for fastening the seats into the concrete stands, he did, however, insist that the trio of extrawide catcher's lockers in the clubhouse be relocated from side by side by side and spread around the room. He did this so rivals for the same spot on the team wouldn't be forced to cohabit the exact same space.

There was Buck the fashion consultant, helping to pick uniform colors and materials. Purple was definitely not his favorite—a far cry from Yankee blue and white—but, hey, he had learned to work with it. And besides, it was "Arizona purple," right?

There was Buck the spokesman, addressing Phoenix business luncheons, chatting on the radio, answering questions over the Internet, pressing the flesh, meeting and greeting the public, showing the colors, flying the flag.

Incidentally, even on the Internet, as Showalter sat in his shirt and tie beside a computer and an operator and watched as the letters popped up on the screen from persons and parts out there in cyberspace, forming into complete sentences, the purple issue surfaced. Buck dispatched his response into the ether: "It has taken me a while to get used to purple. But since it seems to be Mr. Colangelo's favorite color, I have learned to like it. As long as we can stay away from lavender, I'm okay with it." Okay.

Then there was Buck the administrative scientist, who oversaw the development of a "code of conduct" for each and every Diamondback, a manual that would lay out the do's and don'ts of DB behavior:

1. **The Diamondbacks believe that success as a franchise is rooted in team success, not individual exploits. No Dia-**

mondback will ever stage an individual celebration after hitting a home run, striking out an opposing player or winning a game. We will enjoy the moment, but will never "show up" an opponent nor revel in individual accomplishments.

Just like the Ten Commandments, the don'ts outnumbered the do's when it came to attire and attitude.

2. **Emphasis will be placed on the proper wearing of the Diamondbacks uniform:**
   A. **Shoes will be black with white trim; shoelaces will be black. NO HIGH-TOP SHOES ALLOWED!**
   B. **Stirrup socks will be low cut. The length of the uniform pants will allow the stirrups and sanitaries to be visible from the front and back.**
   C. **T-shirts and long sleeves with the uniform will be black.**
   D. **Hats will be worn properly at all times, with the bill in front.**
   E. **When commuting by bus/van, players and staff will be in proper uniform when dismounting and mounting. Only Diamondbacks bags will be used to carry personal gear and uniforms on commuter trips.**

Some of these rules definitely swam upstream. The cap-backward look had become a staple of popular culture, from rap stars to the playground. On the MLB side, Ken Griffey Jr., perhaps the best and surely one of the best-loved players in the game, was not only famous for wearing his cap the wrong way around, he was photographed for the April 1996 cover of *GQ* so attired.

Nonetheless, it was not the way it was meant to be. The bill faced front for a reason—the blurring, blinding rays of the sun. The bill belonged balanced over the forehead and eyes.

And, by the by, high-top shoes, despite being pushed by the shoe companies as a terrific innovation, a must-have for serious athletes in search of ankle support, provided no extra ankle support at all.

3. **During the national anthem, players and staff will stand in a line on the top step of the dugout. If the starting players**

are on the field during the anthem, they will stand at their respective positions and properly face the flag.

Baseball occupied a happy place in the American psyche. Major League Baseball occupied a consequential place in the America world. Professional baseball players—Arizona Diamondback players—had a duty to baseball and America to show their respect for the game and for the country.

4. **Players will always look neat when reporting to the ballpark or to functions at which they are representing the Diamondback organization:**
   A. **Hair will be no longer than medium length and neatly trimmed.**
   B. **Beards are not allowed, but mustaches may be worn to the corners of the mouth.**
   C. **Earrings will not be worn at the ballpark.**
   D. **Tank tops, cutoffs, gym shorts, etc., are not allowed.**
   E. **No cellular phones or beepers allowed in the clubhouse.**
   F. **Sunglasses will not be allowed on top of the hat.**
   NOTE: **As an Arizona Diamondbacks player, you represent the Diamondbacks at all times. Conduct yourself with that in mind.**

The first of those admonitions—the one relating to hair—demonstrated how the Diamondbacks could be specific, explicit, and yet simply, skillfully flexible. No stylistic tips, no length requirement, no mention of whether hair should be above the ear or off the neck or whatever; the Diamondbacks stuck to "medium length and neatly trimmed," which allowed for different hair types and different players. Individual responsibility, within the team context.

No cell phones and beepers was a no-brainer, a necessity, an imperative. It cast out of the clubhouse the unbelievers and money changers (otherwise known as agents), as well as the wives and girlfriends and mistresses, who endlessly distracted and agitated the players, churning and shaking and stirring emotions and problems and dissension.

There were more numbers and more rules, talking about batting helmets and on-deck-circle protocol, and all of it was well and good, and undoubtedly enforceable, but why? Why all the bother? What was ultimately important here—following the rules or winning baseball games?

As an example, Buck was reminded of Jerry Colangelo's All-Star encounter with Barry Bonds and a question was posed: Was it really possible to imagine a professional sports team composed exclusively of good citizens? If that one right fielder or pitcher could win you the division, and he happened not to be an Eagle Scout, did you pass him by?

"I think you saw some of that with Charles Barkley," responded Buck, referring to the ex–Phoenix Suns forward, renowned for his superlative play, outrageous opinions, and party-friendly attitude. Barkley clearly did not qualify for Diamondback status, which, incidentally, would undoubtedly have been fine with him.

"They knew what they were up against," Buck continued, referring to the Suns organization. "They knew what fans would say."

Barkley served the team well for a long time, didn't he?

Buck gave a small smile. "Did they win a world championship?" No.

"That's the bottom line," he concluded, and leaned back in his chair to watch the fog roll in over the ball game in Toronto.

That was too easy. After all, at the bottom line, he was a great player and they did very well with him.

"They might have done just as well without him," Buck said. "You never know. Hey, when you take a Barkley, you know what you're getting—don't complain about it. It's like when you take the job in New York with Steinbrenner. You never heard me bitch and moan about it. I knew the job's a bitch. So what? I knew what was going to happen before it happened. People don't want to hear you bitch and moan about it. Suck it up and do it. If you don't like it, leave."

Both in inflection and manner, Buck acted like the Southerner he was. He spoke quietly and forthrightly, and his opinions were often underscored by a wry sense of humor. He could certainly be tough, but not just for the sake of being tough. His language was peppered with words like *honor* and *principle* and *pride*, words not heard every day in modern America.

In fact, Buck typified a specific variety of the Southern male: he was a Southern gentleman.

And Buck expected his players to conduct themselves like gentlemen, albeit they were free to choose whichever regional or national variety they preferred.

And it didn't matter whether the player was a rookie hoping to hang on with the club or a veteran superstar with his face on a Wheaties box.

"You can get good people," Buck averred. "You can if you're willing to spend the time looking for them. You've got to be ready to play this game seven days a week, and certain guys will take days off on you if you don't watch 'em. And that includes some of the good players on the team."

Buck paused for a moment, with the continuation of the Toronto contest hanging in the balance, as the field started to fade from view due to the fog. "My job is to manage the players. And am I going to say, 'Don't get Barry Bonds, I don't want to have the headaches of having to try to manage him?' Uh-uh. My job's to manage the people. Now if they ask me, 'Who would I go after, who will be a winning player?' I might have a different response.

"But it's still about character and people. One of the most gratifying things about New York was that the people they brought in there weren't the best players, but they were grinders. They were people who would win and would give any effort and do anything— and it was contagious.

"It's a beautiful thing when it comes together in the clubhouse. And the players police themselves. That's the ideal situation. That's what all the coaches want: to have the players police themselves."

So that was, at least for Buck, an underlying rationale: following the rules was about winning baseball games.

"Now you can bring in that player from another organization who's right on the fence attitude-wise," stated Showalter, truly warming to his subject. "Now there's nothing stronger in our lives than peer pressure."

Buck grinned. "Well, there's an argument there, but it's very strong. Anyway, you have a Don Mattingly or a Jack McDowell or a Jimmy Key come over and tap him on the shoulder and say, 'Hey, nothing by it, I know that's probably what you were doing in that other city, but here we don't do it that way. Here we stretch on time, we get on the top step of the dugout when the anthem is played. Here we wear our uniform with pride because we're representing the city, and we wear our hats forward and we tuck our shirts in during batting practice. It's just the way we do things here and we'd appreciate it if you'd do it.'

"And it never gets to me. The players police themselves. For the most part, they want to be disciplined."

Even the casual observer of professional sports might find that a difficult proposition to swallow, contemplating the unique lifestyle choices, on and off the field, that so many athletes favor, but Buck made an attempt to sell it.

"That's what separates athletes, is that they're different. They have to do certain things to be good. It's no accident why these guys are good. The good Lord blessed a lot of them, but to get to this level, the high majority of them have to do these other things. And that's what separates them. Why do you think Otis Nixon played till he was thirty-eight? Why do you think John Smoltz is consistent?

"Because people don't see these guys at two o'clock at the ballpark when nobody's in the stands. I see 'em running. I see 'em in the weight room. I see 'em working. It's no accident why these guys are successful, and why certain coaches and managers are successful. It doesn't just happen—same for writers and anyone else."

By way of illustration, Buck told a story about a writer he knew back in New York who'd dig and dig when he smelled something was up with the club. Many in the Yankee organization complained about the writer to Showalter, wondering what they should do about him. Buck always had the same rejoinder: Would you like to have him on your team? Damn right you would. Because he respected what he did and he worked at it.

But Buck was done talking, because the game on television had stopped now that the fog had been joined by rain. The colorman announced that the retractable roof was going to close and the game would resume.

But the roof wasn't going anywhere, at least not quickly enough to be discerned by the human eye.

Buck sat up straight. "I've got to find out what's going on!"

Mel Didier appeared in the doorway. "Are you watching this? They're closing the roof!"

"They've stopped the game?" Buck said. "That's the first time I've ever seen a game stopped so they can close the roof!"

"Seems the engineer who runs it said they're not allowed by Major League Baseball to change the roof unless it's pouring."

Slowly but surely, the roof began to shut, as Mel and Buck

watched, fairly transfixed by the slow-as-molasses, watching-the-grass-grow progression.

"It'll be a twenty-minute time-out!" Buck said.

Mel Didier was the Diamondback director of player development and, more notably, was one of the wise men that the DBs had collected for the front office. Though he spoke loudly and expansively where Buck spoke softly and sparsely, he, too, could not be mistaken for anything other than a Southerner. Mel had spent the past fifteen years with the Los Angeles Dodgers, but the Dodgers were only the latest stop in a long trek through baseball's front offices and playing fields.

Of all his experiences and teams, two of his former postings held special significance for the Arizona Diamondbacks. Mel had traveled down this expansion road before, with the 1969 Montreal Expos, as director of scouting and baseball operations, and with the 1977 Seattle Mariners, as director of baseball operations. As the DBs entered uncharted territory, it had to be reassuring to have an old hand like Didier along for the ride.

In the meanwhile, the colorman exhausted all the chitchat at his command while waiting for the pieces of the roof to move into place and knit together. Buck and Mel also proceeded to other topics, including what was perhaps their favorite topic—their players.

"What I'd like to see him do is get two hundred to two hundred forty at bats," Mel said about one underachieving fellow.

"That's right," Buck said. "And if he doesn't catch on, then we've got a suspect."

"Exactly."

That settled, they moved along.

"We're going to give him three weeks," Didier said, discussing a player. "And that's it. He's not doing good."

Neither Buck nor Mel was overly impressed with the young man.

"He's got a bone loose in his ankle," Didier added, "that they're going to have to cut and put a steel pin in."

"Can they go a little higher," inquired Buck, "and put a few brain cells in?"

Mel laughed and remembered a funny story of his own. "I got a phone call from an agent."

This tickled Buck's fancy, partly because he was not thrilled with intrusive agents in general, and partly because this particular agent,

143

who represented one of the DBs' minor leaguers, was particularly intrusive.

"I hope that son of a bitch calls me," Buck said with relish. "Send him over to me."

"He says, 'You're pretty excited aren't you?' I says, 'You're damn right.'"

"What'd he want?"

"Move his boy up to Triple A," Mel replied.

"Oh my God," Buck said with a bemused shake of his head.

It was one measure of how much the game had changed that a sports agent—an agent!—believed that he had the right, never mind the expertise, to tell a club how his client should be coached and utilized. Of course, given that the average 1997 salary for major league ballplayers hovered around $1.3 million per year, and the relative ease with which discontented athletes picked up their spikes and gloves and changed teams, the agent—the jock's chosen representative here on earth—had to be taken seriously.

Of course, that didn't necessarily apply to minor leaguers on a Class A team, and it applied even less when that Class A team was overseen by Buck Showalter—or Mel Didier, as he enlightened the agent.

"I said, 'He ain't moving if he hits .500 until he learns how to play left field.'" Mel repeated his brief speech with such delight that his drawl became even more pronounced. "'And we've got a guy who can teach him. And he's really improved and we like him, but he ain't going nowhere.'"

Mel didn't appreciate this new order any more than Buck and later explained why he was willing to pick up and leave the Dodgers and move to Phoenix.

"Buck picks out people of his own character," Didier said. "That's the only reason I left the Dodgers. He's a young man with old-time principles. I wasn't going to leave. At my age, and I'd been with the Dodgers so long . . . I've been in the game forty-five years and he said, 'Why don't you try it one more time?' I've had two expansion clubs, I've started two of them, and they've both been successful, and so he said, 'We need you here to run this player development thing.' I turned him down twice before accepting."

Colangelo hasn't intended to hire a manager for another year or more, sometime before the November 1997 expansion draft, but

Showalter's sudden availability changes everything. Jerry prides himself on his ability to take maximum advantage of his opportunities, and Buck Showalter presents a terrific opportunity.

Showalter's contract with the Yankees expired at midnight, November 1. No more than two minutes later, Buck's phone rang. It was Colangelo.

Now, just days later, Buck is in Arizona, and Jerry is sure he is the right man for the Diamondbacks. Colangelo had spoken to a lot of baseball people before calling Showalter and had only had heard good things about his intelligence, his integrity, his intensity.

For his part, Buck is impressed by those same qualities in Jerry.

At the bottom line, these are two men who, more than anything, want—no, much more than want, expect and demand—to win and recognize how deeply, how profoundly, that competitive streak runs in the other. They have compiled records of competing fair and square, but also with no-holds-barred, no-quarter-given, winner-take-all fervor.

"The whole situation is about the word *commitment*," Buck will tell the assembled media at the press conference announcing his hiring. "One that the state of Arizona, the Southwest, and fans can be proud of. They made it to me, and I, in return, make it to them."

Jerry likes the *commitment* word, too, and shares it with the *New York Times*. "I think my commitment—which is unusual in baseball, it appears—that I made relative to the terms of the contract and in giving him a chance to be involved in the decision-making process. It fit. He fit."

The Detroit Tigers and Oakland Athletics are also interested in Buck, and they already have teams on the field, ready to go, ready to be managed.

It doesn't matter. Showalter is prepared to sign on for the long haul. On November 15, ten days after the Phoenix Suns' opener, Buck inks his name on a seven-year contract worth approximately $7 million.

At his press conference, Buck Showalter removes his suit jacket and puts on a Diamondback jersey and cap. He is now an Arizona Diamondback. In fact, he is the first Arizona Diamondback, and everything he says and does will set the tone and establish a tradition for everything that will follow.

Chapter 11

The Good Book

The Diamondback organization presented a united front, in manner and mission: aggressive, dedicated, determined. But despite this singular similarity in appearance and presentation, a distinct group was apparent within the group. Most people dealt with the administrative side, the business side of the franchise, the marketing execs, the media managers, the community relations reps, the sales force, and so on. At the top of that pile—under Colangelo, naturally—sat Richard Dozer, the president, and Joe Garagiola Jr., the vice president and general manager.

Every club ran its affair in its own fashion, but most GMs ran the baseball operations. Given his legal background, Garagiola belonged in the administrative and business wing.

Besides, baseball was Buck's province. He was hired to build a team his way, from top to bottom. And so he did, starting with his staff, who helped select and train the players.

The baseball side of the organization thus constituted a discrete fraternity within the franchise. Its members were male, experienced, direct, well-groomed, and well-mannered. They were often fit, as befitted old ballplayers, and enjoyed getting out on the field and working with the kids. They were also the happiest people of all to be part of the franchise, precisely because they knew so much about the world of professional baseball. They had been through the clubs and the leagues, American to National to elsewhere, minor to major, the good managers and the bad, the greedy owners and the greedier. They had won and they had lost, each season bringing something new and special, each campaign opening and closing another chapter.

Tommy Jones has spent his entire adult life in professional baseball. He began as a player—"a journeyman utility infielder," in his own words—first in the San Diego Padres organization from 1976 through 1979, then with the Phoenix Giants, the San Francisco Giants' Triple-A club, in 1980 and 1981. Colangelo and his cohorts owned the Giants during Jones's tenure, and he became somewhat familiar with several of the owners. Jones liked both the ownership and the town.

It would have been a terrific place for a major league team, he thought, except for the summer heat, of course.

His playing days over, Jones moved on to the coaching side. He spent six years with the Kansas City Royals, managing in the minors and coaching in the majors. He became the manager of the New York Yankees' Double-A affiliate in Albany. On his days off, he would make the long drive along the Hudson River down to Yankee Stadium in the Bronx. There, he first got to know Buck Showalter.

After the Yankees, he managed in the minor leagues for the Seattle Mariners, the Milwaukee Brewers, and the Chicago Cubs. In twelve years of managing, he won seven manager-of-the-year awards.

Tommy Jones was forty-one when he joined the Diamondbacks. It was October 25, 1995, and maybe ten others had been hired before him. Jones was named the director of field operations, a title later changed to director of minor league operations. That meant he was responsible for the entire minor league system, for the day-to-day care and training and development of hundreds of young players who would pass through the many levels of the Diamondback franchise, on their way either to the big league or out of baseball.

It is easy to believe that a baseball team is basically those people readily identifiable on the TV screen, those nine guys on the field, the other players in the dugout, the manager and the first-base coach and the third-base coach. But that team is really the tip of an iceberg, the end result of a much larger undertaking. Rare is the team that is a collection of all-stars bought on the free agency market. Those that are, like the 1997 Florida Marlins, don't last long.

The dynasties, the teams that are contenders more years than they

147

are not, such as the Los Angeles Dodgers, and now also the Atlanta Braves, are the teams that scout and select and develop their own prospects, drawing them into their systems, teaching them the fundamentals, instructing them in the complexities of the game, bringing them along as players and as people until they not only reach their potential, but reach it as fully incorporated members of the franchise.

So when a team won the World Series and not only the players and manager and coaches ran onto the field and hugged and proclaimed themselves number one, and a whole bunch of people joined in the celebration, some wearing polo shirts and slacks, some even wearing suits and ties, well, those were the scouts and administrators and trainers and strength coaches and pitching instructors and all the other baseball pros who made that team work and win.

Tommy Jones learned soon enough that being a Diamondback meant participating as a Diamondback. Just days after he'd settled into his new corner office on the eleventh floor, Joe Garagiola Jr. walked up and invited him to come over and see the plans for the stadium. Tommy got up and walked into the conference room, where the architects were waiting with the blueprints and drawings. The architects showed what they were thinking, how they envisioned the building and everything inside and out.

Tommy would immediately discover that Diamondback officials were not supposed to simply sit back and accept whatever information and assurances the experts gave them. Joe had his questions and suggestions, and Jones would later watch Buck and others take razor-edged knives and cut up the blueprints and drawings and rearrange the rooms and walkways and offices and shops and all the rest plotted for the stadium.

Back in October 1995, brand-new in his job, Tommy felt a bit tentative about jumping right in at that first meeting. He kept quiet, watching and listening. Regardless, he spotted something that he couldn't let pass, and later, after the meeting, he brought it to the attention of his fellow Diamondbacks. It seemed that the architects had the umpires walking through the visitors' dugout and clubhouse to get to the room reserved for their use. Tommy speculated that this could lead to problems, such as ugly postgame words from managers agitated by unfriendly calls in the just completed contest, ugly words that might incite pushing, shoving, and inevitably, brawling. Tommy proposed that the architects simply imitate other stadiums and put in a door behind home plate, leading to a pathway to the umps' room, creating a safer environment for everyone involved.

And so it was done. Amen.

And so Tommy Jones was launched into the midst of the Diamondback universe.

And so to the manual.

The manual, the player development book, provided the guidelines for the management of the franchise. It laid out in detail both the philosophy and methodology for creating the club, running its operations, handling the players. The manual was the fundamentalist baseball bible, explaining and defining in detail every move and thought, so there would be no doubt and no deviation.

That might sound a trite totalitarian, but it was merely orderly and logical, not sinister. Baseball is not a playground game, a set of particular skills absorbed at an early age that effortlessly fit into the larger sport, because the thrust of the scheme remains on the spontaneous (and increasingly flashy) deployment of those individual skills. In other words, baseball is not basketball, where the apprenticeship into the professional ranks, either through four years of college or a certain span spent on the pro bench, is rapidly becoming irrelevant. Nor is size a prime determinant of success in baseball, as it is in basketball and football.

This is not to claim that one sport requires more athletic ability than another, simply to point out that they require different talents and expertise. In fact, no less august an authority than *Sports Illustrated* contended, in its December 8, 1997, issue, that "Danny Ainge . . . as an NBA All-Star guard, a near-scratch golfer and an infielder good enough to make the major leagues, was actually a better all-around athlete than Michael Jordan," arguably the greatest basketball player of all time, and a baseball washout.

So many dissimilar traits constitute athleticism, beyond how fast one can run and how much weight one can lift—hand/eye coordination, balance, agility, aerobic endurance, vertical leaping, on and on—that comparing sports and athletes is merely a matter of opinion and preference.

Whatever the demands of other sports, baseball is a game of talent and precision and skill and practice. On both offense and defense, each player must anticipate what every other player will do, and everyone must act as a single unit. Though, just like snowflakes, no two plays are exactly the same—the trajectory of each pitch, the bounce of every ball, producing a unique event—all actions invariably fall within general scenarios. Runners on second and third, one out, tie game, bottom of the ninth, and you're the batter, the first baseman, the right fielder: What do you do? Where do you stand? Where do you look? Where do you hit or throw or run?

Baseball requires the inherent talent to get in position to perform whatever task is presented, then the talent plus the knowledge gained from years of practice to attack the task, then, finally, the discipline to use that talent and knowledge to execute that task to the satisfaction of the team plan.

All of which renders baseball a more complicated enterprise than perhaps most would expect.

That was why the manual was important. That was why every team had one. That was why the Buck and his boys worked so long and so hard on theirs.

Tommy Jones grabbed his old copy from the Seattle Mariners off the shelf and dropped it on his desk. The book was typed and not very detailed and, truth be told, not impressive. "It's like a junior high chemistry book," Tommy said dismissively, evidently not a fan of secondary-school science texts.

Tommy pulled out a white loose-leaf binder, with "New York Yankees Player Development Manual" written in gold script across the cover. Below that and to the side was Buck Showalter's name, also in gold script.

This manual had more pages, but it wasn't much of an improvement over the Seattle effort, at least not according to the casual observer, nor, more consequentially, to Mr. Jones.

The Bronx Bombers proposed several approaches for dealing with "dive plays."

1. **Dive at all balls which are hit softly into the outfield and can possibly be caught.**
2. **Be more careful diving at hard hit line drives, especially in the following situations.**
   a. **Runner at 1st with 2 outs.**
   b. **Batter-runner is a run in the game (tie on road, win at home.)**
3. **Dive at tough balls in these situations.**

a. Runner at 2nd base—2 outs.
b. Runner at 3rd base—2 outs.

It seemed rather remarkable that the most storied franchise in sports history would feel it necessary to tell its corps of professional athletes, men who wanted to stand and play in the same outfield where Babe Ruth and Joe DiMaggio and Mickey Mantle had stood and played, that they should try really hard to catch "balls which are hit softly into the outfield and can possibly be caught."

All three recommendations regarding dive balls were sensible, of course, but they seemed obvious, exceedingly obvious, especially to anybody who had played enough baseball to reach the ranks of the professionals.

You might think so, Tommy explained, but the reality was that many ballplayers received little or lousy instruction in high school and even college. Their coaches were often the moonlighting history or shop teacher, lending an enthusiastic but ignorant hand, or, perhaps even worse, the retired ballplayer who knew how to play but had never learned how to teach. Hence, legions of talented young players lacked a solid grasp of the fundamentals, frustrating the full realization of their abilities.

The key was instilling the right lessons in the kids, then repeating and refining those lessons over and over, from the humblest rookie league all the way to the Show.

"Continuity and consistency," Tommy said. "Always say the same thing, the same way."

The Diamondbacks' player-development manual was a handsome affair, a series of bound and printed booklets encased in a ringed notebook, intended for the managers and coaches within the organization. The Code of Conduct, mentioned in the previous chapter, led the parade, along with signed letters from Buck Showalter, Mel Didier, and Tommy Jones.

In accord with his personality, the missive from Tommy was straightforward and sober.

Our objective is to provide a solid foundation upon which to build the most successful player development program in baseball. We can reach our goal by accomplishing the following on a daily basis:

- Teaching individual and team fundamentals in a clear and consistent manner.
- Emphasizing the value of our daily "Early Work Program," realizing this expedites the development of our players.
- Building confidence in our players by helping them become fundamentally sound.
- Committing ourselves to baseball excellence.

No chance to confuse that message. Get down to business, Diamondback chieftains, and show the way.

Mel Didier's message took a different tone, chock-full of that same sound advice, but with more than a dash of spirited motivation, or at least zealous underlining and capitalization.

Discipline is a prime factor in winning. The players may not like you but they will respect you as long as you are fair and your rules apply to ALL of the players. The disciplined player will not "crack" under pressure nor when the "heat is on."

Managers and coaches must believe their enthusiasm on and off the field will be copied by their players. Pride in coaching and selling a WINNING tradition to the players is a BIG part of your job.

Buck's notes included not only their fair share of sound advice and spirited motivation, but also a large dose of unwavering resolution, a surprising inclination for nautical metaphors, and a couple of dubious grammatical choices.

1. There's no limit to what we can achieve if no one minds who receives the credit.
2. When problems cease, so do opportunities. Solving problems was the reason you were hired.
3. Our character is what we do when we think no one is looking.
4. The reward for work well done is the opportunity to do more.
5. Anyone can hold the helm when the sea is calm.
6. Hold yourself responsible to a higher standard than anyone else expects of you. Never excuse yourself.

7. **Harmony is not the absence of problems, but the ability to deal with them.**
8. **You become successful by helping others become successful.**
9. **Respect the game.**
10. **Substance over style, let your substance be your style.**
11. **The approach of "Do this because I say so" falls flat today. Have good reasons for the things you do and have confidence in explaining it to the player.**
12. **Be careful of things that force you to choose sides. There is only one side, we're all in this together. Get onboard, grab an oar and pull!**

We are all protectors and keepers of the game and of the Arizona Diamondbacks way of doing things!

That was enough Diamondback encouragement. It was time to get to the nuts and bolts of baseball. The first series of booklets comprised separate skills and tasks: pitching, catching, infield, outfield, hitting, bunting, and baserunning.

The next section was devoted to team defense, with specific responsibilities discussed: cutoffs and relays, fly-ball priorities, bunt defense, first and third defense, rundowns.

Finally, the last booklets dealt with miscellaneous topics, from an early work program to training room procedures to throwing programs to pregame infield routines to strength and conditioning programs.

The player-development manual was distributed to all twenty-eight managers, coaches, and instructors within the organization. The point was continuity and consistency: everyone working in concert, no matter which Diamondback team he was assigned to, no matter the league, providing the players with the same lesson.

A note within the manual read, "Say it once. Do it one thousand times."

The Diamondback managers and coaches and instructors were to be hands-on teachers and leaders. This was apparent whenever Buck and his colleagues appeared at a DB practice field or ballpark, wearing their sparkling new pinstripes, mixing it up with the players, explaining through example.

"Before too long," Tommy said, "there might not be any coaches or managers who come to the Diamondbacks from the outside.

153

We're hiring great people and we're going to build a tradition. We have some people here who know about winning—Buck and his coaches from the Yankees know about winning. We have some people who've been to the World Series. Don Mitchell came from the Braves. Mel Didier came from the Dodgers. I was with the Royals in 1985."

The Dodgers had set the standard for the past twenty years, Jones declared, hiring perhaps five coaches from outside the organization during those two decades. They had groomed their talent, from players to coaches to administrators, and promoted from within.

The Diamondbacks intended to do the same. They would set a new standard and raise the bar higher than ever: The franchise would provide the best to their players in every way, from uniforms to equipment, practice conditions to playing conditions. That standard demanded a corresponding return from the players in attitude and behavior, on and off the field.

"Show these kids they belong to the best organization," Tommy said, "and they'll give you their best."

And thus more rules, more do's and many more don'ts, from the Code of Conduct:

> **No alcoholic beverages are allowed in the clubhouse (home or away, or on the team bus. . . .) Abusive language, throwing helmets, breaking bats, showing disrespect for your coaches or teammates, being late for practice or appearances, etc., will not be tolerated. . . . Uniforms and equipment will be issued at the beginning of the season. The replacement cost of any item not returned at the end of the season will be withheld from final paycheck. . . . No stereo unless used with headphones. . . . No chains/medallions to be worn on the outside of the uniform. . . . Hustle Rule: If at any time a player does not hustle, he will immediately be taken out of the game. . . . Players will not have conversations with opponents. . . . Players will always be courteous towards fans.**

Every Diamondback player, without exception, was handed the Code of Conduct and asked to sign at the bottom, acknowledging that he had read and agreed to all its stipulations. A copy was made and given to the player. The original was retained by the franchise.

Just in case anybody was disposed to forget about this conduct stuff or wanted to forget, the reading and signing was repeated at the start of each new season.

But when all was said and done, the manual was about baseball, those nuts and bolts, with quite exact and exacting directions.

Sometimes the information had a downright philosophical bent. Consider the introduction to the section on pitching:

> **What is "pitching"? Pitching, in the true sense of the word, is one person's mental, emotional, and physical abilities combined and fine-tuned into a precision machine. It is one's ability to keep the hitter off stride and thus throwing his mechanical timing off in his quest to hit the pitched ball hard. Making the batter understand what you are trying to do, when it is too late to adjust, is putting in a small nutshell what "pitching" is about.**

Within a few paragraphs, the intro gets down to reminding the coaches how they are to act with their young charges, as they bring along the prospects, hoping to turn them from minor into major leaguers.

> **We must treat every pitcher that we have in a uniform like he is going to pitch for the Arizona Diamondbacks in Phoenix. The guy with the 94 mph fastball everybody likes, but it might be that the guy with the 85 mph fastball who will become a Cy Young winner. We don't know; so we have to give everyone the benefit of our instruction, our time, our confidence and our friendship.**
>
> **Some players are more likable than others; that is human nature. We need to find something to like in all of them. It is our job to teach, cajole, and discipline and nurture the player along. Most important, be honest.**

Of course, not every lesson was grounded in philosophy or psychology. The majority of the exercises covered every possible on-field contingency, and the thoughtful prose style was abandoned in favor of a classic outline approach.

Nothing was left to chance or individual interpretation, even in the most basic situations. The following constitute the directions for the shortstop—all Diamondback shortstops—under "Basic Infield Positioning":

1. **Basic—Eight strides from 2nd base and sixteen strides deep of the line.**
2. **D.P. Depth—Walk in four strides and move two strides closer to the base in the double play situation.**
3. **Sacrifice Bunt**
   a. **Runner on First—Move in as the hitter shows bunt. Do not move to the base until the ball is bunted.**
   b. **Runner on Second (or first and second)—Hold the runner on second base in the normal fashion. See shortstop fundamentals.**

The manual not only dealt with the general scheme, but also with specific cases. For example, the amateur might be surprised how much could written by the professional about the evidently dreaded "slow rollers."

The first topic covered was the approved version of the "Two-Hand Technique":

a. **Charge directly to the ball.**
b. **Field ball inside glove foot with two hands and both knees flexed.**
c. **The glove foot should be well in front of the non-glove foot and contacting the ground as the ball is received.**
d. **The ball is thrown as the non-glove foot steps through. Lift the torso with the throw to achieve a more upright arm angle.**

From there, it was only logical to proceed to the proper "One-Hand Technique':

a. **Charge directly to the ball.**
b. **Field ball outside the glove foot with knees flexed.**
c. **The glove foot should be well in front of the non-glove foot and contacting the ground as the ball is received.**
d. **The exchange is made at belt level.**
e. **The ball is thrown as the non-glove foot steps through.**

156

Granted, the procedures for both the two-hand and one-hand pickups did have certain similarities. Actually, points *a* and *c* were the same for both, *b* was close, and *d* in the first definitely encompassed *d* and *e* in the second.

Ah, well, it was the nuances that divided the dilettantes from the working pros. And baseball could be a game of inches and seconds, and the right foot in the right place at the right instant.

With that in mind, it might be somewhat disappointing to consider the sparse advice for the last technique, utilized for those moments when the "Bare-Hand" was required:

a. Used only when ball is slowly rolling or stationary.

That was it. Nothing else. Putting aside the structural problem of having an *a* and no *b* or *c*, the inside info seemed to rely, in this emergency scenario (after all, one would only attempt to grab a ball and throw it in the same motion in the most exigent circumstances), on the player's throwing caution to the wind and improvising on the run. However, more likely, the player was first supposed to follow the schooling for two- and one-hand techniques, and only then improvising where needed.

Another special play covered in the manual was the scourge of Little Leaguers everywhere and was known to one and all as the pop-up. The instructions were as choreographed as a tango; to the aficionado, the play, when correctly executed, was as graceful as the dance:

1. **On balls hit in the infield, middle infielders have priority over corner infielders and corners have priority over the catcher. All infielders have priority over the pitcher. Do not call the ball until it reaches the apex of its flight.**
2. **On balls hit between the infielders and outfielders, the outfielder has priority. Despite the outfielder's priority, the infielder should assume he will have to make the play on these "in-between" pop flies. These are important fundamentals:**
   a. **Full drop step.**
   b. **Sprint back aggressively.**
   c. **Do not get into a "back peddling" mode early in the pursuit.**

  d. **Wave arms when facing the infield and comfortably under the pop fly. Do not initiate a verbal call.**
  e. **Attempt to get to one side of the ball to avoid a directly over the head catch.**

Never mind that "back peddling" was unfortunately substituted for "backpedaling"—this was the word, as it was written in the book. And the word was pronounced well, and the book, same as everything else with the Diamondbacks, was designed to be straight and true.

"I believe in my heart," Tommy said, "that everybody in baseball wants to work with the Diamondbacks."

While not egocentric, that was surely a franchise-centric assessment. Regardless, it was easily verifiable that the young minor leaguers who were Tommy's responsibility were thrilled almost beyond belief that they were part of this new organization.

"The kids can't believe how we do things," Tommy said. "Especially the kids who have been with other organizations."

Other organizations gave their prospects hand-me-down uniforms, either shabby discards from the big boys or simply old, frayed relics from another era. All the Arizona rookies had wonderfully shiny, new uniforms, if for no other reason that that there were no woefully worn, old Diamondback uniforms.

The same was true for the bats and balls and training facilities and ballfields and stadiums.

Much more amazingly, other organizations didn't have the manager of the major league club, and all his top coaches, working with their teenage hopefuls.

Everything was great. Everything was brand-new. Everything was exciting and novel.

Everything was great and nothing was impossible. Nothing had gone wrong. Now no one had blown a big game or sat out during a contract dispute or complained to the media or complained about the media.

Now, still, there was no team, and thus no frustration or disillusionment, only faith and anticipation.

"With the ownership we have," Tommy said, "and the manager and coaches, and all the support, we can't help but be successful."

He looked out his window and across a couple of avenues at the stadium, its metal roof and brick facade glistening in the always shining sun, nearing completion.

"My friends tell me," Tommy said, " 'Boy, are you the luckiest guy in the world.' And that includes the ones who have nothing to do with baseball."

Of course, that is the point: an awful lot of people who have nothing to do with baseball have a lot to do with baseball.

12

Let the Games—or at
Least the Practices—Begin

T alk is cheap, though in the case of professional sports, talk is extremely expensive. Regardless, it is just talk.

Playing is what counts. Getting on the field and showing what you have, what you can do. Getting on the field is why you love the game.

Buck Showalter hadn't signed up with the Diamondbacks just to wear double-breasted suits and sit in his office, and neither had his coaches, instructors, and some of the front-office people, too.

And now the day had finally arrived, the day to put away the formal duds and pull on the pinstripes and cleats and play ball.

June 10, 1996. There would be many opening days, with varying degrees of celebration and significance, but there would never, ever be another day when athletes wore Diamondback uniforms for the first time.

Sixty young ballplayers, twelve coaches, and one major league manager were on the field at the Peoria Sports Complex by 9 A.M. It was an early start, but not early enough, because the temperature would soon be over one hundred degrees.

The boys, mainly teenagers just out of high school, had been chosen in the amateur draft only four days before. Now they were professional athletes signed to contracts with the Arizona Diamondbacks, and the club was treating them like the pros they had suddenly become. Though this might have been only a summer minicamp, the equipment manager was waiting to hand each fellow a Diamondback travel bag and an assortment of clothes to fill it, including not just shirts and pants and a jacket, but also gloves and cleats.

Tommy Jones provided an insight on the franchise's attitude toward its players to the *Arizona Republic,* which also provided an insight into the franchise's attitude toward virtually everything it planned and promoted and intended: "At this level, some teams just roll a couple of baseballs on the field and say, 'Here, you're on your own.' . . . We wanted to make sure we started out the right way, make an impression with the players that we're going to treat them well, especially if they're willing to work hard."

The boys were willing enough, no doubt about that, running from place to place, field to field, listening intently to the advice and admonitions of the coaches. They were split into squads, pitchers and catchers working together off to the side, infielders and outfielders broken into groups.

One coach explained in exacting detail the Diamondback rules for deciding which fielder had priority in a pop-up. "Center fielder over outfield! Outfield over infield! Shortstop has priority over infield! Second base next! Corners have priority over catcher!"

And the proper phrase to employ when encountering a pop-up? Not "Mine!" or "Yours!" but "I got it! I got it!"

To one side, off the diamond, the pitchers stood in a line, throwing to catchers. Almost without exception, the pitchers were tall and skinny, the catchers shorter and more muscular. The pitchers' motions were fluid and graceful, which belied the speed with which the ball moved. The real clue was the sound the ball made on its flight, splitting the air with a sharp hum, like the planet's largest, fiercest bumblebee, diving straight at you.

Another group was at the plate, getting the knack of a hitting drill. A coach tossed a slow strike to the batters, who were to execute two bunts, then swing away four times, then practice a hit-and-run by smacking the ball on the ground and having the preceding batter, already on first, take off for second.

On that same field, Brian Butterfield was giving baserunning lessons. Butterfield was one of the coaches Buck had brought with him from the Yankees. Also in Peoria that morning were former Yankee coaches Mark Connor, Nardi Contreras, and Glen Sherlock.

Butterfield was talking to a young fellow standing on second base, explaining where to look and what to do on a long fly ball. "Turn and analyze. It's a deep, sure catch. The outfielder is deep enough and my speed allows me to make it to third."

Another scenario: "One out. More urgency to score now? Yes. Which ball should you be careful about?" As if on cue, the batter at the plate bunted down third base, but the ball spun backward and died just a few feet from the catcher. "Ball in the dirt to the left, the catcher can come up and block it and throw to third. So we're aggressive but smart."

Another chance: "Playing deep in right, straight up in center, left is cheating to the gap. So boom! I know when to go."

The rookie's expression revealed that he didn't know when to go.

Butterfield's point was that by being aware, always aware, of where everyone on the other team was at every moment, the baserunner would instantly know how to react.

Butterfield watched another player run to first. "Hit that first half of the bag! Nice and easy. Look at the pillow when you hit it. Lean into the finish line. Glance over your right shoulder. The ball may have gotten past the first baseman."

The lesson continued as Butterfield held forth on the proper position off second base. "The lead from second is fifteen feet, topside of the bag. We're playing straight. We're not going to use these wide angles. Arizona players are going to use tight turns to improve the angles."

Butterfield next related how to get from second to third, with an emphasis on keeping the third-base coach in mind. "I make the turn at third and he stops me—boom! I'm going to immediately turn around and locate the ball. Because the play's not over."

The adults were confident they knew the best way to do things, and they were determined to pass along the information to their charges.

And there was so much information, because baseball presented an infinite number of situations and contingencies.

"In a bunt situation," Butterfield said, "you're not getting any help from the coaches. They're going to stand there with their arms folded. It's up to you. You'll double-shuffle to the bag."

And every situation counted, and every contingency had to be anticipated and prepared for.

"Baserunning isn't a little thing," Butterfield said. "Do it right and it'll help you move up a couple of levels."

Butterfield had his style, direct and enthused, and other coaches had theirs. Dwayne Murphy, who had won six Gold Gloves as the Oakland A's center fielder and played twelve years in the majors, spoke quietly, bringing his players into a circle when he addressed them. Chris Speier, who spent nineteen years covering shortstop for the Giants, the Expos, the Twins, and the Cubs and was selected to the All-Star team three times, had a kind of Southern, easy bearing to him, despite having been born in California.

Whatever their individual personalities or techniques, all twelve appeared to take a cue from Buck and stayed calm and encouraging, avoiding extremes either high or low, "setting the temperature for the players," in Mel Didier's felicitous phrase. A comfortable temperature needed setting, for many of the prospects were as skittish and dazed as newborn puppies. To underscore just how jittery some of the boys were, Buck had to sit down and convince one overwrought player not to leave camp and quit the team at the end of the first day.

Not everyone's excitement translated into discomfort, as demonstrated by Josh McAffee. Upon finishing catching one of the pitchers, a Dominican boy who spoke virtually no English, McAffee jumped out of his crouch, dashed over to his fellow DB, and communicated by hugging him.

McAffee was from Rock Springs, Wyoming. Same as so many other Americans, his first exposure to organized sports was in Little League, starting at the age of seven. He progressed through the ranks into Junior Babe Ruth and on to American Legion ball.

For McAffee, his last year in high school was critical. High school seniors were commonly scouted and signed by MLB teams, to begin the long climb through the minor leagues. This was not the only path open to prospects; many attended college and then were drafted by the pros.

Still, Josh wanted to be a professional baseball player, and he wanted to start sooner rather than later. But he faced a serious obstacle—baseball opportunities in Rock Springs were, at best, extremely limited. His school didn't even have a team.

The McAffee family decided that Josh had only one option, and that was to find a school with a vibrant baseball program. Josh's American Legion team coach, Russel Haigh, contacted the coach of Farmington High School in New Mexico. Farmington was a frequent stop for baseball scouts on the Southwestern circuit, known for producing promising players. Josh transferred to Farmington, and his parents regularly made the journey from southwestern Wyoming to northwestern New Mexico to check on their son.

Their son did well enough to be drafted in the fourth round by the Diamondbacks. Now the eighteen-year-old was in Phoenix with the team, and his parents and paternal grandparents were with him, watching with smiles that would not end.

Josh's good fortune had made the news back home. In fact, McAffee's grandma was willing to part with a copy of the *Rock Springs Daily Rocket-Miner*, dated June 8, 1996, which featured a picture of Josh on the cover and a story on page six. "I would like to thank my family," the paper quoted Josh, "without them none of this would have been possible. The sacrifices they made really helped me get here."

Another picture of Josh waited inside the newspaper, this time seated beside Louie Medina, the Arizona scout who had promoted McAffee to the club. "Josh is the prototype of the future catcher," Medina said of the six-foot-one, 215-pound athlete. "His body size is good and he has the best arm strength I've seen this year. He could throw a ball through a brick wall."

"This is most definitely a dream come true for me," Josh said.

It was a dream for a lot of other boys as well, including the other seven catchers in camp. One of those seven other catchers was the young man chosen just ahead of McAffee in the third round, eighteen-year-old Mark Osborne.

Osborne was also a big fellow, standing six four and weighing in at 205. A left-handed pitcher in high school back in Sanford, North Carolina, Osborne had the requisite arm strength needed to be a catcher. "I've wanted to be a catcher since I can remember," Osborne would say a bit later. "At some positions, you can go two or three innings without ever touching the ball, but as a catcher, you're in every play. You're in control of the game."

One of the players who would be throwing what McAffee and Osborne would be catching was the Diamondbacks' number one selection in the amateur draft. Nick Bierbrodt was a six-foot-five, 190-pound pitcher from Long Beach, California. It would seem that as the two new boys on the block, either the Devil Rays or the Diamondbacks would get to choose first. Major League Baseball, or the team owners who constituted Major League Baseball, did not view the issue with such benign reason and decreed that the Devil Rays would choose twenty-ninth and the Diamondbacks thirtieth, dead last. That made Bierbrodt the thirtieth player conscripted overall, a spot worth a $525,000 signing bonus, a figure that would eventually balloon to $1.046 million, based on a formula that adjusted the amount according to the percentage increase in first-round bonuses from 1995 to 1996.

That wasn't bad money for an untested teenage athlete, but it was small change compared to what John Patterson received. Patterson was also a pitcher, also eighteen, and also long and skinny—six foot six and 210 pounds. The Texan also went in the first round, taken by the Montreal Expos, selecting fifth. The difference arose in how he was handled after being drafted, and that made all the difference in the world.

Bierbrodt had signed his deal with the Diamondbacks six days after the draft. The Expos, however, didn't offer Patterson a contract in five days nor in ten days nor in fifteen. And that was a mistake, because after fifteen days, the rules stated that the draftee was now a free agent.

"That's the way things worked out," said Montreal's general manager Jim Beattie. "I have nothing against the kid and wish him the best."

Suddenly liberated from any commitment to the Expos, Patterson, in the form of his agent, Randy Hendricks, entered the marketplace, and the marketplace responded with vigor. Hendricks claimed he fielded offers from twenty-six teams, and the Diamondbacks won out with a tender of $6.075 million.

That was an awful lot of money, but Hendricks maintained that it wasn't even the top bid. The money couldn't have been too far off the mark, because Patterson settled on Arizona. "I want to be one of the players who helps build the tradition of the team from the beginning," John told the media, providing a reason beyond dollars for choosing the Diamondbacks.

But even Patterson's bonus paled next to that given to Travis Lee. Rather incredibly, the Minnesota Twins also failed to sign their first pick, the number two selection in the entire draft, first baseman Travis Lee, within the prescribed fifteen days. The Diamondbacks immediately leapt into the hunt for Lee's services and won out, for a cool $10-million bonus.

When the smoke cleared, the Diamondbacks had managed to snag three first-rounders, a stunning accomplishment with terrific long-term implications for the franchise.

Of course, it wasn't a numbers game alone. Sometimes the number one flopped and the walk-on became an All-Star. Sometimes it was physical: a sensational college shortstop was a step too slow to compete at the next level. A great hitter with an aluminum bat, which they used in high school and college, might not be able to get the heavier, differently weighted wood bat, with its sweet spot one-third the size of its metal counterpart's, around quickly enough. Sometimes it was mental: the kid who had played the game with mastery and flair since he was old enough to strap on a glove couldn't take the pressure of the daily grind of pro ball. Or the hometown hero hated being on the road and away from that hometown.

Or, perhaps worst of all, an injury ended all the dreams before they could really begin.

On and on, innumerable pitfalls and hazards and problems were gathering to waylay each player on his quest for success.

There were precious few sure bets, can't-misses, guaranteed winners, in baseball. Deciding on everybody else was an educated crapshoot.

Kevin Sweeney had to be considered a crapshoot. He was selected by the Diamondbacks in the twenty-ninth round, hardly a stirring endorsement. The twenty-two-year-old outfielder from Cheektowaga, New York, would be assigned to the Lethbridge Black Diamonds, the club giving him a chance to produce. And while some of the higher-priced ballplayers would do better than expected and some would do worse, Sweeney blew any and all expectations away, leading the Pioneer League in hitting with a .424 average, and finishing first in on-base percentage, slugging percentage, runs scored, and tied for first in RBIs. He was named the Organization Player of the Year, the Pioneer League's Most Valuable Player, and the awards kept coming.

It was still early in his professional career, and even Sweeney's outstanding performance didn't guarantee how far he'd go, let alone if he'd make it to the Show. Still, one thing was certain: Kevin Sweeney was better than a twenty-ninth pick.

It was hot and getting hotter, and some of the boys weren't used to an Arizona summer. However the players were doing, Buck and his coaches were loving it, even loving wearing those polyester uniforms and wool caps.

Baseball is the only sport where the managers and coaches wear uniforms. To many, it is a strange sight, seeing wrinkled men with their stomachs hanging low over their belts and their wispy, white hair poking out from beneath their caps, shuffling around the grass. Even if they weren't wrinkled and fat and white-haired, isn't there an age when it's time to leave the costumes to the younger set?

"My wife says that all the time," Buck replied. "She says I should wear a tie in the dugout like the NBA coaches."

Not surprisingly, Buck had an answer: "In football, you wear pads and everything because you're going to be hit. In basketball, you wear shorts and sneakers so you can move around faster."

And don't baseball players wear uniforms so they can play?

"No," Buck said. "You wear a baseball uniform because you're representing your team."

Though resolved to Buck's satisfaction, the utilitarian-versus-representation debate had the smell of an intellectual construct to allow men past their playing days to continue to put off adult attire for yet one more season.

And if so, well, there was nothing wrong with that, right?

Meanwhile, the Diamondbacks continued to build their club with their trades and free agent signings and more drafts.

Garry Maddox Jr. joined the franchise two months later. About to start his senior year at the University of Maryland, Maddox was an accomplished outfielder and hitter, twice named Atlantic Coast Conference Player of the Week in his junior year, despite missing part of the season due to injury.

One more thing: Garry Jr. was the son of Garry Sr., who spent fifteen years in the majors with the Giants and Phillies, winning eight Gold Gloves for his command of center field. Yet despite a father's pride in his son's ability and achievements, Garry senior was totally opposed to Garry junior's leaving school for pro ball. The two Garrys spoke, and then Garry senior talked with Luis Medina, the Diamondback scout who had found Maddox, and eventually the father softened his hard stance and the son put his autograph to a contract, promising to finish his degree at Arizona State.

Jason Goligoski wasn't a high draft pick and he wasn't nineteen. On the other hand, he was most probably the only ballplayer on any club at any level of Major League Baseball who was also a painter and furniture artisan. And that wasn't the end of his talents. Growing up in Hamilton, Montana, fifty miles outside of Missoula, GoGo, as he was known, learned all there was to know about hunting and fishing.

He also learned something about baseball, won a scholarship to Washington State, and was later selected by the Chicago White Sox in the eighth round in 1993.

Unfortunately, GoGo didn't find happiness, or enough playing time, with the White Sox, and he asked to be released from his contract. His next stop was with the Colorado Rockies, but GoGo again felt underutilized and got out of there, too. He signed with the Diamondbacks on February 5, 1997.

Twenty-five years old, married, and with two children, he was frustrated by his progress in the professional ranks. "I know I'm good enough to play," the shortstop told the *Arizona Republic*. "You have to think that way or you're never going to make it. I'm not happy just to put on a pro uniform. My goal is to make it to the big leagues."

Both Maddox and McAffee had expressed remarkably similar sentiments, separately asserting that each would never rest on his laurels, but would work until he made it to the majors. That shouldn't have been much of a shock; after all, to reach this first step on the pro ladder required an intense level of dedication and determination.

GoGo was different from Maddox and McAffee and everybody else on the team in one respect: he had an artist's eye and touch. In his minor league wanderings, he'd realized that all those baseball bats broken in the midst of games were simply tossed away. He'd also realized that he could take those remnants and fashion them into bed frames. And that's what he did, producing and selling bed frames in the off-season.

GoGo has branched out to include hockey sticks, shotgun barrels, tennis rackets, and whatever else in his carpentry business. Now and then, for a change, he would also sell one of his wildlife drawings.

Goligoski had lots of talent, in lots of ways. The question was, would his future be in crafting bats or swinging them?

Mark Davis must have felt as if he were swinging back and forth in this, the later stages of a successful career. His career began in 1979 with the Philadelphia Phillies, as a first-round draft pick. The left-hander eventually pitched not only for the Phillies, but also for the Giants, the Padres, the Royals, and the Braves. In 1989, Davis won the Cy Young Award, when he saved 44 games and had an ERA of 1.85 for San Diego.

However, a series of arm injuries put him out of commission in 1995 and 1996, and he underwent one operation on his elbow and another on his left shoulder. Attempting a comeback, he signed with Arizona on February 2, 1997. At the age of thirty-six, older than not just the players, but also several of the coaches, Davis was sent to the organization's High Desert Mavericks of the Class A Advanced California League.

His young compatriots quickly seized upon the chance to pick up whatever tips they could from the old pro. "We ask him what pitches he likes to throw in certain situations," Ben Norris, not much more than half Davis's age, told the *Republic*, ". . . what being in the major leagues is like. It kind of gives you an extra boost. When you see him out there pushing it . . . you know that he's won a Cy Young and that's what all pitchers want . . . you see that hard work can pay off."

"I've been doing this for a while now," Davis said. "I think it's part of the job. You should want to share things like that. . . . I tell them that one day, it will all fall into place and they'll get to the majors and they're going to go, 'Wow! The guy didn't hit that! Hey, these guys are no different from me. They're just like me.'"

Still, for all his good work with the youngsters, Mark was here to pitch, to get back to the Show. He was still a player, not a coach.

"The doctor says I'm going to have good days and some not so good," Davis said. "I just have to keep working at it and be smart about it."

He pitched well enough to compile a 3-1 record, with a 2.66 ERA, good enough to get him promoted to Triple A, as the Diamondbacks loaned him to the Milwaukee Brewer's Tucson Toros of the Pacific Coast League.

Davis must have impressed the Brewers, because on August 15, 1997, he entered Diamondback history when he was traded to Milwaukee for a player to be named later, in the Arizona franchise's first major league deal.

"This is a terrific opportunity for Mark," Joe Garagiola Jr. said, "and we wish him nothing but the best."

Professional baseball could be a cruel mistress—and one with a twisted sense of humor, too. For at the end of the 1997 season, the Diamondbacks signed Davis, one more time, to one more minor league contract, for one more shot.

One year after that first amateur draft, and that first minicamp, the Diamondbacks selected another sixty young prospects, consisting of thirty-four ballplayers from high school, eight from junior college, and eighteen from college. The first choice was Jack Cust from Flemington, New Jersey, a six-foot-two, 195-pound, eighteen-year-old outfielder labeled by *Baseball America* as "the nation's premier left-handed high school power hitter." He hit .592 as a senior for Immaculata High School, which included 15 home runs, 7 triples, 9 doubles, and 51 RBIs. For good measure, he also stole 12 bases and walked 48 times.

His exploits, as befitted all legends-in-the-making, were captured in isolated moments. Jack Cust smashed three balls into the upper deck of hallowed Yankee Stadium while displaying his talents for all interested. Jack Cust hit a home run in high school that traveled 460 feet. Jack Cust hit another home run in high school that traveled almost 500 feet.

"Jack is excited about getting his professional career off and running," Garagiola said in the official Diamondback press release, "and we're excited to have a player with his potential."

Jack Cust could turn out to be an All-Star one day, and so could Garry Maddox Jr. and Josh McAffee and Kevin Sweeney and Nick Bierbrodt and John Patterson and Mark Osborne and Jason Goligoski, and maybe Mark Davis would get back on top again, but it was a long road—on average, a player who did actually make it to the Show put in four years in the minors—and Mel Didier was available to put the situation into some perspective.

"The truth is," Mel said, "maybe one, maybe—*maybe*—two will make the big-league team next year. The year after that, maybe five. The year after that, maybe eleven."

Didier paused. "Are they that good? We hope they will be that good."

Those were probably optimistic numbers, maybe very optimistic numbers. Regardless, the Diamondbacks were intent on building a club from within, developing their own high-priced talent, instead of buying other people's high-priced talent. Of course, they would end up doing a bit of both. Whether the franchise would wind up doing more developing or buying over the long haul would depend on how intelligently they chose in the draft, how cleverly they drafted, and how smartly they coached.

But on that first day of the first Diamondback minicamp, June 10, 1996, all the Arizona franchise had was a bunch of eager kids who, whether they were million-dollar bonus babies or walk-ons just happy to be there, were all getting the MLB-prescribed $850 a month for first-year minor leaguers, all hoping to live a dream, all scratching and sweating and working to make the team, this team, and then the next and the next, all the way up.

Perhaps as Didier said, one would make it, perhaps eleven. Were they that good? They, the players, would soon find out—and so would the Diamondbacks.

And that would be that.

Chapter 13

Youth Must Be Served . . .

The baseball establishment professed shock.

"I think it's insanity to pay that to an unproven college player," Kevin Malone, the assistant general manager of the Baltimore Orioles, told the *Los Angeles Times*, "even though he's one of the highest-profile guys closest to being ready. It's another sign that the game's in trouble and another sign that the industry can't control spending. . . . It's shocking."

"I have only two words," said Bud Selig, owner of the Milwaukee Brewers and acting baseball commissioner. "I'm shocked."

MLB was falling over itself in shock over the $10 million the Arizona Diamondbacks paid twenty-one-year-old Travis Lee.

On the other hand, one had to wonder how shocked Major League Baseball really was; after all, twenty teams in addition to the Diamondbacks had bid for Lee's services. In fact, according to Jerry Colangelo, four teams were willing to match Arizona's offer, and two teams upped the ante by half a million each after Travis agreed to the Diamondbacks' proposition.

Actually, what was more shocking was that the Minnesota Twins had somehow failed to get it together to send the second selection in the 1996 amateur draft a formal, written contract within fifteen days of the draft, violating Major League Rule 4 (E), thereby setting Lee free and setting off the scramble to sign him.

171

Travis had proved his ability on a variety of stages. The 1996 graduate of San Diego State and winner of the Golden Spikes Awards as the best amateur baseball player in the country, Lee hit .416 over forty games for USA Baseball, including driving in ten runs in nine games at the Atlanta Olympics to help the American club win the bronze medal.

"We have told our fans that we are going to become competitive as quickly as we can," Colangelo stated in the press release of October 11, 1996, announcing Lee's signing. "This is an example of that commitment. Travis Lee can be an outstanding big-league player for a long time."

The Diamondbacks generously allowed Lee's agent, Jeff Moorad, space in their press release to compliment the franchise on its comportment throughout the wooing and negotiating: "From Jerry Colangelo on down, the Diamondbacks impressed us with the way they are building both an organization and a team. Travis liked what he saw here and wants to be a part of this from the ground up."

Travis spoke for himself at his coming-out press conference at the America West Arena. Standing six foot three, weighing in at 205 pounds, Lee possessed the square jaw of a proper sports hero, and the by now inevitably seriously sincere manner of a Diamondback player speaking to the media. No, he didn't regret not signing with the Twins, who hadn't accorded him "the respect" he believed he deserved. Yes, he was overwhelmed by touring from city to city as he showed his skills and his agent fielded offers. Yes, he was thrilled to be in Arizona and felt "right at home here."

Buck helped him on with his very own Diamondback cap and Diamondback jersey, with his name and his number, sixteen, on the back of the shirt. With the jersey fitting badly over his black polo shirt, his cap pulled low on his forehead, and his hands shoved inside his pants pockets, Lee finally looked like the big kid he really was, his lopsided grin showing his guileless glee at becoming a Diamondback.

Travis told how, during a tour of the new Diamondback facilities and stadium, he walked into one of Arizona's minor league locker rooms and there was that same jersey, hanging up in what could be his locker—if he signed on the bottom line.

"I saw that number sixteen with my name on it," he recalled, "and I was like, all the hairs on my body jumped up."

A nifty visual, and it worked, at least when combined with 10 million large: Travis signed.

Those who might really have been shocked by Arizona's investment would have had reason. Professional baseball was littered with the hopes of can't-miss prospects who somehow missed.

Nonetheless, from the start, Lee was impressive. Days after joining the Diamondbacks, Travis was working out with his new mates who were already playing in the Arizona Instructional League at the Peoria Sports Complex. On command, he hit to one field, then the other, then bunted, then hit away, smacking the ball out of the park. Done with displaying his slugging prowess, he showed off his fielding skills, exhibiting a nimbleness rather startling in a big guy.

Watching, Buck smiled, quite content with his newest player.

In short order, Travis was playing for the High Desert Mavericks, Arizona's farm team in the California League, on the Class A Advanced circuit. Lee adapted well to his new surroundings; in May alone, he hit .404, with 7 home runs and 31 RBIs in 28 games. Not surprisingly, he was named California League Player of the Month.

After watching Lee crack a pitch some 450 feet straight away for a grand slam, not to mention collect another two hits in the same game, Mel Didier was quoted in *Sports Illustrated* as saying, "In my forty-five years, Travis is the best hitter I've ever seen."

In 61 games, Lee hit .363, which included 18 homers and 63 RBIs, outstanding, league-leading totals.

The Diamondbacks were ready to move Travis up to Double A, but they encountered one snag—the Diamondbacks didn't have a Double A team, not yet anyway. So Arizona arranged to "loan" Lee to the Milwaukee Brewers' Triple-A Tuscon Toros. Lee would benefit from facing new challenges, and the Diamondbacks would be close enough to keep an eye on their future first baseman, playing just two hours down Interstate 10.

"In a normal environment it's a big jump," Toros GM Mike Feder told the *New York Times,* "but this is a player who probably in a normal year would not have started in Class A. I can't speak for the Diamondbacks, but he's conquered that league. He'll face better pitching and players with a lot of experience up here."

Lee took to the Pacific Coast League with gusto. In his first 30 games, he was batting .283 with 9 home runs and 25 RBIs. By the time he was through, playing in 59 games, he hit .300 with 14 home runs and 46 RBIs. In fact, combining his final tallies in Class A and Triple A, Travis batted .333 with 32 homers and 109 RBIs.

In the same *Sports Illustrated* article in which Didier was cited regarding Lee's ability, the magazine noted that "of all the prospects toiling away in the minors, perhaps none is more deserving of a shot at the big leagues this summer than first baseman Travis Lee."

Unfortunately, the Diamondbacks were a year away from their inaugural major league season.

The Arizona Fall League, the top of the minor league ladder, was next on Travis Lee's journey to the majors.

October 21, 1997: Another game in the Fall League, another chance for Travis Lee to show his stuff, another chance for Travis Lee to sign autographs and answer questions.

The left-hander is a star on the rise, and both the kids and the professional autograph hunters know it. They lean over the railing around the dugout, holding out their baseballs, clamoring for his notice. The children are thrilled to snag the signature of any Diamondback, but especially thrilled to get Travis Lee's. The adults are another breed altogether: male, in their midthirties to midforties, almost always overweight and disheveled, each carries a case full of baseballs and baseball cards, some lug bats, and all are armed with lists of names that they check off as they nab another player's John Hancock. In between player sightings and hunting expeditions, they sit separately from the crowd, and even from one another.

It is one thing to see children rushing to get close to the players, calling out their names, begging for their cooperation—it is quite another to watch adults jumping and pleading, a little too determined to collect those signatures, a little too excited when they get their prizes. They might be smart businessmen, hoarding their trophies for the day when they might be worth millions, or at least hundreds or thousands, but they are a creepy bunch.

On this autumn day, the autograph hunters remind one observer of child molesters, as though they are too old to be hanging around the playground, as though they are someplace they shouldn't be.

Regardless, the hunters are in pursuit of Travis, for they know his signature will be worth something, and probably soon. In fact, word in the park is that a Travis Lee baseball card, heralding his minor league achievements to date, is already worth $20. In contrast, Mark Davis's rookie card, the card of a former Cy Young winner, a card that is almost as old as Travis Lee, can be had for a cool 50¢. Such are the vagaries of athletic glory.

Lee, along with most of his teammates, is ready to sign for the kids, but is leery of the adults. The problem with these guys is that they're never satisfied—one autograph is never enough, there's always another card and another cap and another program in the case to scribble on.

His teammates are finishing up batting practice and fielding, and Travis wants to get out there. So he goes through the line, picking and choosing, moving fast.

He's getting good at this.

As he signs a couple more, he turns down a request for a quick interview. "Talk to you after BP's totally over," he says. "Otherwise I'll get in trouble." He says it nicely enough, sincerely, just as a kid would say it.

Travis jogs out to the outfield. Most of his bulk appears to be from the waist up, and he jogs leaning forward, his arms methodically pumping; not the most graceful sight, but decidedly efficient. Anyway, Lee reaches the outfield, where he mainly stands around and talks with the other guys and shags the occasional fly ball.

Schmoozing completed, Travis gets another turn at bat. He places a weighted donut on the end of his bat; he warms up his swing. He slices heavily downward, and the sound of the bat cutting through the air is clearly audible all the way into the first rows of the stands.

Travis takes a handful of whacks at the ball, each pitch, without fail, crashing to the back of the center-right fence or over it. Afterward, he remains to the side of home plate, bat in hand, knocking down the balls thrown in from the outfield, assisting the coach standing nearby. He's agile with the bat, having fun blocking and bunting, even abandoning his post to play a little field hockey with a couple of other players.

Fun over, Travis returns to the sideline and to the writer patiently waiting. Travis is definitely not a publicity hound. Some of the players relish the attention from the media—one young fellow has had a half-page article in his hometown paper about his baseball exploits laminated, and is at this moment proudly displaying it to his teammates and anybody else who's willing to take a look.

Not Travis. A press manager from the Fall League, who has handled an awful lot of media requests for face time with Travis— many more such requests than for any other player—says that he is a good guy, a bit overwhelmed by the demands of the media.

The manager explains that Travis is still a big kid, a real baseball fan, who was as excited as any other fan would be when he met Frank Robinson, the Hall of Famer from the Baltimore Orioles and the current commissioner of the Arizona Fall League. Lee always refers to the commissioner as "Mr. Robinson," though Mr. Robinson tells all the young players to call him Frank. "And he could hardly believe it when he was called over to have his picture taken with [former Chicago Cubs great] Ernie Banks," the press manager recalls.

Unfortunately, those glad moments are behind him. As the first original Diamondback star, unsullied by other teams and their rules and uniforms, he must rise yet again and satiate the media monster. So he stands and speaks.

The autograph seekers, young and old, are only a few yards off and continue to cry out for Travis's signature. "I want to sign for kids," Travis says. "Baseball has a long tradition of signing autographs. But these collectors . . ." He shakes his head. "When a kid comes up to you and asks you to sign it on the sweet spot of the baseball, you know he doesn't know about that."

Travis is right. A batboy, probably around ten years old, for one of the Fall League teams can be seen before every game entering the locker room to ask the players to sign an assortment of bats and balls. From his approach, one might assume that he is helping out some of the spectators. Sadly, the truth is he takes all the signed objects and hands them over to his father, waiting in the stands. The father checks to ensure that his son has gotten the names he has wanted, before passing to him another load of paraphernalia.

A minor league version of child abuse.

All right, nothing he can do about any of that, and Travis is nothing if not a baseball realist. He has already learned to accept everything with a certain ease, which translates some of his answers into a greatest-hits collection of sports clichés, inevitably delivered with an unconcerned shrug.

Does he mind talking to the press? "It's just part of the job."

Is he excited about one day soon playing in the major league stadiums in front of huge crowds? "Same old game anywhere you play. Same bases and lines and grass."

Any ballplayer you want to emulate? "Just want to be Travis Lee."
Shrug, shrug, shrug.

He talks about how long his baseball year has been, and his surprise at the toll it's taken on him. "I never thought I'd get so tired," he says. "I played sixty games in college, mainly on the weekend. Now I'll have played something like over two hundred games this year."

He took six months off from baseball last year and doesn't plan on touching a glove or bat again when this season's over until spring training. Nevertheless, Travis plans on staying in shape during the

MOST INFLUENTIAL

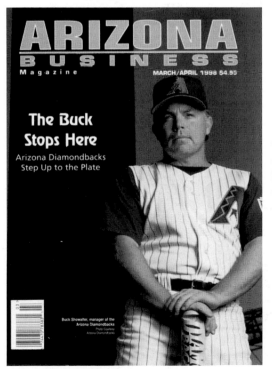

Jerry Colangelo, the most powerful man in Arizona.
(The Business Journal/*Scott Foust*)

Whether the title of an article or a chapter in a book, this headline is too apt to ignore. (Arizona Business Magazine/ *Arizona Diamondbacks*)

Travis Lee of the Scottsdale Scorpions, at bat before a fairly typical crowd in the Arizona Fall League, only months before he would become a major-leaguer and start for the Diamondbacks.

Tucson Electric Park, at dusk at the Diamondbacks' first spring training game, February 27, 1998.

Bank One Ballpark halfway to completion.

The spot reserved for the swimming pool in right field.

BOB, before . . .

And after. Note the city's controversial, opulent garage in the foreground in the early stages of construction.

The view from the completed pool, literally overlooking the warning track. The hot tub sits on top of the pool, separated by the tile.

On top of the world, ma! A view from the one-dollar seats, the best bargain in professional sports—as long as you don't mind heights.

The perspective from the lower floor of Jerry Colangelo's two-story suite.

Where all your consumer dreams come true—the team shop in Bank One Ballpark.

Break open that piggybank, kids. Marketing to toddlers: the one-piece on the right is $20, the socks are $5, the hat is $10, and the bib is $5.

Two signatures that autograph hunters, as well as ordinary fans, covet: Manager Buck Showalter and rookie Travis Lee.

Your intrepid correspondent, in sunglasses and helmet, at BOB, for newly signed Andy Benes's introduction to the media and Arizona. Benes somehow gets away with skipping the safety helmet for a Diamondbacks cap. *(Irwin R. Daugherty/*The Tribune)

Opening Day, March 31, 1998. The first fans flow inside as batting practice is already under way. More reporters than players are on the field. To the right, a knot of eager correspondents surround Buck.

The knot, up-close and personal. Buck feeds the ravenous press.

Batting practice for the servers: Checking those handheld computers one last time in preparation for feeding the fancier fans.

A not-quite-traditional Indian blessing: Asked to grace the ballpark, this visitor from Oregon issued a political statement on behalf of the American Indian Movement, upsetting the local tribes in Arizona more than the bemused fans.

An emotional Jerry Colangelo welcomes one and all to Opening Day.

In the killing-two-birds-with-one-stone category: the Diamondback coaches and trainers during the Pledge of Allegiance—first to the US of A, and then to Buck, up on the JumboTron.

The Opening Day line-up for the Arizona Diamondbacks. In batting order from right to left: Devon White, standing beside Buck, then Jay Bell, Travis Lee, Matt Williams, Brent Brede, Karmin Garcia, Jorge Fabregas, and Edwin Diaz. Pitcher Andy Benes is in the bullpen, warming up.

off-season. "Fifty years ago," he says, "it was different, but the game is for the big and strong now."

It's the middle of the World Series, but Travis says he isn't much of a television viewer and hasn't caught many of the games. Like a lot of professional athletes, he plays so many games himself that he doesn't really enjoy watching.

Travis doesn't have much to say about the money, but the incredible sum sits out there, like an elephant squatting on the pitcher's mound. He hasn't run out and blown it on wine, women, and song. He has bought a car for his mom, and one for himself. His is a BMW and has four doors, Travis explains, because his fellow minor leaguers usually don't have vehicles of their own, and so it falls to him to give his teammates rides around town.

Money is providing Travis with a crash course in the difference between the haves and the have-nots. He talks about how he discovered that some of the Dominican Diamondbacks weren't eating lunch in order to save their per diem to send home to their families. There is a trace of both sadness and surprise when he relates this.

"Sometimes I'll be in the room talking on the phone with a lawyer or financial adviser," Travis says, "and the guys will be in another room pooling their money for a pizza. That's not so great."

He really is a nice guy, really in it for the love of the game. Maybe he'll even stay that way, even after he makes more money and becomes more famous and is handed all the privileges and perks that go along with the life of a successful professional athlete. There's no reason to think he'll change, as so many have, and become obnoxious and greedy and self-consumed and vile. Just the opposite— given his strong family ties and college degree and solid grasp on what he cares about and wants to accomplish, he could set the standard, at least for young Diamondbacks.

It is nice to think so.

Travis says he doesn't want to be a celebrity. "I'm not looking for that," whatever *that* is. But then an interesting point is brought up to him: professional athletes tend to date models and actresses and other fellow celebrities.

"Hey," Travis says, a crooked grin blossoming on his face, "I'd like that."

On that final, happy note, it's time to batter up and play ball.

Chapter 14

. . . And So Must Experience

A reporter from a Phoenix television station buttonholed Matt Williams, the Cleveland Indians' stellar third baseman, at the 1997 All-Star Game. The reporter asked Matt what he thought of the advent of the new Arizona team. Matt said he was sure the Diamondbacks would work out great, and he was sure a lot of players would like to play there, because a lot of players owned homes in the area.

Matt and the reporter both laughed, because everybody knew that Williams was one of those ballplayers happily residing in the Valley of the Sun.

Still smiling, Matt noted that his own contract was going to be up in a couple of years.

The date was June 7.

Matt Williams wasn't the only baseball player to call Arizona home. Approximately fifty of his fellow pros and almost two hundred and fifty former big leaguers lived in the general neighborhood. The boys headed down for spring training, breathed in that warm winter air, drank in the gorgeous mountain vistas, played golf, played more golf, and never left.

"You can do anything at any time of the year here," Williams told the *Arizona Republic.* "You really can't beat it."

Randy Johnson of the Seattle Mariners also had something to say to the local paper. "I've got two years left here, and then I'm coming down, playing with the Diamondbacks," he said at the start of spring training, 1996. That was quite a bold statement, coming from the game's most intimidating pitcher, the six-foot-ten southpaw and Cy Young winner.

This sort of player enthusiasm, expressed by others as well, excited some supposition that the greats and near-greats would be banging down the Diamondback door, begging to play within commuting distance of home. It was just the sort of supposition that Buck Showalter, not interested in raising false expectations, was quick to disparage.

"People say a lot of these big free agents want to come to Phoenix," he said sometime after Johnson's comments to the newspaper. "Randy Johnson, for example, talks about it. Okay. Let me ask you a question. You're Randy Johnson. You say you want to come to Phoenix. You want to come? Well, how bad do you want to come?"

Buck's folksy, Southern voice was in full throttle. "Will you want to come for two million dollars less? 'Well, no, now I'll come, but for the same money I can get anywhere. All things being equal, I want to come.' "

Buck smiled. "Oh, so you *don't* want to come."

Point taken. Nevertheless, perhaps Matt Williams was a different story, different from Randy Johnson or any other ballplayer, different because his wife of nearly eight years had filed for divorce in March earlier that year. The split occurred just as Williams was starting his first year in Cleveland after a ten-year career with the San Francisco Giants, a career that saw him win three Gold Gloves, smack thirty or more home runs in four of those seasons, hit one hundred–plus RBIs two times, and make four All-Star teams. Between the split and the move to Cleveland, the thirty-two-year-old Williams found himself separated from his three young children, ages five, seven, and eight, far more than he could bear.

Williams did the best he could. The divorce decree gave Matt joint custody, and his kids flew to Cleveland for every single home stand. All that flying back and forth was hardly an ideal situation. During an interview on-line for the Diamondbacks' Web site—yes, the Diamondbacks have a Web site, just like every other forward-thinking business—Matt went into more detail:

"I just missed my kids terribly. I think it was more difficult on them. Kids have routines, and as parents you need to stick with those

179

routines as much as you can. It's important that they enjoy themselves and enjoy their life," which hardly seemed possible if they were consigned to an exhausting round-trip every couple of weeks.

"They got sick of it, man," Williams said. "It was almost as if they didn't want to come—not because they didn't want to see me, but they just hated that flight so much, and it was like, 'Hi, how are you?' and I'm off to the ballpark. Then I got to see them at night a little bit before they went to bed and a little bit the next morning, and it didn't seem like I got to see them at all. It was tough on them, extremely tough."

And sufficiently tough on Matt that he told Jeff Moorad, his agent, sometime after that 1997 All-Star Game, that it sure would be nice if he could play in Arizona the following season.

Nice indeed.

In the meantime, Williams enjoyed a personal-best 24-game hitting streak and finished the season with 32 homers and 105 RBIs, ending the year with 297 career home runs. He also earned his fourth Gold Glove, committing just 12 errors in 402 chances. The Indians made it to the World Series, losing by the length of an outstretched hand in the seventh game to the Florida Marlins.

Bad feeling, losing the big game—in this case, the really Big Game. Not exactly in a celebratory mood, Matt decided to fly straight to Phoenix to be with his kids instead of returning with the team to Cleveland, where a parade was planned.

Matt went to his hotel room and found the message light blinking. It was from Jeff Moorad, who was staying in the same hotel. Williams phoned him and his agent stopped by for a visit with his friend and client. It was one in the morning. When they finished talking, it was a quarter to six, just enough time for Matt to jump in a cab and get to the airport for a 7 A.M. flight to Phoenix.

Back on the Internet, Matt recalled their discussion: "We went through a number of different things, weighing the pros and cons. We wrote down a list of Cleveland versus Arizona, and there were good things on both sides. I mean, Cleveland just played in game seven of the World Series and had a very good chance of going back. As far as my baseball career went, Cleveland was great, but it always came back to my children, and that outweighs anything. I'd rather be with my children than go to a World Series, and if that's wrong, then that's wrong, but that's the way I feel. That's what made my mind up, and we went to work on it. It was emotional. It was one of those points in your life where you have to make a decision."

Of course, the decision—any decision, either way—wasn't entirely Matt Williams's to make.

And so Jeff Moorad went to work.

The Indians were quite content with their third baseman. In fact, they wanted to sign him to a contract extension. Regardless, the club received his request with singular compassion. Actually, it seemed to Williams that John Hart, the Cleveland general manager, was half-anticipating such a petition.

Matt expressed the attitude of the Indians' front office: "They saw past the baseball part of it."

Then again, Cleveland wasn't a charity, and the team wanted fair value for their prize player.

And what of Arizona? How did the Diamondbacks feel about Matt Williams, yearning to go home?

Matt Williams was not only a terrific player but also a solid citizen and dedicated father as well, qualities that marked him as just the man for a franchise that promoted itself as the natural harbor for solid citizens, dedicated fathers, and other all-around good guys.

Even more important, the team had to relish the notion, the vision, of their corners anchored by Matt Williams at third and Travis Lee at first, All-Stars present and future.

Vision aside, just as Cleveland wasn't parting with Williams without receiving appropriate compensation, Arizona wasn't about to throw out all its plans and hand over all its prospects to acquire one player, no matter how rare and right.

Cleveland and Arizona talked, but not much could possibly come of it, not yet, for one undeniable reason—the Diamondbacks didn't have any players to trade for Williams, nor would they until the expansion draft. And so all the conversations and propositions and ideas remained just that—talk.

On the eve of the draft, Williams was asked by a journalist what he imagined it would be like playing for the Diamondbacks, beating sun and all. Williams's rosy response appeared on another Internet site:

"Arizona is going to be a great place to play baseball. I have had spring training there for most of my career until I was traded. I live in Arizona in the off-season and I do not mind the heat. The rising temperatures towards the afternoon tend to wear you out a bit, but most of our games will be played at night and the temperatures will drop into the nineties, which is perfect baseball weather. Afternoon games will be draining, so players might have to take it easy before game time. On days that it is extremely hot, players might not take extra batting practice or do so much running before game time. You do need to save yourself for the game."

Look! Matt Williams does not mind the heat. Hark! Perfect baseball weather. Heed! Save yourself for the game.

He belonged. He really belonged.

It was time for the draft.

The Diamondbacks won the coin toss and elected to choose second and third, giving the Tampa Bay Devil Rays the first pick. The idea was that if the Devil Rays didn't upset the applecart by taking one of the players Cleveland coveted, the Diamondbacks might be able to use their consecutive selections to strike a two-for-one deal for Williams.

Specifically, the Indians wanted to hold on to their young pitcher Brian Anderson, whom Cleveland had to leave unprotected. Of course, the Devil Rays had to first pass on Anderson, which they did, instead taking pitcher Tony Saunders from the Florida Marlins. That left Anderson for the DBs, and they nabbed him.

The draft proceeded in fine form for the Diamondbacks, and speculation ran rampant through the draft that Williams would be wearing the purple and turquoise before the day was out.

Alas, it was not to be. The Indians wanted too much, five players for one.

Perhaps three for one was the correct calculation, because Arizona traded Gabe Alvarez, Matt Drews, and Joe Randa, all three picked up in the draft for Travis Fryman. Twenty-nine years old, Fryman was far from a marginal third baseman, not at a $6.5-million salary. In 1997, he had batted .274 with 22 home runs and 105 RBIs. He actually had an ever so slightly better fielding percentage than Williams, .978 to .970, committing just 10 errors in 448 chances.

Matt Williams was disappointed. He had believed it was going to happen, but then it hadn't. He was resigned to playing out his contract in Cleveland.

But Jeff Moorad kept prodding, and the Diamondbacks and the Indians kept talking. And just two weeks later, the Indians dispatched Williams to Arizona in exchange for Travis Fryman and relief pitcher Tom Martin. Players were one thing, but Cleveland also wanted money—$3 million, to be exact, a tidy sum that was turning out to be a bone of contention.

Moorad called Williams and told him the problem, which Williams solved with one dramatic stroke. "I told him at that point that money was not a factor with me," Williams said, "and that if they needed money, I'd take care of it."

So he did, chipping in $2.5 million, the Diamondbacks willing to contribute the remaining half million.

The deal was done.

On December 1, Williams appeared at his very own Diamondback coming-out press conference inside the America West Arena, complete with the traditional awarding of the DB cap and personalized jersey. Williams said this was "the most important decision of the rest of my life." He had nothing but praise for Cleveland, the town and franchise, "a great team with tremendous teammates and great fans."

But the town and the franchise weren't the issue. "Given all that, I had to trade it all for a chance to have a good relationship with my children. They are the most important thing, without a doubt, in my life."

"We recognized the uniqueness of the request," Moorad told the *New York Times*. "The professionalism of the Indians absolutely stunned Matt and me. We were blown away by the spirit of cooperation. Teams don't do this for players."

"It's going to be good to be able to stay at home," Matt Williams said.

It was a unique situation, made all that much more exceptional because Williams agreed to take $4.5 million instead of the $7 million due him in 1998. At first blush, the giveback seemed to contradict Buck's confident "All things being equal, I want to come" assertion. However, first blush quickly gave way to reality.

In bringing Williams to Arizona, the franchise welcomed him with a five-year contract extension worth $45 million. The extension meant that Williams would average $9 million per season, finally earning $10 million, at the age of thirty-seven, in the year 2003.

One might say that it had paid Matt Williams very well to be generous.

Truly, though, for once in the modern sporting world, money wasn't the start and finish of the tale, the end-all, be-all. Perhaps that was why it worked out so well for everyone involved. Perhaps this small, lonely, individual act would light a spark that would herald a new day in professional sports, a day when family and personal responsibility and values would take precedence over ego and cash.

And perhaps it worked out so well for everyone involved simply because the deal—when the dust finally settled and the negotiators considered the players and contracts and clubs—ultimately made baseball and business sense for all parties.

Either way, one fact was indisputable: on opening day, March 31, 1998, and for a long time thereafter, the Arizona Diamondbacks would have a hell of a ballplayer holding down third base.

PART IV | The Show's Sideshow

Chapter 15

Working with Others—Jerry's Way

Everything had to be decided. It was so easy, so natural, for the eye to become accustomed to things the way they were, for the mind to forget what had come before, that all the landmarks of our world—all the symbols and names, beliefs and traditions, people and places—can seem inevitable, unchangeable, permanent. But there was a time when they had to be conceived or designed, hired or built. They had to be chosen. Someone had to decide.

Jerry Colangelo decided for the Arizona Diamondbacks. He decided the big things and he pretty much decided the little things, too.

Choosing the name of the new team topped the list of the basic and undeniably consequential issues. While a rose was still a rose by any other name, and a collection of professional baseball players constituted a professional baseball team, the name of that team captured the history and heroes, heart and soul, past and future, of the franchise in a few letters. And if those few letters held significance, then the visceral nature of sport, the emotional pull that bonded fans to a team, empowered a team's logo with symbolic force.

In short, in war, soldiers followed the nation's flag to victory. In sports, fans followed the team's logo to the team shop, where the merchandise awaited conquering—and fans were buying $3 billion worth of licensed Major League Baseball merchandise every year.

Let us pause a moment to really drink in that figure—$3 billion. Three billion American dollars.

Now let us pause the next moment to wonder why. Why so many billions spent on baseball badges and stamps and insignias—baseball stuff—and billions more on football stuff and basketball stuff, not to mention stuff from Disney and the Hard Rock Cafe, the Grand Canyon and Planet Hollywood, Ralph Lauren and Calvin Klein, the Gap and Banana Republic?

Everybody likes souvenirs. They remind us of good times and fond memories. However, at a certain point, at a certain level of expenditure and effort, souvenirs become more than remembrances of days past or tokens of glad associations. Souvenirs become identities.

People love flags and symbols and logos, because people want to belong. We need to belong, because we are social creatures, and belonging to groups gives structure and identity to our actions and history and beliefs. Belonging proves that each of us is not totally alone in an unfeeling cosmos. Belonging affirms that together we are part of something more, something finer and greater than any individual. Belonging gives meaning to our lives.

Unfortunately, pervasive public cynicism, both earned and unearned, has robbed our most powerful institutions of much of their ability to inspire and reassure us and bind us to them and to each other. While Americans are surely among the most vocally patriotic and religious people on the planet, our institutions of state and government have suffered devastating losses in public confidence and trust. Other valuable institutions, from volunteer organizations to political parties to unions, have also found their memberships and support in critical decline.

At the same time our essential organizations and systems have become diminished, the two modern industries of communications and entertainment (whose corporations and personnel are frequently though not necessarily one and the same) have increased in autonomy and power. As will be discussed later, the very nature of the media, as we can roughly call the marriage of these two industries, might well be fatally hostile to the stability and success of traditionally vital institutions—fatally hostile to the health and well-being of our society.

But that is for later.

Now the focus will not be on this great, overwhelming issue, this matter of national stability and welfare, but on a smaller, more immediate concern, which asks exactly what is filling the void left by the demise of the old institutions. Of course, the answer is the same to both queries—communications and entertainment.

Actors and athletes have taken the place of statesmen and explorers, philosophers and scientists, as our society's heroes, "heroes" in the sense that these celebrities are the most watched, admired, privileged, and imitated people in America today. Similarly, the institutions these people inhabit and represent are not merely immensely wealthy and powerful, but command center stage with amoral authority, interested in gaining influence and fame not to effect societal change but to sell products. And the cynical public, having forsaken and been forsaken by the old institutions, gladly seizes upon this substitute, a substitute that might not provide a lot in real benefits, but doesn't require a lot in return either, aside from unconditional love.

So that, at least in part, is why.

Three billion dollars.

Jerry Colangelo, Major League Baseball, and Greg Fisher had certainly not reflected upon these ideas when ruminating over a name and a logo for the Arizona baseball team. Nonetheless, they had probably reflected long and hard upon the intense loyalty that fans displayed for the teams most cherished, and how the media could help transform any club's fan base from the hometown to the national and even international stage. And as professional sports continued to gain a bigger, more global stage, the $3 billion expended upon sports merchandise was only going to increase.

All of which made the new name and the logo very important indeed.

Based in Phoenix, Campbell Fisher Ditka Design had established a reputation from New York to Los Angeles. Even more important, the firm had already done work for two of Colangelo's teams, the Suns and the Rattlers.

Greg Fisher was tall and thin, spare in dress and manner, a perfect match with his postmodern office, stark and subdued with art and angles and high-tech equipment. Both Greg and his environment looked as if they belonged more in California than Arizona. But looks must have been deceiving, because Campbell Fisher Ditka Design was comfortably ensconced on Camelback Avenue, Phoenix's most fashionable boulevard.

The firm was hired to lead the search for an identity for the new club, with Greg taking the lead position for the company. The task began some nine months before Major League Baseball actually awarded Jerry Colangelo and his investors a team. This might have seemed a bit presumptuous—a name without a team—but the franchise had to be ready, assuming there was going to be a franchise.

Besides, Jerry was never one to play it safe.

A contest was announced, and Colangelo's investment group invited the public to submit suggestions. The response was enthusiastic, and the ballots piled up.

Regardless, all those postcards and letters, all that postage, didn't really matter that much. Colangelo had hired Fisher, a professional, and it wasn't to sort through other people's recommendations. Even so, Fisher's ideas weren't the final word. That only belonged to one man.

The choices were quickly whittled down to five: Coyotes, Barracudas, Scorpions, Rattlers, and Diamondbacks. A committee of designers and future Diamondback executives regularly met to thrash out the candidates, though it is a bit difficult to imagine the progression of the discussion: "Coyotes are fast! Like a fleet center fielder!" "But barracudas have rows of sharp teeth! Like a ferocious reliever intent on closing out the side in the bottom of the ninth!" "Hey, but scorpions . . ." And so on. Perhaps.

Fisher did have sketches for the group to examine: *Rattlers* spelled out, with the *t*'s pointed at the ends, like a snake's fangs; an *A* with a giant scorpion drawn inside, its tail curled upward; an *A* inside a baseball, and the ball was also a sun, with flames around the circle; and many more sketches.

Major League Baseball was going to reveal its two new cities in just three short weeks, and Colangelo and company had to be ready.

The committee—Jerry Colangelo, Bryan Colangelo, Joe Garagiola Jr., Rich Dozier, Scott Brubaker, and Greg Fisher—narrowed the field to the Scorpions and the Diamondbacks. Greg prepared five logos for each name.

The committee met and met yet again. Finally, the moment arrived to stand up and be counted. It was time to vote.

Jerry stated that everyone was to cast one ballot. Jerry and Joe preferred Diamondbacks. Bryan, Rich, Scott, and Greg wanted Scorpions.

The campaigning had been hard and well fought, but now the election was done. And now Jerry had one last thing to say.

I forget to tell you, he announced. I get seven votes.

And then Jerry tabled any decision until after his vacation.

Colangelo took his family to California for two weeks. While he was away relaxing, the members of his defunct committee were, figuratively and maybe literally, sweating out the finale.

In due time, Jerry phoned Greg and told him it was the Diamondbacks. After all, Greg had to know. He had work to do, and not much time to do it.

The others knew that Fisher knew, and they started to call—and call. Colangelo had sworn the graphic designer to secrecy, and Greg would not, could not, relieve his comrades' suffering.

Dozier phoned one night at eleven, but hung up with his curiosity unsated. Colangelo happened to call shortly thereafter, and Fisher informed him of Rich's tortured state. Jerry rang up his future team president and chatted awhile—but refused alleviate his misery and give him the word, one way or another.

Fisher needed a break. Besides, it was a Sunday afternoon, and Jerry was still away. Greg decided to take his wife and two kids to watch the Suns play the Charlotte Hornets.

Jerry called in the middle of the game. He had interrupted his vacation and was back in Phoenix. He was ready to let his men in on the decision. That day. So they convened after the game and learned from Jerry that Diamondbacks was it.

There was one week and two days to go.

Jerry flew back to California to resume his vacation with his family.

The real work was about to begin. The club had a logo: a slanted *A* with a stylized purple snake running up one of the letter's green supports, an equally stylized purple reptile's head and fangs forming the link between the two supports, copper lines outlining the snake's separate body and head, and also the entire *A*.

The predominant purple wasn't just ordinary purple—it was "Arizona purple," which would have been a meaningless term except it was Jerry Colangelo's concept of the richest purple available. Aside from being a color favored by Jerry, aside from showing up well on television and under stadium lights, purple was the hottest color in sports merchandising.

191

The contrasting or highlighting colors could claim a more legitimate Arizona legacy. Both turquoise and copper—the mineral and the metal—were indigenous to the state; fortuitously, their colors worked extremely well with purple.

March 9, 1995. Jerry announced that Arizona had won itself a team, the people cheered, and Diamondback caps and other souvenirs went on sale in Phoenix Suns stores and other retail shops.

Phase one completed. Now the Diamondbacks needed uniforms.

Baseball, in the corporate structure of Major League Baseball, did not permit its teams to simply venture out and design uniforms willy-nilly. Major League Baseball was there to advise and consent at every turn, on every color, every style, every stripe and lettering.

Baseball expected to provide a designer to assist Arizona, but Jerry scotched that notion from the start. He was paying for the uniforms, and he would have his designer on the job. Round one to Colangelo.

Color: Pro caps were wool and pro uniforms were polyester, and purple turned out to be a difficult color to match in both wool and polyester. It took Russell Athletic, which made every team's uniforms, some time to hit upon the right combination of dyes to find a shade that wouldn't bleed in the wash.

The chosen copper color also faced an uphill battle. The metallic bits of copper flaked under playing conditions and didn't show up well under the lights anyway, so a coppery brown was substituted.

Stripes: Jerry wanted stripes, but Joe Garagiola Jr., a baseball traditionalist of the first order, believed that pinstripes should only be worn by the Yankees. Stripes it was. Next, Colangelo wanted them to be one and three-quarters inch apart. However, the baseball fashion authorities dictated that the stripes must be separated by no more than one inch. Yankee stripes were one inch apart. Jerry went with the same. Round two to Major League Baseball.

Colangelo would win round three and the match with his final masterstroke. Most teams had three uniforms—one for home games, one for road games, and one for batting practice. The Florida Marlins had four. But the Diamondbacks, the Arizona Diamondbacks, would have no less than five.

Two for home, two for away, and one for batting practice. Three different caps were mixed-and-matched with the uniforms.

On the road, the team would be garbed in a gray jersey and pants set—league-sanctioned Baseball Gray, gray tinged with blue—with purple pinstripes for the road, or the same gray pants topped with a purple shirt. At home, the choices were a cream set with purple stripes, or the cream pants with a sleeveless purple vest worn over a purple shirt. For batting practice, the jersey was a black mesh, while the pants remained either the gray or cream standards.

They looked terrific.

The uniforms were constructed of 100 percent polyester. Polyester was hot under any conditions, but in Arizona it could be absolutely, painfully, murderously suffocating.

A few months before the start of the 1998 season, Buck Showalter offered his evaluation of polyester: "There's nothing in the uniform that allows you to play baseball better. To be quite honest, it's one of the most uncomfortable uniforms in sports. The hose kill you, the pants have the elastic stuff in the material that's very binding . . ."

So why were the uniforms made of such strange, artificial fibers?

"Because that's what Major League Baseball wants," Buck said. "It looks good, it's easy to take care of. And it's the easiest for the company to make. They say they customize them? Every year when the uniforms come in—after they've tailored them, in the spring—it's a brutal time, because they're all screwed up."

The giant corporation shuts its eyes to the discomfort of its workforce for the sake of profits—nothing new there.

But still, why design so many uniforms? Simply to have more than all the other teams? Was that the point?

The answer was so obvious that the question was an embarrassment, and Jerry, with his customary bluntness, did not hesitate to explain his motivation to one and all in the pages of the *Wall Street Journal:*

"From the standpoint of marketing, the more styles you have, the more you sell."

Of course.

It all came down to that tag hanging from every sanctioned pair of briefs and every approved pair of socks, the tag that explained the complex and crucial important relationship between professional sports and merchandising, value and values:

"Congratulations on your selection of this genuine article—a product officially licensed by Major League Baseball. It takes hard work and commitment to make the Major Leagues. Every Major League Baseball product is designed and crafted to meet the highest standards of quality and performance. This product represents America's long baseball heritage. With the purchase of this article, you bring home a part of Baseball you can call your own. The Major League Baseball Genuine Merchandise logo is your assurance of authenticity. Accept no substitute."

It was November 3, 1995. The uniforms would be in the stores by Christmas.

Chapter 16

The Glory of the Rockies

The Boeing 757 was waiting in a closed hangar away from the main terminals. A crowd was gathering outside on a lovely spring morning in May. The Diamondbacks were almost two years away from having a team, but they already had a plane. In truth, it wasn't exactly the Arizona Diamondbacks' plane, it was an America West aircraft painted to represent the DBs.

America West Airlines was headquartered in downtown Tempe, not too far from Sky Harbor Airport. The company had done business with Jerry Colangelo before, putting up $800,000 per year to acquire the naming rights to the arena where his Suns played. They also had the basketball team's charter business, which returned a few dollars back into the airline's coffers.

As Arizona's homegrown airline, America West wanted to be part of the Diamondbacks, and the Diamondbacks wanted America West. The contract finally signed covered a lot of ground and a lot of money.

America West purchased one unit in the team, which initially cost $5 million, later rising to $6 million. Another $2.5 million of the airline's funds was to be spent each year on buying advertising time during DB games and other media opportunities, and on a suite in the stadium.

The deal made sense to AW on several levels. The team was a good investment; successful sports franchises were *very* successful franchises, with substantial returns. The association with the team spurred brand recognition at home and across the country, so when the consumer thought of the Arizona Diamondbacks, he would almost have no choice but to think of America West. Hand in hand with that goal, virtually all of the airline's advertising was "retail," direct to the consumer in newspapers and on TV, promoting their ticket prices. The deal guaranteed that no other airline could advertise during the DB games, which promised AW an unobstructed shot at gaining the attention, and hopefully the business, of an audience expected to be reasonably demographically desirable.

In addition to the suite, America West was getting fifteen seats on the field behind first base, twenty in the loge, and the opportunity to buy unlimited quantities when available.

America West would also have a small store inside the stadium selling tickets, and also bits of AW merchandise.

Which all led up to that Boeing 757 secured behind the shut hangar doors on a spring day in 1996.

Officials from America West and the Arizona Diamondbacks mingled with members of the media, a large contingent of DB investors, and forty lucky civilians who had won a radio promotion. They had all been invited not only to witness the unveiling of the plane—but to take a ride.

Before long, the moment arrived. The hangar doors were opened and the great beast was slowly towed out, its turquoise fuselage gleaming in the blue sun. The body was trimmed in red, and a giant Diamondback *A* was painted behind the main passenger doors. A huge, white baseball with red and black stitches covered the tail.

It was no exaggeration to say that there was nothing else like it in the skies. America West had commissioned five other theme aircraft before (including one honoring the Phoenix Suns, three for AW's hub states of Arizona, Nevada, and Ohio, and the last, to quote a press release, "a child's concept of teamwork . . . designed by the daughter of an America West pilot"), but this was the first jet dedicated to a Major League Baseball team.

A five-man Dixie band played an up-tempo version of "Take Me Out to the Ball Game" while the media rolled their cameras and snapped their photographs and interviewed the beaming airline and baseball representatives.

"On behalf of the hometown airline," Bill Franke, America West chairman and CEO, told the crowd assembled in the reviewing stands, "I'm extremely proud to dedicate this aircraft to the hometown team, the Arizona Diamondbacks. This beautiful Boeing 757 aircraft will fly the Diamondbacks' banner across the skies of North America."

Jerry Colangelo spoke next. "The Arizona Diamondbacks' family is honored that America West Airlines would recognize the franchise in this way," he began, but soon, as was his wont, he veered off onto a topic that he felt needed illuminating, then and there. On this occasion, he folded a few words about how wonderful the plane was into a couple of lines about his ongoing effort to have the DBs placed in the National League instead of the American by the other owners. This plane will carry the team to many away games, he said—to a lot of National League cities.

"If they put us in the National League," added Colangelo, "we'll say that's exactly what we wanted. If they put us in the American League, we'll say we fooled 'em."

That said and done, it was time to board the plane. It seemed clean and even new inside. The AW and DB officials had the first-class section reserved for themselves, and everyone else settled into the open coach seating. One had the definite impression that many of the passengers cramming themselves into the small, uncomfortable seats weren't used to this second-class reality. After all, these were the investors in the club, and this mainly male, mainly older, frequently well-fed group were people who had sufficient disposable income to drop half a million dollars or much more into the Diamondback kitty. People with that kind of cash were also often (particularly when their companies were paying) used to flying first-class.

Regardless, spirits were high, because this was a free trip to Colorado, where buses were waiting to take the group to Coors Field in downtown Denver to watch a baseball game.

The Colorado Rockies were one of the franchises that the Diamondbacks readily listed as a model to emulate, on and off the field. Instantly and immensely popular from opening day, 1993, the team drew 4.5 million fans their first year in baseball, the highest attendance in the history of sport. In their third year, the Rockies made the playoffs as a wild-card contender. In 1995, the club moved into Coors Field, a terrific new stadium designed just for baseball—after signing a most advantageous deal with the city, which had paid for its construction—and the Colorado brewer had contributed handsomely to the club's pot for stadium-naming privileges. The Rockies would pay no rent for five years, and a token amount thereafter, and receive all of the income from luxury boxes, parking, concessions, and advertising. In return for keeping the facility in running order, the Rockies would also pocket all revenue derived from concerts, meetings, and other nonbaseball events.

Coors Field was a beauty, in the classic baseball-ballpark style that had been updated so triumphantly in recent years in Baltimore, Cleveland, and Dallas. No Astrodome here, and no AstroTurf either, nothing to gawk at and be intimidated by, but rather a welcoming, intimate theater for fifty thousand fans to come and partake in the game. But old-fashioned did not mean old, and modern conveniences, and modern temptations, abounded. For watching the game wasn't the only thing to do in the stadium named for the local beer company in exchange for a generous check. The kids had a play area, with a batting cage and a speed-pitching venue. An enormous store beckoned young and old to enter and buy Colorado Rockies polo shirts in a wall-full of patterns and colors, from $39 to $59, as well as a complete array of geegaws and garb for the logo-loving fan.

When the boys and girls and men and women needed succor from all the watching and playing and shopping, food and drink awaited consuming. Not just peanuts and Cracker Jacks anymore, not just rubbery hot dogs and flat soda; that would not do for the patrons of Coors Field. Instead, the choices would have made a mall food-court proud. Lines of carts lined the walkways. One stand sold foot-longs for $4.25, and bratwurst for $4 even. Taco Bell held aloft the standard for fast-food joints.

While many more food choices lured the hungry fan, the real focus seemed to be on beer. Beers of the World offered Amstel Light, Killian's, Blue Moon, Corona, Sam Adams, Beck's, Newcastle, and naturally, Coors, for $4 per. Competing with all those beers was a microbrewery selling concoctions called Right Field Red and Squeeze Play Wheat.

A segment on HBO's sports magazine show, *Real Sports,* extolling the virtues of Coors Field, revealed another reason, aside from the amenities, for the stadium's selling out every game since June 1995. Anywhere between five and six hundred "hospitality" employees were always on duty, there to help fans in any manner possible.

HBO interviewed Jerry McMorris, the owner of the Rockies.

Asked about the future, it was his opinion that Phoenix was the "next special place."

Phoenix had journeyed to Denver on this day to both learn and celebrate. While the investors and contestant winners were enjoying the game, some of the Arizona officials were having meetings with their Colorado counterparts, picking up ideas. Despite the Rockies' mastery of the business end of baseball, this was one area where the Diamondbacks required little advice.

Scott Brubaker had invited a bunch of the team's sponsors on the trip, and executives from many had accepted, such as Miller Brewing and Bank One. David Evans was also along for the trip, representing Pepsi-Cola.

It had taken five months to negotiate the deal between Pepsi and the DBs, and Evans was content. The Phoenix office and plant of the giant drink manufacturer was south of the airport, in a series of unattractive, squat buildings that might have looked modern in the 1960s. The pool in front of the one-story administration building needed cleaning.

Jerry Colangelo called in August 1995. Evans was not surprised to hear from the Diamondbacks' owner, and he and his Pepsi bosses were eager to do business. In the company's eternal battle with Coca-Cola, it was number two Pepsi always chasing number one Coke. In Phoenix, Coke already had the pouring rights, as the soda people called them, to the Phoenix Suns and the Arizona Cardinals.

Pepsi had already lost basketball and football. Pepsi wanted the Diamondbacks and baseball.

David Evans was a jovial fellow who believed in his commodity: "Pepsi is a great product. It gives people refreshment, a lift in their day. It's enjoyment everyone can afford."

Evans summed up his Pepsi philosophy with three effervescent words: "It's positive fun!"

Generally speaking, Pepsi liked celebrities promoting its lines. Since the 1980s, they had signed up a bunch of the most famous athletes in the world to push soda: Michael Jordan, Magic Johnson, Shaquille O'Neal, and Deion Sanders, for starters. The company evidently believed professional athletes presented the proper image of good, clean, positive fun.

The DBs sounded like fun, too—and no one could doubt that they would be positive, image-wise.

The exact amount Pepsi paid to join the Diamondbacks' team was not announced, but it was in the millions. Pepsi got exclusive pouring rights, meaning no other company—meaning Coke—was allowed to sell beverages inside the stadium. Pepsi also received the usual signage franchise. Other potentially exciting opportunities included Pepsi sponsorship of a "coach's corner" TV show. Such programs were staples in many markets, and they were more often than not stultifying, boring affairs, as the head coach of the town's college or pro team was handed an out-of-prime-time half hour by a local station during his team's season to sit on a bare set and run some videotape while droning on about what went wrong in his club's performance that week. Since Buck Showalter would be occupying that host's chair for the DBs, the show had a sliver of a chance of being amusing, and a surer hope of being informative. Time would tell.

In any event, a better promotional bet for Pepsi was its plans to put the big Diamondback *A* on soda cans, along with some reduced-ticket-price offer.

The game was ending and it was time to return to the buses and take the long trip to the airport. The group had been fed and feted and entertained and was going home tired and happy.

Randy Suggs was happy. He was one of the team investors, joining a group that had purchased one unit. In total, five hundred units had been sold, which added up to a cool $250 million.

Considering that Randy had a piece of one piece, and there were so many pieces, he didn't expect to have a major impact on draft choices, game strategy, etc. He just wanted to have some fun and make some money. So far he had definitely had some fun—and he had no doubt he was going to make some money.

The Rockies had taken only three years to pay back their investors. The Phoenix Suns had paid back their investors many times. Randy was confident the DBs would do well, and not too far in the future.

Randy was president of Suggs Homes. The motto of the company was A Heritage of Quality.

Randy enjoyed baseball. He took his young family to the Cactus League spring-training games. He had bought into a luxury box in the Bank One Ballpark, a fine setting with an excellent sight line to the field and a perfect stage to dazzle clients and other business folk. However, Randy had also signed up for four seats down near the field, where the real fans resided.

Randy was a local boy, born and bred, but Tom Jorishe, the owner of Camelback Volkswagen/Saab/Suburu, was originally from Pittsburgh. He had played catcher at Penn State, even starting on the freshman team. Unfortunately, the next year another catcher arrived at the university, who not only jumped ahead of Tom on the team, but wound up being drafted by the Mets.

The Mets might not have wanted Tom, but the U.S. Army did and sent him to Germany. While in the service, he started selling cars to his fellow GIs; after his discharge, he stayed in Europe and stayed in the car business.

Eighteen years later, he returned home and, after hearing how great Phoenix was from a friend, moved his family to Arizona.

Europe might have had its charms, but he missed sports and jumped back in, buying season tickets to the Suns and the Cardinals. However, baseball was still his first love, and he went so far as to attend a Pittsburgh Pirates fantasy baseball camp, where adults paid cold cash to put on a uniform, pull on their glove, and play hardball with major leaguers for a few days. Jorishe liked it so much he went off to camp not once, but twice.

Tom was definitely interested when the possibility of buying into the Diamondbacks arose. He did his financial due diligence—because there is passion and then there is business—and Tom soon became one of the distinctly minority owners in the club.

Tom was happy with his investment. One way or another, he had made it to the major leagues.

It was a smooth ride back to Phoenix on the DB Boeing 757, which would now join America West's regular flight rotation. The painting job cost America West $80,000 but planes had to be periodically painted anyway, so it wasn't too bad. The trip to Denver and back would cost the airline another $20,000. Since a full-page ad in the *Arizona Republic* cost $15,000, the extra five grand was worth it if the media treated the purple-and-turquoise plane like a legitimate story.

The trip made all the Phoenix TV stations. The plane was the main thrust of the story. American West's sponsorship had paid off.

So that made it complete. Now everybody was happy.

Chapter 17

South of the Border,
Down Mexico Way

O vershadowed by the massive airliners of the international carriers, lost among the pack of sleek corporate jets, ignored within the horde of green military craft and polished private craft and news station helicopters, were a pair of old propeller planes. Old and none too scrubbed. None too inspiring.

They looked as if they belonged on the fog-shrouded runway in the final scene of the movie *Casablanca*, their rusty propellers whirring away, instead of idling in the brilliant winter-blue sunlight outside a hangar at Sky Harbor Airport.

It was Super Bowl week 1996, and a companion piece was about to get under way: the Sonora Bowl. Yes, while the Dallas Cowboys and the Pittsburgh Steelers were gearing for battle before a global audience, the Arizona Hispanic High School All-Stars were preparing to take on the boys (or men) from Tech de Monterrey, the number one college football squad in Mexico.

The planes had been sent courtesy of the Mexican state of Sonora. The young players, their coaches, a gaggle of media, a handful of former and current NFL players, and assorted Phoenix officials and business types boarded the plane and headed south, down Mexico way.

Among those business types were two fellows representing the Arizona Diamondbacks.

It was a short trip past Tucson and Nogales, over the border and through some rugged terrain. From the air, Hermosillo was a sprawling city of corrugated buildings and haphazard avenues and crowded streets.

The airport was modern, maybe twenty-five years ago, its terminal small and squat. Three buses were waiting to take the Americans into town, escorted by police motorcycles. A throng of small children, probably not more than four-year-olds, were standing just off the runway, egged on by their teachers to welcome the visitors. The kids, drafted into service by an overeager political functionary, couldn't have had the tiniest notion who these strange people were, but yelled and clapped enthusiastically nonetheless.

The road into Hermosillo was a vista of junked cars and old cars and Volkswagens and Dodge pickup trucks and Pemex gas stations. Sonora Bowl pennants hung from almost every lamppost.

The caravan pulled up before a hospital in the middle of the city and the Americans disembarked. At this stop, the cheering pre-schoolers had been replaced by cheering "Tecate girls," attractive young women in extremely short shorts and equally tight tops, representing the Mexican beer company. The guests were led up the stairs to the second floor. Most of the Americans, who had been so ebullient on their modest adventure till now, suddenly fell silent, their faces revealing their shock at the stark rooms and thin walls and old equipment and sparse supplies.

The band was led by a smiling doctor into a chamber where seven babies were crowded around one respirator. The Americans had brought souvenirs from the Super Bowl, hats and pins and other stuff, but no one in this room would appreciate the trinkets. The doctor quickly progressed to the next room, where six older kids, obviously rather ill, lay in their beds while worried relatives sat beside them. This was more like it, and the visitors, especially the older, more experienced fellows, moved from bed to bed, handing out this and that. The kids happily accepted the gifts, even if they didn't grasp this Yankee form of commercial campaigning.

The Americans were falling behind schedule. They climbed back on the buses.

The soccer field had been turned into a football gridiron. The stadium's cement stands were supposed to hold twenty-five thousand fans, and they were filled to capacity and beyond, filled with young people, screaming and laughing.

The NFL veterans, who included Oscar McBride and Terry Samuels of the Arizona Cardinals, and Efren Hererra, the ex–Dallas Cowboy kicker and Mexican native, conducted a brief, frenzied clinic with hundreds of the local children, running them through some rudimentary catching and running drills.

A slew of Phoenix TV stations had dispatched crews to collect a bit of footage. Better yet, the game was about to be broadcast live on Mexican television throughout Sonora.

The festivities began with a cadre of red-jacketed five- to nine-year-olds playing their instruments, ranging from flutes to saxophones to guitars to drums to electric pianos. A military unit, armed with M16s, marched about, as did a man encased in a costume resembling Barney, the purple TV dinosaur.

But that wasn't all, not by a long shot. A drum corps in red velvet appeared and banged away. A couple of hundred cheerleaders, armed with balloons, and scores of young girls in native costume danced around. The music and noise were deafening.

Cops were everywhere, some in standard tan uniforms, others in more ominous white shirts and black vests, still others in SWAT, urban camouflage and matching berets. Finally, dozens of police cadets in bombardier jackets and black combat boots were lined around the interior of the stadium, facing the stands. The police presence seemed inappropriate, to say the least; after all this wasn't a soccer match, which had a history, from Latin America to Europe, of flaring into riots.

The Mexican flag was carried out by six girls in maroon outfits with gold epaulets and white stockings. Behind them was Miss Arizona, in a sparkling silver suit, and Miss Sonora in glittering green.

The Mexican national anthem was played and the whole stadium shouted, "Viva Mexico!"

There was more of the same and more of the unexpected: a walking cactus wearing a helmet, a Tecate coyote zooming around on a dune buggy, trumpets and more drums, parachutists landing in the stadium bearing the game balls . . .

Beating all the other attractions, and a truly extraordinary sight, were the one thousand or more twelve-year-olds in the center section who held up cards and flashed messages in perfect unison. H-O-L-A spread across the stands when the teams first appeared, followed by U-S-A. The words continued throughout the afternoon:

T-O-U-C-H-D-O-W-N required the most letters. The kids must have practiced for weeks.

The game eventually commenced, and the older, larger, more practiced college team jumped out to a 17–0 halftime lead, on its way to a 30–6 victory.

The outcome wasn't much of a surprise—nor was the halftime extravaganza, featuring more dancing girls and bands and parachutists—but the game was only a component of the pageant. The more important contest was raising the profile of the American sport in Mexico, as the two nations, culturally and economically, increasingly mingled and swapped and merged their identities and interests. So it was on this day, as the American football powers worked not only with their Mexican counterparts, but also with the state of Sonora, to build a solid foundation that the NFL would need to broaden its fan base, create more markets eager for its merchandise, and ultimately, establish a franchise in Mexico City. Sports was a global business, and the NFL pursued its opportunities wherever they appeared.

Which also explained why two officials from the Arizona Diamondbacks were in Hermosillo, enjoying the show.

Actually, Scott Brubaker and Blake Edwards, number one and two in DB sales and marketing, did more than just watch. They brought along some Diamondback pins and caps and handed them out in the hospital and to anyone else they encountered. They were spreading the word, the good word about the Diamondbacks, because the franchise was convinced that Mexico, particularly northern Mexico, was fertile ground for future DB loyalists.

It might have seemed a long way to go to distribute bits of memorabilia, but, hey, the trip was free and arranged by somebody else, and business had to be slow during Super Bowl week anyway, so there they were.

Imagine, millions of Mexicans, primed to purchase the wide assortment of paraphernalia proffered by Major League Baseball and its newest franchise, the franchise just a few hours drive over the border, Nogales to Tucson to Phoenix.

The Diamondbacks' interest in Mexico, in all of Latin America, wasn't only about merchandising. The region was a wealthy source of player talent. In 1995, for example, citizens hailing from the Dominican Republic, a small country of some 8 million souls occupying half the island of Hispaniola, accounted for seventy-seven players on major league rosters, 6 percent of the total. By 1997, that figure had risen to eighty-eight players, accounting for almost 10 percent of all major leaguers.

Other Latin countries were also well represented. Mexico had twelve ballpayers in the majors, Cuba had five, Puerto Rico twenty-seven, and Venezuela thirty-seven. Counting up all the Latin athletes playing in America's national pastime in 1997, one arrived at no less than 184 major leaguers, or fully 16 percent of MLB's rosters.

In 1998, that figure would rise to about 20 percent, or one out of every five Diamondbacks and Yankees and Cubs and Dodgers.

Baseball transcended sport in the Dominican Republic, and elsewhere throughout Latin America. It was more than a game, it offered a way out, a chance at a better life—a chance at an incredibly, unbelievably better life—for desperately poor young people.

Accordingly, most American franchises sent scouts to the island or relied on Dominican scouts to scour the land in search of baseball talent. Most of the teams had training facilities of one kind or another in the country, from no-frills operations, consisting of a cinder-block dorm erected beside a rough, rocky diamond, to the seventy-acre facility the Los Angeles Dodgers called home, where some one hundred players lived comfortably enough while working on their skills with the help of two full-size fields, two practice fields, batting cages, and exercise equipment.

These were the places where the scouts brought the young boys for a tryout, hoping to get the players signed for a couple of thousand or maybe eight or ten. If that sounded a bit unsavory, pawning off the boys for a pocketful of change, particularly in comparison to the huge bonuses American ballplayers demanded, well, the price differential was simply a function of the respective markets. What was better, what offered more hope: going into the sugarcane fields to work all day for pennies, or being paid—and paid well by Dominican standards—and fed and housed, too, to play baseball and maybe one day make it to America and the majors?

The contest of capitalism had its own definite set of rules, same as baseball.

And though it was a long shot, whether in the Dominican Republic or the United States, that any one player would go all the way, from the playground to the minors to the Show, it was certainly possible. Sammy Sosa signed with the Texas Rangers in 1985 for $3,500. In

1997, he signed another contract, this time with the Chicago Cubs, this time for $42.5 million for four years. The Dodgers claimed that 13 percent of the players who have trained at their facility have made it to the big leagues.

It could be done, and so they kept trying, because they loved the game, because they desperately wanted a better life.

Poverty wasn't the only measure of desperation. Cuban ballplayers fled their home to find freedom as well as fortune. Pitcher Livan Hernandez left Cuba for the United States and prospered in every way, earning the Most Valuable Player award for leading his Florida Marlins to triumph in the 1997 World Series.

The Diamondbacks signed two Cuban players early on in their history. Vladimir Nunez and Larry Rodriguez defected from Cuba to the Dominican Republic together, then offered their services to American baseball. Unlike most of their Latin compatriots, Cuban ballplayers preferred not to head directly to the United States. This was not a political decision, but financial. American athletes, as well as American-based athletes, had to enter the baseball ranks through the amateur draft. However, by remaining offshore, by offering their services as Cuban refugees residing in Venezuela, Costa Rica, or wherever, they became free agents, permitted to accept bids from all interested teams.

Once again, capitalism giveth and capitalism taketh away.

Nunez was twenty years old and Rodriguez twenty-one. They were both pitchers, deemed a Diamondback priority from the start. Nunez was six foot four and weighed 220 pounds. Rodriguez was six foot one and 190 pounds. The former's fastball was clocked in the midnineties; the latter's was reputedly a tad slower, but graced with better control.

They were excellent prospects, and each signed a two-year deal. Nunez cleared $1.75 million. Rodriguez received $1.25 million.

That was on February 1, 1996. Thirteen months later, they had gotten a full taste of the American experience. The Diamondbacks believed in hard work, from the front office to the field, and quickly put the Cubans to the test. His very first year with the franchise, Nunez was dispatched to the Class A California League, the short-season rookie Pioneer League, and the Arizona Fall League. After a 1-6 campaign in Class A, he lived up to expectations, going 10-0 in the Pioneer League in Lethbridge, Canada, and was named Pitcher of the Year in the league.

Rodriguez also started slowly, ending up 2-5, and also rebounded in Lethbridge with a 7-1 record.

Nunez and Rodriguez had something else in common: they both got married, and both to Latin women—Nunez's bride was from the Dominican Republic, Rodriguez's from Venezuela. And one more thing: the Nunezes soon had a baby boy, and the Rodriguezes had a daughter.

Not everything went according to schedule. Nunez gained thirty pounds—undoubtedly from his first exposure to American fast food—and needed to get his weight down. Rodriguez had a more serious problem, partially tearing his rotator cuff while pitching in Lethbridge. Rodriguez was able to avoid going under the knife, the doctors deciding that a long course of rest and physical rehabilitation could repair the injury.

The waistline and the rotator cuff would be repaired and corrected. Both pitchers would return to shape, long before they would needed by the Diamondbacks. They would continue to work and improve and maybe get their shots at the big time.

Despite the progress of and focus on the two Cubans, the Diamondbacks' Latin effort remained solidly centered in the Dominican Republic.

By the age of thirty, Milciades Arturo "Junior" Noboa was a veteran of professional baseball at a variety of levels. He had bounced around the majors as an infielder with five teams and had spent time in the minors as well. Returning to the Dominican Republic, Junior followed in his father's footsteps and became a star on his home turf. He played in the Dominican Winter League for twelve seasons and also served as the general manager of the Escogido Lions.

He was perfect for the Arizona Diamondbacks. In the summer of 1995, Noboa was contacted by Don Mitchell, flown to Phoenix for a couple of days of interviews, and promptly signed, sealed, and returned to his island to begin working.

Noboa wasted no time, and so let it be recorded for prosperity and baseball statisticians that the first two Diamondback ballplayers in the history of the franchise were a pair of young Dominicans signed by Junior, seventeen-year-old Jonathan Leyba and sixteen-year-old Jose Luis Bido, the former a six-foot, 180-pound catcher, the latter a six-foot-three, 155-pound pitcher. They were determined, they were gifted, they were optimistic—and time would tell how far they would go.

More players followed, and then more, and soon twenty-six players were in the Diamondback camp. The camp, or academy, as DB officials preferred, was at first a makeshift affair outside Santo Domingo, especially with a practice field bordered by garbage and glass and graffiti. The boys lived in a dorm, and a cook on staff prepared hot meals. Despite the academy's shortcomings, the entire situation, from playing to living conditions, instruction to nutrition, was undoubtedly an improvement over what most of the kids were used to.

The poverty endemic in the Caribbean nation could not be discounted. In fact, Mel Didier was so moved by what he saw on a trip to the baseball academy that he started a clothing drive when he returned to Arizona. Diamondback employees donated thirty-six crates of used clothing, which was shipped to the Dominican Republic.

"This was our way of trying to be a good neighbor," Didier said.

Buck and his coaches often made the trip to the academy to check on the kids' progress, invariably putting on their Diamondback uniforms and getting on that broken, bumpy field.

On one of the visits, Noboa borrowed a friend's oversize four-wheel-drive vehicle and piled the cadre of high-ranking DBs inside for a ride. It was an all-star group, comprising Buck, Roland Hemond, Joe Garagiola Jr., and Tommy Jones, just the group Junior wanted. He drove them some twenty-five miles from Santo Domingo, the capital, off the road and into a field.

Noboa stopped the car and everybody climbed out. This was the spot, he said, in so many words. This was where he was going to build a first-rate, first-class baseball academy.

The Americans were not quite sold; they were in the middle of nowhere, and a rolling, uneven nowhere at that. Still, the Americans didn't have to be sold, because Junior had gotten some wealthy Dominicans to invest.

The academy in Boca Chica was built around four ballfields laid out in cloverleaf fashion. An observation tower in the middle provided panoramic viewing of all fields. To the side were another two half-diamonds and extra pitching mounds and batting tunnels. An exercise center was housed in a separate facility, the free weights and exercise machines selected by Jeff Forney, the Diamondbacks strength and conditioning coach. Another building served as the kitchen and dining area. The academy's main structure was a long, two-story hall, complete with dorms, locker rooms, and conference rooms.

The complex was large enough to service not one but two teams, and so it would, the Diamondbacks and the Blue Jays splitting the rent and all the facilities. The main hall was designed so it was simply split in half, assignment-wise, the DBs in the east wing, the Blue Jays in the west, the two franchises connected by a ground-floor walkway and a second-story patio. Each wing was large enough to accommodate fifty players and coaches.

Junior Noboa was proving not only a smart baseball pro, but perhaps a savvy businessman, too.

They held a ceremony to formally open the academy on November 16, 1996. Joe Garagiola Jr., Rich Dozer, and Don Mitchell flew in for the event, and so did officials from the Toronto Blue Jays. The Dominicans trumped that with a delegation that was led by Pres. Leonel Fernández and Baseball Hall of Famer and Minister of Sports Juan Marichal. Official America responded with our woman in Santo Domingo, U.S. Ambassador Donna Jean Hrinak.

The Diamondback and Blue Jay players watched as Garagiola presented President Fernández with a Diamondback jersey with El Presidente's name emblazoned in teal on the back, spread above a turquoise "98," a reference to the franchise's inaugural season.

In precious little time, the Diamondbacks had gone from having no presence in the Dominican Republic (or anywhere else, for that matter), to fielding a squad of some forty-five young prospects, trained by experienced coaches, overseen by perhaps the best young mind on the island, occupying perhaps the finest training facility on Hispaniola.

And so the Arizona Diamondbacks, Dominican Republic branch, were in business, bringing players from Panama and Venezuela and Mexico and Curaçao and Cuba together with their colleagues from the DR. It was expected that well over half of the players in the academy would spend at least one upcoming campaign on one of the Diamondbacks' American-rookie or Class A teams. Out of those players, perhaps five would move on to the next minor league, and then maybe a couple would continue up the ladder, until one, two— or none—reached the promised land.

In the meanwhile, as usual, the business side of the Diamondbacks kept apace with the baseball side. On May 13, 1997, the Diamondbacks announced that a Spanish AM radio station, KPHX, would broadcast all eighty-one home games. A few weeks later, on June 10, 1997, the franchise made a three-year deal with KDRX, Channel 64, the Phoenix area's Telemundo affiliate. In the first year, the Spanish station would broadcast thirty games, increasing to fifty games during each of the next two years of the contract. By 1999, the Diamondbacks expected that some games would be telecast into Mexico.

The franchise wouldn't depend upon these deals to strike up Diamondback loyalty among Hispanic fans. Just to offer one small example, the club sponsored Fiesta de Béisbol III, a high school game featuring Arizona's best Hispanic ballplayers. "Fiesta de Béisbol III is a continuation of events the Diamondbacks have sponsored in the Hispanic community," declared Richard Saenz, the DB director of Hispanic marketing, through a press release. "We want people to know that the Diamondbacks are Arizona's team, especially our young baseball players. Who knows, they may be wearing a Diamondbacks uniform someday."

That was exactly so, as borders crumbled and baseball slowly went international. The Diamondbacks were among the major league leaders in searching the world for players, finding Paul Weichard, a seventeen-year-old outfielder, in a baseball tournament in Alice Springs, deep in the Australian outback.

The huge Mexican market remained the prime international market. Roland Hemond had long had ties to Mexico and helped arrange a Diamondback affiliation with the Monterrey club in the Mexican Summer League. Unlike the situation in the Dominican Republic, Mexican rules required that before a Major League Baseball franchise could sign a player, that franchise had to be in business with a Mexican pro team that already had that player under contract.

The DBs were forging ahead on the marketing front, too. The club was putting together weekend group sales from several of the larger Mexican cities. The sales slogan sounded a bit like an ad for the newest soft drink: *"Sábados con los Diamondbacks—Ilenos de sabor Latino,"* which translated to "Saturdays with the Diamondbacks—a total Latin flavor."

The Diamondbacks weren't waiting for the Mexicans to travel north to check out the American brand of baseball. Indeed, the

Arizona Diamondbacks and the Milwaukee Brewers announced that they would journey to Hermosillo, Sonora, on March 15, 1998, smack in the middle of spring training, to play an exhibition game.

"The baseball fans in Sonora are enthusiastic about the Diamondbacks," said Rich Dozer, "and we are excited about their support. We want the people of Sonora to consider us their team."

The game would be staged at Hector Espino Stadium, a thirteen-thousand-seat arena. The contest was to be an annual event, with some of the proceeds pledged to helping local baseball programs.

So Scott Brubaker and Blake Edwards, lone Diamondback representatives virtually lost in the midst of another sport's promotion, would now be replaced by a squad of Diamondback players proudly wearing the purple and turquoise, playing before a cheering, packed house. And all those Diamondback pins that Brubaker and Edwards had handed out like candy to anyone willing to take one would now be overrun by an avalanche of Diamondback merchandise and tickets, none of which was tendered free. And the Diamondback presence, once a sideshow to a high school football team, would indisputably be the main attraction on this particular day, and maybe for many days to come, not only in Hermosillo, not only Sonora, but throughout Mexico and probably far beyond those borders as well.

Globalization. The new name of the game, for baseball and business, and culture and commerce, ideas and ideologies. While the Arizona Diamondbacks were surely small players in this breaking down of barriers between Mexico and the United States—particularly small when one considered such factors as illegal immigration and NAFTA—the franchise held the potential to be a potent emotional lever. Particularly potent when one considered that as a significant component of the entertainment industry, the Diamondbacks were a product to be exploited as programming by the media.

The exploitation of that product was an increasingly consequential matter, for baseball and beyond.

For while the breaking down of borders had its immediate, undoubted benefits—increasing understanding, tolerance, and cooperation, decreasing confusion, tension, and conflict—it also held the seeds of long-term problems. The same factors that caused the breaking down of external differences could also promote the breaking apart of internal similarities, those ties that bound a people and a nation together. And once those ties were severed, what would remain?

Of course, while there was a rational progression from baseball's self-interest to the end of civilization, the length one had to travel from home plate to Armageddon rendered the entire scenario irrational.

Nonetheless, while not specifically indicting baseball, it was a major component of the sports industry, which was a vital part of the entertainment industry, which was a key element of the media confederacy.

Chapter 18

The Stadium

O n November 17, 1995, the first page of the sports section of the *Arizona Republic*, in keeping with its fascination with the countdown, ran the following headline: "D-Backs' Opener Only 891 Days Away." The accompanying story concerned the groundbreaking ceremony for the Bank One Ballpark and came with a photo of Gov. Fife Symington, Jerry Colangelo, and Steve Roman, senior vice president of Bank One, all wearing Diamondback player jerseys over their shirts and ties, happily shoveling a little dirt with silver shovels to symbolically start the construction. That dirt was the first of some 336,000 cubic yards of dirt that would eventually be removed from the site, to be replaced by 427,000 cubic yards of concrete.

One thousand invited guests—"investors, sponsors and civic leaders," according to the newspaper—were provided with the choice seats to the affair. Another three hundred fifty fans, uninvited, ordinary baseball fans, "stood on the fringes, craning their necks to catch a glimpse."

One more constituency could be found at the proceedings, solely represented by Bruce Bateman, who held aloft a cardboard sign that read, "Taxpayers Voted Stadium Down." The sign referred to previous stadium proposals that had been voted down by the electorate.

"I'm not antibaseball," Bateman told the newspaper, "but I don't like being forced to pay for a stadium with a tax gun pointed at my head."

Bateman was not allowed too close to the gala event, which included a hamburger and hot dog meal for the invitees. Instead, he was positioned outside the rear stairwell of a nearby parking garage.

Work on the stadium began immediately, which meant digging a deep hole at the southwest corner of Seventh and Jefferson in downtown Phoenix. Workers dug during the day and hauled away the dirt and stones at night, dumping much of it into the Salt River. A little more than two months after the groundbreaking ceremony, excavation was completed. The hole covered 22.5 acres. Construction could now commence on the huge footings that would support the towers that would hold up the retractable roof. The footings, four and a half feet thick, would rise to ground level and then another sixty-three feet higher. The towers would sit on top of the footings, and all together they would soar twenty stories in the sky. It promised to be an astonishing sight.

Some items were uncovered in the dirt, pottery and such, artifacts that belonged to the Hohokam tribe. The Hohokam were the original Phoenicians, migrating into the region three hundred years before the birth of Christ and staying for seventeen hundred years before mysteriously vanishing. The assumption was that a sudden and extended drought had rendered the Hohokam's sophisticated system of canals and irrigation useless and had forced the tribe to flee the land and never return.

The Hohokam artifacts were turned over to an archaeological consulting firm, which planned to exhibit them at Arizona State University. There was talk that the items might eventually be put on display somewhere in the stadium.

The Hohokam weren't the only people to have spent time in the area. Much more recently, the lot had also been used by neighborhood kids to play baseball. But the Hohokam had had their day, and so had the kids. Drought had run off the ancient tribe, and bulldozers had done the job on the kids. At least for the latter group, the children, the irony was inescapable—their sandlot field had been obliterated in the name of baseball. Irony aside, that was the nature of change; some people win and some people lose.

* * *

On April 5, 1995, months before either of these events, Bank One Arizona had sent a press release into the world announcing "the establishment of a long-term marketing partnership with the Arizona Diamondback Franchise enabling the Corporation to secure naming rights to a downtown baseball stadium."

In other words, the bank bought itself a stadium. Not a whole stadium, actually, but surely one of the most important parts: the part where they plaster up the name. The bank laid out a million dollars per annum to ensure that the bank's logo appeared—and "prominently" at that—throughout the facility.

The bank was definitely in for the long haul, and that $1 million base fee would be collected every year for thirty years, with annual escalations.

All that money constituted just the beginning, because the bank wasn't stopping at a few big, bold signs. Oh, no.

The announcement went on to state that the bank was in for another annual million for other unspecified advertising, marketing, and promotion opportunities, for the same three decades with the same annual escalations.

When all was said and done, Bank One would pay $65 million for the naming rights, plus another $65 million for other marketing opportunities.

The bank's announcement continued with the usual publicity blather about the benefits the partnership between Bank One and the Diamondbacks would bring to Arizona and all the good the bank does sponsoring other local events and so on.

But then, the typically confident tone of this typical press release (and a bank's press release at that) seemed to falter just a bit at the end. Suddenly, in the last line, the self-congratulations veered off for a brief discussion of an obvious issue that begged for a word or two.

"In recent years, naming rights to businesses have become commonplace in professional sports, such as the Delta Center in Utah, the Arco Arena in Sacramento, the Great Western Forum in Los Angeles, Busch Stadium in St. Louis, and Coors Field in Colorado."

Translation: Even we admit that Bank One Ballpark doesn't have the romantic ring of Yankee Stadium or Candlestick Park, but, hey, that's how the real world works.

The first thing to be considered, before the money, before the tax, before the corporate sponsors, before all the politics and business, was the sheer size of the project, the almost unimaginable scope of the enterprise. Bank One Ballpark (instantly known by the friendly acronym BOB) was going to be so large that eight America West Arenas would fit inside with the roof shut.

The statistics were daunting, beginning with the structure: six acres in size, rising 220 feet into the sky, the stadium was slated to contain 3,500 tons of reinforcing steel and 11,700 tons of structural steel.

The 5.25-acre folding, retractable roof would use up most of the six hundred thousand square feet of metal deck built into the stadium and weigh 9 million pounds. It was composed in part of six hundred-foot spans of steel and four miles of steel cable, A pair of two-hundred-horsepower electric motors, each backed up by another motor, would be required to open and close the roof's two sides in about five minutes. With the roof shut, eight thousand tons of air-conditioning would cool the stadium in four hours.

A steel truss, curved in the manner of a bridge, would be situated on top of the stadium, supporting a fixed portion of the roof and half of the retractable portion. Five hundred seventeen feet long, fifty-two feet high, eighty feet wide, and weighing 2.4 million pounds, the truss was to be painted a traditional ballpark dark green. The truss and the retractable roof represented not only the stadium but the entire thrust of the Diamondback organization, the mix, the uniting, of tradition and technology of the past, the present, and the future, too.

The stadium's interior would assuredly be equally impressive. Administrative offices occupied much of one floor, as well as conference and meeting rooms. Some of the meeting rooms had terrific views of the ballfield, allowing the focused Diamondback official to make the deal and catch the game at the same time.

To get to the statistics once again, *Arizona Business* magazine, its pages positively glowing in anticipation of a downtown business bonanza, provided a quick run-through as part of a special supplement dedicated to BOB: "Its insides are where the real fun starts. For instance, there is 30,000 square feet of administrative offices and a 20,000-square-foot home team clubhouse. Visitors are sardined into 7,500 square feet. Members of the press will enjoy an 18,000-square-foot area.

"Bank One Ballpark has four public entrances, a pair of VIP gateways and 43 turnstiles. . . . There is a playground for kids, a 10,500-square-foot interactive baseball theme park and a 2,000-

square-foot Hall of Fame and a same-sized team store. There is also a 4,000-square-foot team store. . . .

"Also, there are 12 novelty stands, 212 concession points, 650 televisions, 121 lockers and 12 passenger elevators with a pair of freight elevators. For the club crowd, the lower deck restaurant seats 500. There are 69 luxury suites and two party suites."

The bathroom situation deserved special note. City of Phoenix constructions codes required five toilet fixtures for every one thousand men, and eight for every one thousand women. The stadium would double that percentage, with a dozen for every thousand men and fifteen for every thousand women. In hard numbers, that counted up to 340 toilets for women, and 55 toilets and 218 urinals for men.

Some innovations are truly blessed.

One more bathroom fact: In an innovation of truly modern conception, single, unisex toilets, equipped with changing tables, would serve the needs of a parent taking care of a child of the opposite sex.

Other distinctive features demanded notice. Eighty-five percent of the 48,500 seats would be located between the foul lines (and in a move so obviously right—obvious once one saw it implemented, that was—all the seats were to be angled so they faced home plate), leaving most of the space beyond the outfield walls for some more innovative flourishes. These innovations included 110 picnic tables, so the fans could eat and watch in comfort, and the swimming pool.

Not surprisingly, the notion of a swimming pool in the right-field bleachers attracted a great deal of attention. It was Scott Brubaker's idea, who said he was inspired by the shower that the late, great showman and Chicago White Sox owner, Bill Veeck, had erected in his stands of his stadium. The Diamondback pool, at 385 square feet, was not intended as some useless—or profitless—showpiece. Rather, with space for about thirty-five people, the pool and its surrounding attractions would be available for renting. Guests could splash in the pool or sit in the hot tub, which sat above and on top of the pool, or pour a drink at the swim-up wet bar or cook at the barbecue—all the while keeping an eye on the game, while those in the surrounding bleachers perhaps kept an eye on the bathers. The pool was equipped with changing rooms and bathrooms.

Brubaker had little difficulty rounding up sponsors for the pool, officially called the SUN Pool Party Pavilion. Paddock Pools and Spas designed and built the entire site, with Aqua Clear Industries providing the chemicals for the pool and the money for the construction. Aqua Clear manufactured SUN pool products—hence the name. For its efforts, Paddock would receive signage and other promotional opportunities.

The pool, maintained at eighty-two degrees, was ready-made for television, an irresistible setting for interviews, another symbol of the stadium's unique identification with Arizona and the sun-bleached West.

Attracting yet more attention to the pool were the two fountains just behind it that would shoot jets of water five stories into the air for fifteen seconds whenever a Diamondback hit a home run. Whatever water hadn't already evaporated would fall back into the pool.

Just another show at the Show.

The first of the stadium's five levels, the field level contained much of the ballpark's guts, including storage facilities, loading dock, kitchen, security headquarters (along with booking and holding cells), and building operations. On the baseball side, there were locker rooms for the Diamondbacks and their visitors, as well as batting tunnels for both sides. The exercise room and trainer's rooms for the Diamondbacks were located beside their lockers.

Not surprisingly, Buck's office was nearby, close to his players.

That wasn't the end of it: the umpires' dressing room, interview rooms, and the Strike Zone Lounge and the Hot Corner Lounge, only accessible to the fans sitting behind home plate, were also on the field level.

And then there were the six massive "chillers," which would cool the stadium on those 110-degree days, sure to come.

One floor up was the main concourse, formally named Fox Sports Arizona DiamondTown, with shops and food stands and the picnic area and the swimming pool and the Cox Clubhouse, housing Cooperstown West, the ballpark's baseball museum, along with interactive games and attractions. The Clubhouse, named after Cox Communications, a local cable-television provider, would be open even when no games were on the schedule.

Entry to the Clubhouse, where the kids could measure how fast they threw and how high they jumped and how fast they ran—as well as hit in an old-fashioned batting cage, get videotaped practicing their best sports-anchor chatter, and pose for their own rookie baseball cards—would cost extra, game or no game: for those with game tickets, $4 for adults and $2 for children, and for those without tickets, $6 and $3.

Eating options were numerous on the concourse, though heavily weighted to the fast-food side of life: Little Caesar's Pizza, Ben & Jerry's, Blimpie Subs, Juice Haus Yogurt, Garcia's Mexican Food, Desert Ice, Carla's Crazy Corn, and McDonald's, which the Diamondbacks proclaimed to be the only McDonald's inside a major league stadium.

Happily, in addition to the hot dogs and pretzels, Fielder's Choice would offer fresh fruits and vegetables.

Finally, video walls showing the action on the field, or, at other times, classic baseball footage or player interviews, would be joined by graphic time lines and three-dimensional exhibits, creating ten theme areas featuring baseball history.

The third level was all business: administrative offices for the Diamondbacks, the press box, broadcast booths for TV, radio, and public address, and postproduction facilities.

The fourth level was dedicated to luxury, from the suites to 4,400 club seats, which were reached by passageways between the suites. The Stadium Club and Friday's Front Row Sports Grill were here, the latter's terraced seating open to all fans, and also on nongame days.

The fifth level, the upper deck, held twenty thousand seats, four party boxes, and a banquet room. The party boxes would be rented on a per game basis for $2,200 to $3,500—and food was extra.

The stadium guaranteed terrific amenities for everyone, but especially terrific for season-ticket and suite holders. The Diamondbacks prepared handsome folders for prospective buyers, explaining all the options, from how the seats could be selected to a listing of the services and comforts to the prices. Season tickets in the upper level started as low as $283.50, which sounded like a remarkable bargain in this era of $1,000-face-value floor seats to professional basketball games.

Those $283.50 seats could be purchased for $3.50 per single game, which was precisely the price of a season ticket divided by eighty-one, as in eighty-one regular-season home games. The same held true for all the season tickets, no matter the expense level. Thus, unlike most group rates, season tickets offered no discounts, just a secured pew in the cathedral.

The most expensive seats in the upper deck were $13.50 per game, or $1,093.50 for the duration.

Jumping down to the choice seats, right down near the field, top single-game rates were $45 and $50, which translated into $3,645 and $4,050 for the season. Taking into consideration that most people wanted not one but two or four tickets, the total package price for seats near home plate—or anywhere else in the stadium, for that matter—could quickly escalate to significant sums.

Many and perhaps most of those who purchased season tickets reduced their financial outlay by splitting the seats among a group of people, each person or family paying for only a certain number of games.

Regardless, for those season-ticket holders in the more expensive sections, known in ascending order as the Diamond, Dugout, and Clubhouse seats, the franchise offered more than the game. These additional benefits helped render the entire experience not only more enjoyable, but also . . . fuller. The fifteen hundred reserved parking spaces in the covered garage, linked to the stadium by a secured walkway, ensured that these special fans didn't have to waste precious moments searching for spots for their cars, nor mix with the hoi polloi on their way in and out of the park. Access to the private lounge and the business center, as well as the assistance of the concierge staff, allowed them to take care of private or professional matters between innings. Complimentary game notes saw to it that they had an official record of all the action.

For sustenance through this busy day, they were accorded membership in the Stadium Club Restaurant. If these fans didn't want to leave their comfortable seats—and their seats would be larger than the norm, with extra leg room—to troop to the restaurant, waiters would attend them at their seats and bring them food.

Finally, looking ahead, these season-ticket holders were guaranteed seats when the Diamondbacks brought the playoffs and World Series back home.

In short, good seats came with their own rewards.

In early 1996, the Diamondbacks started accepting $50 nonrefundable deposits to get on line for the opportunity to pick seats. Before long, the franchise had deposits on about 44,000 seats.

By March 31, 1998, the Diamondbacks had sold close to 36,000 season tickets.

But one didn't have to spend a king's, or even a princeling's, ransom to delight in an afternoon or evening at the ballpark. On a per game basis, 17,000 seats, more than a third of the stadium's capacity, were priced at $9 or less. Helping to keep that average down were 350 seats in the upper deck that the Diamondbacks were offering for one dollar each. These buck tickets would be available only on game day, and it was hoped that younger people would be the prime beneficiary of the team's gesture to hold down prices.

However, those big spenders were the first target of the Diamondbacks, just as they were with every sports team and stadium manager. And more profitable, vastly more profitable, than even those Clubhouse seats were the sixty-nine luxury boxes encircling the stadium's midsection.

Eight different suite styles and sizes could accommodate between twelve and twenty-four people. Prices ranged from $95,000 to $125,000, with two different lease options available. The first option was a ten-year contract with a 4 percent annual price increase. The second plan was for seven years, with annual price increases of 7 percent.

A brochure provided by the Diamondbacks spelled out some of what was offered:

"The standard decor of the Bank One Ballpark Luxury Suites will be provided by the Arizona Diamondbacks as part of the Suite Agreement. This will include wall and floor coverings, custom wood cabinetry, appliances (refrigerator and ice maker) and plumbing fixtures. Each suite will also be prewired for two (2) television monitors (to be provided) and in-house television service.

"Each Suiteholder will have the opportunity to 'customize' their suites [sic] by selecting from a wide array of furniture options. In addition, Suiteholders are welcome to add a personal touch by adding any additional approved accessories (i.e., wall hangings, corporate identifiers, etc.)."

That was only the beginning, and the brochure enumerated other suiteholder advantages, such as a private concourse with a private elevator and escalator, private rest rooms, exclusive catering services, premium reserved parking, more and more, on and on, so many desires and whims ministered to, some even before the well-heeled fan could imagine them.

Why, the suiteholder even received a complimentary subscription to the Diamondback magazine.

Whether these suiteholders were actually fans was debatable, because the prime customers for luxury suites, in Arizona and elsewhere, were corporations. Corporations leased them for prestige and for pork—as a prestigious place to take clients, and as pork for the bosses to sit back in and drink in the privileges of success.

It seemed that the beloved ballpark was large enough to simultaneously encompass both the spiritual consciousness and capitalist reality of our American experience.

On August 8, 1997, the Diamondbacks invited the media to the "topping off" of the roof, the raising of the final piece of structural steel into position, the lifting of the last of the six movable trusses. The procedure had taken longer than expected. The delays couldn't have entirely been a surprise; huge projects were often delayed, particularly huge projects that had no real precedent.

To underscore that fact, the Diamondback press office had wasted a lot of paper diligently informing the media of the raising of the truss for this day and time—bring your cameras and notepads—only to have to send another notice announcing a delay:

"*Media Alert*—Bank One Ballpark Truss Will Rise on May 28"

"*Media Alert*—Bank One Ballpark Truss Lift Postponed"

"*Media Alert*—Bank One Ballpark Truss Lift Begins Today"

"*Media Alert*—Bank One Ballpark Truss Takes Successful First Step"

"*Media Alert*—Bank One Ballpark Truss Goes Up, Comes Down"

"*Media Alert*—Bank One Ballpark Truss Lift Begins Again"

While the press office hustled back and forth to the fax machine, the project managers and project directors and engineers and other experts and workers figured out whatever they needed to figure out, and the enterprise continued.

The 2.4-million-pound east roof truss was raised only a few feet off the ground, allowing the steel cables, over three inches thick, to lose their slack, stretch, and test their integrity and strength. The truss remained in this position overnight.

In the next stage, the truss was lifted 174 feet off the ground by four four-hundred-ton-capacity hydraulic jacks to the top of its support towers. With all the checking and inspecting and complications, the procedure took two weeks longer than expected.

The west roof truss underwent the same operation and was finally lifted onto its towers, 149 feet in the air.

After that, end pieces were attached to each truss to secure them to the top of the towers.

So the stadium arrived, with some fits and starts, to the day of the "topping off."

The Diamondbacks turned it into a celebration. The workers, still dusty from their morning labors, were treated to a catered lunch and given miniature baseball bats, emblazoned with "Bank One Ballpark," as souvenirs. The men and women thrust the bats into their back pockets as they loaded their plates with food and sat down on the concrete where some of the steps would be installed, facing the podium.

The podium had been set up because speeches were to be made, commemorating the occasion. It was quite a setting, the stadium a shell of steel and metal and concrete, the interior a pockmarked crater of dirt and rocks, littered with trucks and machines and no less than six giant cranes.

"These boys have big toys," muttered a Diamondback official.

A small tree and an American flag had been hoisted upon the truss. The tree was said to symbolize the groundbreaking, while the flag signified the collective pride in country and stadium.

The chief of steel from Schiff Steel, the subcontractor for the roof, commended Colangelo for the "guts" required to build the ballpark, and other people said other complimentary things to the workers and the Diamondbacks. Naturally, Colangelo delivered a few words commending everyone for their efforts, etc., etc., and then the construction workers applauded and a large number lined up to get his autograph.

This was a touch startling, not only because Jerry Colangelo was at the site more days out of the week than not, checking up, thereby rendering his presence hardly uncommon, but also because one didn't really expect to see a bunch of mainly large construction workers interested in the signature of a businessman.

The ceremony was a success, and the ballpark was, to every appearance, thundering forward to a triumphant completion. However, not everything associated with the stadium—away from the construction site, that was—had gone so smoothly.

Two events in particular stood out. The first was the great cooler flap.

In the middle of May 1997, a Diamondback PR spokesman announced that fans would be banned from bringing any food and drink into the stadium. The Diamondbacks reached this decision through consultations with the stadium concessionaire, Restaura, a subsidiary of Viad, which not only had the concession contract for America West Arena, but was also a corporate investor in the franchise.

"The decision was a slam dunk," declared the flack. "If you're selling a product, you don't want to let the same product come in."

That unfortunate "slam dunk" comment was destined to be repeated ad nauseam, as proof of the Diamondbacks' arrogance and greed. Only three teams out of all thirty—the Braves, Marlins, and Astros—had instituted such a policy.

This was an issue tailor-made for the media. The situation was easy to grasp, with families carrying paper bags filled with peanut-butter-and-jelly sandwiches and juice boxes on one side, and security personnel frisking people and forcing them to buy overpriced, cholesterol-laden Big Macs and giant souvenir cups of teeth-rotting soda on the other.

Newspaper columnists raged, talk-radio hosts railed, and the public wrote letters and phoned, condemning Colangelo and the franchise. Those who were still angry about the stadium tax felt that they were being robbed twice. Those who weren't angry about the stadium tax had now been given reason, albeit rather flimsy reason, to doubt the sincerity of the Colangelo and the Diamondbacks when they continually asserted their concern for the community. After all, a trip to the ballpark was touted as the quintessential family outing, and the Diamondbacks and their stadium as the standard-bearers of Arizona family values.

A couple of days later, Jerry Colangelo, who had been out of town when the flap erupted, responded in a written statement:

"In the last week, while I was pretty much out of the office because of the loss of my mother, a story broke regarding the Arizona Diamondbacks' policy regarding food and beverages and coolers at Bank One Ballpark.

"For the record, we are busy building a baseball organization and Bank One Ballpark, and have yet to finalize any specific guidelines or policies regarding the operation of Bank One Ballpark."

Jerry Colangelo wasn't always so calm in addressing the issue. *Republic* columnist E. J. Montini, who had frequently opposed Colangelo's plans and had roundly criticized the food ban, wrote that he had received a call from the Diamondback managing general partner. Jerry, reported the columnist, first stated that he had spoken to the publisher about said columnist, then alleged that the columnist was abandoning his roots by attacking a fellow Italian, and finally noted that the columnist was a miserable SOB.

Colangelo was never hesitant to call journalists or their bosses when he was displeased. According to several reporters, he has passed along this trait to certain other Diamondback officials and son Bryan at the Suns, along with the notion that the local media should seriously consider serving local interests, which included local sports teams.

Sports teams, went the basic reasoning behind this idea, not only brought joy to the public and profits to the merchants, they also were a rich source of civic pride to the entire community, a source of unity without controversy, just good feelings all around . . . so why wouldn't the press line up behind them and their well-intentioned management?

In Phoenix, and probably everywhere else, the press usually did just that (as long as the team was winning), and Colangelo and his minions grew accustomed to the media's cooperation. But *usually* did not mean always, not on every occasion, not without fail, and that deviation from the norm often led to a problem.

In this instance, the rules of peaceful coexistence, never mind active cooperation, were definitely out the window. And that was why seven months after the initial rumpus, Jerry Colangelo conducted a press conference to reveal the new policy. In brief (though it remained a topic of conversation for some time in Phoenix), coolers that could fit under the seats would be permitted, as would bagged food, sliced fruit, sealed or empty water bottles, fruit juices in boxes, and baby food and formula. What remained out-of-bounds were glass bottles, alcohol, soda, thermal containers, whole fruit, or any other object that could be used as a projectile to toss onto the field.

The franchise added a little comedy to the affair, having two actors who had been used in Diamondback commercials loudly interrupt, walking in with a huge cooler, a beer keg, and a large, cooked turkey in a pan. Colangelo played his part, denying the cooler and the keg entry, but okaying the turkey—once it had been properly sliced.

Jerry had one final comment, seeking to close the circle on the matter. Referring to the Diamondback spokesman who had so badly misspoken in the first place, Colangelo said, "I told him we're missing one prop here, and that's a rope. Because if we had one, we'll probably hang him, not in effigy, but for real."

The great cooler flap was still four months from resolution when the second unpleasant, and considerably more serious, event occurred.

On August 13, 1997, Larry Naman walked into a county building, pulled out a .38 revolver, and shot Mary Rose Wilcox. A security guard jumped on Naman just as he was firing, possibly shifting the direction of the barrel and the bullet. Naman shot Wilcox from behind, as she was leaving a Board of Supervisors meeting, and the bullet lodged in her left pelvis, or, less delicately, in her butt.

Wilcox was whisked off to the hospital and Naman to jail. Just a few hours later, Naman appeared before the media in his new attire, black-and-white stripes, and read a statement:

"I shot Mary Rose Wilcox to try to put a stop to the political dictatorship of Jerry Colangelo, the Maricopa County Board of Supervisors, and the Arizona state legislature in pushing the baseball stadium tax. And to try to force them to demolish the Bank One Ballpark so that it will restore the vote of the people as the bottom line and to restore the public's faith in their democratic election system and to restore democracy on the noncandidate side of the ballot in Maricopa County."

Naman declined to answer questions.

Though some briefly speculated whether Naman acted as part of a conspiracy, with other politicians and Diamondback officials in danger from violent comrades still out there, armed and hiding in the bushes, the more mundane truth quickly became clear—Naman had gotten it into his head that shooting a Maricopa County supervisor was the thing to do.

The whole business rapidly took on a hint of the ridiculous. Never one to miss a media opportunity, Mary Rose, clutching her rosary beads and describing herself as "heavily sedated," summoned the press the day after the shooting. She used her new forum to blame talk radio for instigating the attack: "I think they've wound people up in a frenzy. . . . I hope the hate that's spewed out of these stations will stop."

Naman hadn't mentioned talk radio in his statement. There was no reason to believe he had ever listened to the radio. Even if he had, the idea that a lunatic—a certified lunatic, in fact, considering his stint in an Oregon state mental hospital—had decided to shoot somebody because of overheated political dialogue, or that any logical connection could be constructed between what Naman might have heard and what he did, was simply stupid. Perhaps worse than stupid,

Wilcox's comment was clearly a political calculation on the part of either her or her equally ambitious husband to turn this literal pain in the ass into martyrdom.

In other words, if this were not a random act of insanity but a deliberate political statement, then Mary Rose herself was elevated from victim to cause.

It didn't work. Wilcox's little spiel got thrown back in her face quickly enough, recognized for the fraud it was.

When Wilcox left the hospital shortly thereafter, it was in a wheelchair, escorted by the sheriff of the county and surrounded by dozens of his men—just in case Naman's secret anarchist army was waiting in ambush.

Mary Rose made it safely home.

Naman appeared before the press again in November, claiming that he only intended to wound, not kill, "to put a stop to the political dictatorship" of Jerry Colangelo, the Board of Supervisors, and the Arizona legislature.

Speaking of Colangelo, Naman said, "If Jerry had been available, I most definitely would have shot him."

Naman wanted to represent himself at his trial, because he believed that he had an "excellent" chance of getting the jury "to approve of me shooting Wilcox."

The following month, Naman was ruled competent to stand trial.

Not long after, Naman refused a request for an interview from a writer. He explained that while he intermittently courted the media, from newspapers to television, not enough people read books to make an interview for a book worth his while.

Maybe Larry Naman was sane after all.

With the topping-off ceremony completed, it was time for the workers to get back to business and for the media and other guests to depart.

As they walked around Jefferson Street and back to their cars on Fourth, they passed the murals that covered the outside of the construction site. The murals, representing scenes from baseball history, had been drawn and painted by elementary-school children from different Phoenix schools. It was interesting to see what choices the kids had made, what they knew about baseball, and what they cared about.

One mural was the labor of a boy named Scott, judging by the picture of a young man, also named Scott, with a bat on his shoulder, preparing to hit. Bubbles floating above his head, depicting his thoughts, were filled with pictures of Babe Ruth, Jackie Robinson, and a rather improbable member of that company, Jose Canseco. Another bubble personified his vision of himself in the future, holding a trophy that read, "Arizona Diamondback, 2018."

A different mural celebrated the career of Mickey Mantle, showing him in various poses on the field, listing the World Series records he held: 18 home runs, 40 RBIs, 42 runs, 26 extra-base hits, 123 total hits.

Murals hailed Mike Piazza, the 1993 Rookie of the Year, Ken Griffey Jr., for having "100 RBIs in a season twice before the age of 23," Roberto Clemente, Willie Mays, and Babe Ruth again. The Babe and Jackie Robinson—the greatest player and the greatest pioneer—were the most popular subjects.

In between all the action drawings and painted statistics, one group of school kids had displayed a fine sense of humor by honoring not athletes but Abbott and Costello, and their magnum opus of baseball routines, the opening of which was writ large around the border of the mural, the two comedians depicted in the center: "Who's on first, What's on second, I-don't-know's on third . . ."

The murals were a humanistic touch in this massive amalgamation of steel and concrete and bricks and mortar, a small reminder that the success of this extraordinary expenditure of intelligence, energy, and money was ultimately dependent not upon steel and concrete and bricks and mortar, but upon the sustained passion and respect for the game by the players, coaches, and also the fans, however young.

Chapter 19

The Media

J anuary 1998. The Arizona Diamondbacks were entering the final stretch to the start of major league play, the last buildup to their grand appearance on the world stage. An appropriate moment to step back a moment and consider the ultimate thrust of this baseball juggernaut.

As has already been proposed in these pages, we can regard modern professional sports as a component of the entertainment industry, which in turn is a component of the media. The sports industry is a product with a definable time scheme, nonstop action, and recognizable personalities, which permits it to be easily and profitably showcased on global communications outlets. This utility guarantees that Major League Baseball will eventually expand overseas, if for no other reason than to suit the media's growth patterns.

While the Diamondbacks were soaring high, Major League Baseball faced some problems. Attendance was just now climbing to the level of the strike-shortened 1995 season, when baseball played 11 percent fewer games. Two other worrisome trends: (1) Though MLB trumpeted the fact that over 63 million people attended a game in 1997, more than pro football, basketball, and hockey combined, the actual number of baseball games played roughly equaled the games played by all other major sports, though baseball took in only one-third the total ticket revenue; (2) That very same MLB projected that approximately 10 million kids would attend a pro game in 1998, which sounded promising until one realized that that forecast meant that less than 15 percent of the fans in attendance would be nineteen years old or younger, not an encouraging comment on the ability of baseball to market itself to the sports-crazed youth of America.

Therefore, the impetus of the media (as well as some of the more forward-thinking teams, such as the Diamondbacks with their Mexican connection) to expand around the world becomes even more undeniable.

Accordingly, in contemplating baseball and its driving role in society, it is only reasonable that we must also contemplate the very media that drives baseball, and all pro sports. Only by first understanding each institution separately can we appreciate the full impact of their combined force. We've spent some time considering baseball; perhaps it would be advisable to take a few moments to consider the media.

This is where it gets interesting because, unlike baseball, it is arguable that the *very nature of the media* is poisonous to the health and future of America. Not for any of the usual reasons given—some ridiculous, nonexistent "media conspiracy," or any particular political bent, liberal, conservative, or otherwise, or even the endless propagation of sex and violence. No, this discussion concerns the inherent, irresistible nature of the media, leading us all to an unavoidable and ruinous day.

Begin to understand the media through the historical example of the oil industry. The oil industry in America started as exactly that, an American industry, and grew rapidly with Wall Street money and Southwest oil, soon expanding overseas with more Wall Street money and U.S. government assistance. And though the business was now international, it was still an American industry, composed of large corporations that approached the world on an American basis, working to benefit their American stockholders and bankers and directors in order to further the American interest. Of course, the American interest was ordinarily uncomplicated—revenue for the companies and plentiful, cheap oil for the citizenry.

But then the large corporations became extraordinarily large, then became transnational, meaning their wealth and power became global, and their stockholders and bankers and directors were as likely to be Saudi and Dutch and Taiwanese as American. And thus the corporations were no longer American, nor Saudi or Dutch or

Taiwanese, but totally self-serving, self-interested entities, concerned not with war and peace, or politics and justice, but only with the welfare of the industry itself. And when that interest conflicted with the American interest, the American interest no longer held any significance whatsoever.

American corporation to independent state, a state without allegiances or politics or principles—national to international to transnational—independence without purpose, a state without faith.

And we are left with oil crises and high prices and economic dislocation.

How dissimilar is professional baseball? The *Rocky Mountain News* asked Bowie Kuhn and Jerry Colangelo whether corporate ownership was good for baseball. Kuhn, the commissioner of MLB from 1969 to 1984, and Colangelo responded in separate columns. Kuhn's reply was entitled, "NO: Uphold Integrity Not Profits."

The courtly ex-commissioner held that individual owners protected the game because of their regard for its rich traditions. Kuhn believed that baseball's preservation demanded such reverence, because baseball fans are the most conservative of all fans and don't want to see radical changes.

Corporations, on the other hand, "are more apt to vote on baseball matters in accordance with the interests of the corporation.

"I'm not criticizing corporate ownership. But more often than not, corporate owners are driven more by the profit motive.

"For instance, to them, interleague play is good because it means we can sell more widgets, not necessarily because it's good for the fans.

"What we're going to see if corporate ownership continues to grow is that baseball will be converted into a new kind of game. It will be highly successful, and it will draw numbers in the future that you can scarcely imagine today. It will be internationalized, and the marketing will be intense. But somewhere down the line, there may be a fatal flaw. The traditional values may be put aside, and I see signs of that already."

Bowie Kuhn's opinion was shared by some of the leading baseball thinkers. Conservative, in this instance, was not a political label, but referred to conserving values and institutions, conserving the best that the game has to offer.

Columnist George Will, in writing about the new group of owners, noted, "Perhaps one reason today's ownership group scants base-ball's traditions is that the group is new. Once the sale of the Dodgers to Fox is consummated, Jerry McMorris of the expansion Rockies will be the senior owner in the NL West. In the last eleven years, nineteen of the twenty-eight teams playing this year have been sold. In those eleven years, the average career for a player now active, who has played at least two years, is 7.5 years. That is longer than the average tenure of the thirty owners whose teams will play next season."

On the other side, Jerry Colangelo's essay was headlined, "YES: Mom-and-Pop Era Is Over." In his typically direct manner, Co-langelo stated that corporations were taking over because of the tremendous investment required to purchase a team, and then the tremendous cost of maintaining it year after year. Colangelo used his own Diamondbacks to illustrate, listing the $130 million expansion fee, plus the $20 million future TV-revenue giveback, plus $50 million in start-up costs, plus $100 million in stadium construction costs, all of which added up to an even $300 million.

"All that," Colangelo concluded, "is kind of pricey for any indi-vidual."

Then Colangelo talked about who, or what, would be most interested in spending all that money. "You see conglomerates, like those in the cable-television industries, making purchases for various reasons but, first and foremost, for programming. So we see these conglomerates like Rupert Murdoch and Ted Turner. You see people who recognize professional sports as much more than sport. They're part of the entertainment world, and it's just another piece of the puzzle."

While Bowie Kuhn's argument relied perhaps more on emotion than fact, Colangelo's view, entirely monetarily based, was already a reality.

In any case, we can see how the sports industry, in its still early evolution, expanding, changing, is not following a path already trod by the oil industry. Other components of the media, older than sports, more developed and established, have pushed the oil-company example several steps further.

The modern media is a relatively young industry, same as oil. Newspapers were joined (and then increasingly supplanted) by radio and then TV, at both the local and national levels. The film industry grew even more quickly, soon establishing itself as the dominant cultural force in the country. Taken all together, news and entertainment combined (and as an entertainment subset, the sports industry is included here), the media expanded in wealth and fame, decade after decade, through the twentieth century. While the media changed during that time in many ways, in one fundamentally crucial way the media remained the same, the media remained the *American media,* owned and operated by Americans, for an American audience.

That is no longer the case. The entertainment industry has gone global, designing and marketing its products for foreign consumption as much as for the home front, and reaping huge profits for its efforts. As entertainment has embraced the world, so it has been embraced in return, attracting investors, artists, athletes, and pretenders from everywhere.

This trend reached an apparent (or, more appropriately, a very public) zenith when Japanese corporations started buying U.S. film studios. The cry went up, from Main Street to radio talk shows to Congress, that the new owners would impose their own values and ideas on their properties, i.e., their movies, and subvert this uniquely American enterprise, implanting some sort of Japanese message in films. This did not happen, of course, and the furious debate subsided and disappeared. But what was not discussed or understood was that the genuine problem was not that the movie business would adopt Japanese values, but that it would abandon American values. (The oft-repeated concern that the Japanese would attempt to rewrite the less savory aspects of their history, such as World War II, through the movies seemed rather ironic when it was an American, Oliver Stone, who abused American history with his paranoid fantasy, *JFK.*)

Television has also ventured beyond our shores. Three networks have spawned hundreds of producing and distributing outlets, many of which sell their programs overseas. At the same time, U.S. outlets buy shows from different countries to broadcast here, while others, with increasing frequency, go into partnership with foreign networks to produce programs for airing in many nations at once.

From U.S. networks selling programs *to* foreign countries, to U.S. networks buying programs *from* foreign countries, to U.S. networks joining in producing partnership *with* foreign countries, the next step is obvious: U.S. networks will combine with foreign networks in permanent partnerships, seeking to maximize their collective ability to bring together as much money and technology and influence in order to garner the largest possible planetary audience and grab as much profit and power as feasible for these new global networks.

As the American television marketplace becomes ever more diffused and competitive with the addition of new production companies and channels, the share (and hence the revenues) of the major networks, which once had the whole game to themselves, must continue to diminish. Hence, the major corporations, to maintain and then enlarge their audiences, must find new markets. And that overriding search will point them in one direction, in the only direction left—over there.

Now think back to baseball; as other sports and other entertainment media splinter MLB's once dominant position, it, too, is seeking opportunities overseas.

So the entire media—TV, films, sports, news, and entertainment—will go the way of oil. The media industry will become transnational, with consequences that could prove grave indeed.

At its soul, a nation is a myth agreed to by its people. All the other material factors, social, political, and economic, are tied together by the underlying belief and value system to which all citizens voluntarily and consciously subscribe.

America is a faith, as tangible as a church and as mysterious as the ideas and ideals that inspired its construction.

America is also a tribe, permitting the supplicant to join or separate from the nation with relative ease. Once accepted into the tribe, one is instantly, totally American, no generational probation required. Try that in China or Germany or in a hundred other countries.

It is no accident that we call those who led the American Revolution our Founding Fathers, a stirringly intimate, personal identification. They are all our fathers, whether our families were here in 1776 or arrived last week, because we are all equally American, all possessing legitimate claim to our collective history and glory. We have no royal titles to hand down, no familial privileges or special rights; all Americans originate from the same mythic parentage, from the beginning, from the ribs of our political Adams, our Founding Fathers.

This secular faith, this voluntary joining, comes with a high price. Since nothing is defined by unalterable factors such as race, the national consensus of what it means to be an American must be affirmed over and over, through stories and lessons of valor and virtue, sacrifice and achievement. We must be taught and reminded what makes America special, and what it means to be an American. This unending renewal is accomplished first at home, then at school, and always through the media. The media assume an even more pivotal role in our lives when we recognize how many of our families have broken apart and how many of our communities are fractured and isolating.

From Thomas Paine's *Common Sense* to Edward R. Murrow's radio reports, from Jimmy Stewart in *Mr. Smith Goes to Washington* to John Wayne in *The Sands of Iwo Jima*, the media have not only reported the facts but also explained the world to Americans, anecdotally and emotionally, in American terms, on American terms. Sometimes co-opted by the government, sometimes determinedly independent, the media have operated as an indispensable part of America.

Does not the same hold true for baseball, bringing us together on its field of dreams, conjuring an image, teaching us about fair play and sportsmanship and competition, lessons applicable to all Americans equally?

Times have changed. Partly it is due to all parts of the media growing so large and so rich. Partly it is due to our declining trust in literally all our major institutions, which by default raises the profile and importance of the media. Partly it is due to the ceaseless media presence, demanding our attention, drowning us in sensation. Partly it is due to the media's relentless, vainglorious self-promotion.

All these parts construct a media that gorge on cynicism and criticism, controversy and scandal, distrust and exploitation, every component of the media fighting each other for attention and profits, a swelling black-hole continuum that manipulates and uses and discards people and ideas and hopes.

And consider this: all this controversy and ill will and mistrust from the *American media*. Now let us imagine the day when the media are no longer really American, but transnational. Imagine the constant pounding of images and ideas, the contempt and conspiracies, the different values and "truths," when the media, telling a thousand different tales in a thousand different voices, are anchored not to America but only to the global market.

George Orwell was wrong in his classic novel *1984* when he

postulated a world in which governments would control the media and destroy freedom. The reality is that the many arms of the media are approaching the day when, without intent but with a reckless disregard for the truth or purpose or consequence, they will possess the capacity to overwhelm civilization, and thus enfeeble governments and shatter nations, as a normal course of business.

This is the world into which Major League Baseball is moving, an unfamiliar, dangerous world for an industry based on a perfect patch of green grass. Baseball is a relatively minor player in the overall media scheme—"just another piece of the puzzle," in Colangelo's phrase—but a player nonetheless.

Major League Baseball is going global, as are the media, as are all of us. As 1998 dawned and Diamondback frenzy grew in Arizona, perhaps this was our last chance to pause and consider what all that meant before opening day.

PART V | Spring Training

Chapter 20

Spring Training, for Real

Phoenix to Tucson is a short trip, a straight shot south down Interstate 10. When the federal government raised the speed limit to seventy-five miles per hour, the determined driver could make the trip in under two hours. It is not an especially interesting trip, not comparable, say, to heading north a roughly similar amount of time, the altitude steadily rising, passing from one climate zone into another, the bare terrain giving way to rolling mountains and lush green forests, eventually ending in Sedona, set amongst the glorious Red Rocks.

Phoenix to Tucson can't match that wondrous transformation, but it does have one distinct advantage, at least for Arizona baseball fans: Tucson Electric Park, the spanking new spring-training home of the Arizona Diamondbacks.

The approaching visitor first encounters the farms, warehouses, junkyards, and other landmarks familiar to all urban outskirts. The highway doesn't permit a good view of the handsome city, but one cannot help but be amazed by the mountains, topped with snow, that press against the city itself.

El Niño had disrupted Buck Showalter's meticulous plans for the perfect training camp. As usual, his attention was captured by details small and large. He persuaded a local artist to paint the team logos on the clubhouse walls in exchange for game tickets, which, on one locker room wall, resulted in a long snake twisted into the shape of a large *D* staring out at the players as they dressed. Despite Buck's commitment to extracting the most from spring training—the Diamondbacks brought 7,200 baseballs with them, intending to use them all in a month and half—despite Buck's rising at 4 A.M. to be at his desk by 5:30 in preparation for the 7:30 staff meeting, the unusual season of persistent rain and wind had on occasion forced the Diamondbacks off the training track. Sometimes they took throwing and batting practicing indoors, in the facilities' tunnels built expressly for those purposes.

One way or another, Buck's players got their work in, as the manager split the sixty-two players into two squads, purple and turquoise, allowing him to effectively double the workday, and double his opportunities to see everyone do everything.

"I've asked the coaches to suck it up," Showalter told the press. "It's only for seven days."

However it got done, the manager and his coaches seemed pleased by the team's progress. All the same, Buck was intent on dispelling any illusions that the Diamondbacks were on an inevitable march to quick success. "It's a great time for baseball," Showalter told the TV audience back in the valley, "before the reality of how good you really are sinks in, so I hope everybody in Phoenix comes down."

Buck also had a message for his players, which he delivered with something less than subtlety via another television interview: "I might be biased, but I think this is the finest training facility in baseball, and we'll have no excuses. If our players can't develop here, then they probably aren't players."

Buck wasn't going to entice everybody in the valley to come to Tucson, but the crowd was already building up outside the gates of Tucson Electric Park. TEP was located on the twenty-acre grounds of the Kino Veterans Memorial Sportspark, spring training center for both the Diamondbacks and the White Sox, and was as new as the home-state team. The complex was supposed to cost about $25 million, then $28 million, but a couple of years, a few design and construction miscalculations by the government, and a handful of expanded clubhouse and practice-field requirements by the Diamondbacks and the White Sox added more than another $10 million to the scheme.

"When you're putting together the cost of a large facility, everything is an estimate," Pima County administrator Chuck Huckelberry assured the press. "Anyone will tell you that preliminary cost estimates for such projects are usually at least ten to fifteen percent off."

Ten million dollars plus on top of $25 million was quite a bit more than 10 to 15 percent, but, hey, who was counting?

Tucson Electric Power Company bought the naming rights to the stadium for ten years. In a press release Colangelo stated, "We are very proud that Tucson Electric Power Company, a local organization with a strong commitment to its community, has chosen to become a major supporter of Pima County's spring training program. This partnership will create unique marketing opportunities that will result in a great experience for baseball fans all over southern Arizona."

"This agreement brings together local business, county government, and two new entities in our community, the Diamondbacks and White Sox, with a common goal—to ensure Pima County benefits from spring training," said Charles Bayless in the same press release. Bayless was not only listed on the page as chairman of TEP, but also president and CEO. "The naming of Tucson Electric Park sends a strong message that TEP is serious about its commitment to our community, and about marketing our business in a competitive environment."

Kino Veterans Memorial Sportspark contained thirteen and half practice fields, two clubhouses each almost forty thousand square feet in size, a golf course, and a lake. TEP had room for more than 11,500 spectators, with 8 luxury boxes, 469 clubhouse seats, bleacher seating for 8,006, and space for 3,000 on the grass surrounding the outfield.

The county was funding the place primarily through a bond issue, and a visitors' tax, which captured in its net rental cars, hotel rooms, and recreational vehicles, at least when they parked in RV parks. Perhaps the Pima County politicians had learned a lesson from their Maricopa County counterparts and, determined not to annoy their constituents, instituted a bond issue, which wasn't a tax, and imposed a tax only on out-of-towners, who headed home to vote.

Despite all that, the bond issue, the taxes, and also the revenues generated by the stadium would not be sufficient to pay for the operation of the Sportspark, sticking taxpayers with the rest of the bill.

No one should have been too surprised. These things happened, again and again.

Regardless, tonight was the big game, the first game, curtain rising on TEP and the Arizona DBs. It was shaping up to be a cold night— El Niño again—with temperatures already in the forties and dropping fast, but the crowd, building for hours, would not be deterred. A radio reporter walked up and down the line, asking the usual questions: Are you excited? Are you glad the Diamondbacks are here? Fortuitously, the reporter concentrated on children, who were surely more willing than adults to indulge such simplistic queries.

Back in Phoenix, the Arizona organization closed its offices early and dispatched two busloads of employees down to Tucson to take in the festivities. Buck greeted his fellow Diamondback laborers, many lightly dressed, with some official DB jackets to ward off the chill, which was only going to get worse as night fell.

When the gates finally swung wide, the people rushed inside, each of these early-bird ticketholders receiving a commemorative T-shirt and pin. The Diamondbacks had finished their warm-up and the White Sox were on the field.

Not surprisingly, most of the 11,298 fans were in attendance to cheer on the Diamondbacks, not the Sox. They rushed past the gates and into the stadium, pouring into the gift shops and concession stands, buying memorabilia and hot dogs.

Down in the Diamondback clubhouse, the schedule and some of the rules were tacked on different walls. One paper near the door and across from Buck's office spelled out with military precision the day's agenda:

2:45–3:25: Commissioner's Office Talk
3:30–3:50: Agility Run and Stretch
3:50–4:00: Throwing Program
4:00–4:15: Team Defense—Bunt Defense
4:15: Starting Line-Up Transported to Stadium for BP
4:15–4:30: Non-Starters Take Infield
4:30–5:30: BP for Non-Starters
4:30–5:10: Pitchers—Offensive Fundamentals
5:10: Conditioning—2 20-minute rotations (cages, bunt, hit, T-work)
Game pitchers to stay in stadium.

A sign on the inside of the locker room's door spelled out the next day's first marching order: "Dressed and ready to go—9:30 A.M." The same message was repeated in Spanish: *"Todo el equipo en la uniforme completo—9:30 de la mañana."*

The clubhouse was solid-block construction, which suited its utilitarian purpose and bunkerlike mentality. The clubhouse contained, in addition to Buck's office and a spacious locker room, a conference room, a video room, a laundry, and an equipment room. On the wall in the hall was a framed quote from Teddy Roosevelt: "The best executive is the one who has sense enough to pick good men to do what he wants done, self-restraint enough to keep from meddling with them while they do it."

That was hardly in the inspirational vein of "Win one for the Gipper!" One might have thought that TR's "I wish to preach, not the doctrine of ignoble ease, but the doctrine of the strenuous life" better suited the demands of training camp. Or perhaps Teddy's "The first requisite of a good citizen in this Republic of ours is that he shall be able and willing to pull his weight" would have aptly expressed the teamwork concept.

Evidently, Buck had chosen the framed quote—and it really wasn't necessary to check with anyone to know that Buck had taken it upon himself to select the proper lesson—presumably as a declaration of faith from the manager to his players not only in their athletic abilities, but also in their mature dedication to their profession and their individual and collective professional goals.

Notwithstanding the care that must have been taken to select such a relatively obscure quote, for a message that was not only starkly direct, but so on point as to cause one to stop and blink, it would have been nigh impossible to beat the most famed of the Rough Rider's many exhortations: "Speak softly and carry a big stick; you will go far."

Back in the stadium, a run was on in the shops for baseballs, hats, and sweatshirts celebrating the Diamondbacks' first year in the major leagues. The Diamondbacks had designed yet another logo—a stylized snake's head grasping a ball in its teeth—just for this inaugural campaign. The Diamondbacks would be wearing the logo throughout the coming year, and so could any adult or child lucky enough to purchase this potentially collectible item. Nor would this be the last new item available to a waiting public, for a big *D* (the same *D* that was painted on the locker room wall) would adorn the batting helmets of the team during season number one—and perhaps only during season number one, which rendered buying that batting-helmet replica all the more pressing and precious.

However, on this game day, competing logos aside, sweatshirts and jackets were definitely a hot item on this cold evening. It was almost 6 P.M. and the sun was beginning its descent behind the Catalina Mountains. The sky was turning pink and purple, the palest shades emerging first, softening and warming the heavens, the hues steadily deepening, the colors intensifying, the action on the field increasingly secondary to this magnificent spectacle. But inevitably, and before too long, the sun disappeared and the colors vanished into the blackness of night, and attention was more easily redirected to the field, where the tall lights penetrated the darkness and the teams were preparing to play.

The stadium was filled with senior-citizen ushers and ticket-takers. Like the paying customers, the attendants were giddy with excitement. Also like the customers, most of the attendants didn't seem to know their way around the grounds just yet, checking their guides to escort people to and fro.

Down on the field, the two teams were either in or around their dugouts. The Diamondbacks looked loose and ready. A TV reporter from a Spanish station was doing his stand-up in front of the dugout, giving that camera his solemn, this-is-history-in-the-making gaze, while young children just a few yards away ignored him, instead lying on top of the dugout, reaching their arms over the top and tossing down T-shirts for the players to autograph. A few players were on hand and obliged, signing and tossing the T-shirts back up.

Brian Anderson, one of the more amusing interviewees on the team, was leaning against the dugout railing, one foot on the top step. He was talking with Amy Bender, a TV sports reporter who had been hired by the franchise as the host for the Channel 3 Diamondback pregame show. Almost all of Amy's shows were going to be on the weekends, so as not to disrupt the station's normal weekday schedule. Independent station Channel 3, out of the running for the sitcoms, soap operas, and one-hour dramas that were the networks' prime fare, maintained a profitable lineup by buying a host of syndicated talk shows and those pseudo-news/information programs known as infotainment.

In fact, Channel 3 didn't just play them once, they showed some of them twice in the same day, *Jerry Springer* and *Oprah Winfrey* in the morning and then again at night. Since most Diamondback games started at 7:05 P.M., due to the summer heat, for a pregame show Channel 3 would have had to preempt its six-thirty showing of *Entertainment Tonight. ET* was a big ratings winner, a lucrative property—lucrative enough to also be granted that twice-a-day exhibition, five days a week—and Channel 3 wasn't about to sacrifice *Entertainment Tonight,* not even on the altar of professional baseball.

In any event, Brian Anderson was making fun of Amy's pants, which in his rather dubious stylistic judgment he deemed too short. He referred to them as "flood pants," indicating that they would stay dry even when the water rose high. Amy gave as good as she got; noting the grass stains on Anderson's knees, she wondered whether the pitcher had received the green marks in the performance of a certain sexual act. Amy learned a long time ago that, as a woman breaching this male bastion, shy and sensitive wouldn't cut it. Indeed, not knowing how to give as good as one got would quickly get one cut out of the loop in the no-holds-barred sports world. For a beat reporter, who spent more time with the players than with colleagues back in the office, that could make for a lonely time.

"Hey," Anderson said, grinning, "I'll do whatever it takes to get in the big leagues."

In the meanwhile, Matt Williams walked out of the dugout, glove and ball in hand. He headed to one end of the dugout while another DB, too far away and not well-known enough to be recognized, headed in the opposite direction. The two started tossing the ball back and forth. Even though it was a most casual exercise, a last warm-up before the game, the speed with which the ball zipped through the air was striking, the ball smacking the gloves with a solid thump. The next throw was a bit off the mark, forcing Williams to take a step to the right to catch it. This caused the writer standing beside Amy to gently nudge her closer to the dugout and a pace farther out of harm's way. Out of the corner of his eye, Williams noticed this sideways movement.

"You don't trust me?" he asked as he threw the ball back.

"I don't trust the other guy," the writer graciously replied.

"You hear that?" Williams called out, mildly amused. "He doesn't trust you."

The unidentified Diamondback barely grunted his unappreciative response.

247

The introductory ceremonies were appropriately brief—despite the significance of the moment to the Diamondbacks and their fans, this remained just a spring training game. The highlight of the pregame rites was the announcement of the starting lineups. Though Chicago and Arizona shared TEP, when they played, one had to be the home team and the other the visiting—after all, somebody had to hit first.

No surprise, this being the Grand Canyon State, the Diamondbacks were accorded the honor of hosting tonight's contest.

The White Sox went first, jogging from the dugout when their names were called, assembling along the first-base foul line. The crowd greeted the players with enthusiasm, though an enthusiasm that appeared to be well under control.

Then it was the Diamondbacks' moment. One by one, they trotted out in their purple hats, purple shirts with *Arizona* stitched across the front, and gray, pin-striped pants. They mirrored the White Sox, lining up between third base and home plate.

Their reception was excited, the applause punctuated by shouts and yells. The loudest cheers were bestowed upon the usual suspects, meaning those who had won the biggest contracts and the most publicity: Matt Williams, Jay Bell, Travis Lee. Perhaps the most thunderous roar was reserved for Buck Showalter.

Interestingly, Jerry Colangelo, wearing long underwear beneath his clothes in deference to the weather, stayed off the field and out of the limelight.

The national anthem was sung, a few fireworks were shot up over the outfield wall, and it was time to play ball.

The Diamondbacks took the field, Willie Blair on the mound. Blair was another high-priced player, having signed a three-year, $11.5-million deal on December 8, 1997. Blair was thirty-two years old and had already been with Toronto, Cleveland, Houston, Colorado, and San Diego for a total of seven not entirely impressive seasons, recording 25 wins and 41 losses. Because of his performance through the 1997 season, however, with the Detroit Tigers, when he went 16-8, people had begun to take serious notice. What was even more impressive was that after suffering a fractured jaw from a line drive hit by Cleveland's Julio Franco in May, Blair had returned in July to go 13-6 for the rest of the season.

Blair was penciled in as the number two man in the Diamondbacks' pitching rotation. The first spot belonged to another right-handed free agent, Andy Benes, formerly of the St. Louis Cardinals. The Diamondbacks had paid out more than $18 million for the six-foot-six, ten-year veteran. Benes was regarded as one of most durable pitchers in baseball, never missing a scheduled start before the 1997 campaign. In 1996, after getting off to a dismal 1-7 start, he won 17 games while dropping 3, finishing 18-10. In 1997, Benes had to skip the first month of the season due to a rib-cage injury, then had to forgo his last five turns in the rotation after breaking a finger on his pitching hand while trying to lay down a bunt. He finished the season 10-7.

Once again, a lot of baseball people thought Arizona had overpaid for the pair. (Of course, George Steinbrenner, the Diamondbacks' most persistent critic with regard to their spending habits, shelled out $20 million for pitcher Kenny Rodgers. Before too long, the Yankees were so eager to get rid of Rodgers that when they traded him to the Oakland A's, they agreed to pay $5 million of his new contract.)

Maybe the Diamondbacks had spent too much, but the club needed some durable, reliable starters, and now they had them.

Blair and Benes were both fine citizens, married and with children. In fact, Blair's wife, Trina, had given birth to their third child only a couple of weeks before.

For their part, Andy and Jennifer Benes had four kids. Husband and wife met the media after the signing in Bank One Ballpark, still a couple of months away from completion. According to government regulations, everyone on the stadium grounds had to wear a hard hat and work shoes. The construction managers were used to visitors touring the grounds and had both extra hats and shoes waiting. Nonetheless, as the inaugural season neared, and media interest rose, more and more hats were required to handle the additional sightseers. (So many pairs of shoes had mysteriously disappeared early on, evidently appropriated by the first rounds of guests, that it was decided not to keep buying these relatively expensive work shoes.)

However, though the many members of the press were decked out as prescribed by the Occupational Health and Safety Agency, Department of Labor, Diamondback officials Jerry Colangelo, Buck Showalter, Rich Dozer, and Joe Garagiola all flouted the regulations, every one of them wearing tasseled loafers, all holding their hats in their hands.

Andy wore his new jersey over his shirt, answering questions in a voice so soft-spoken that one had to push in close to hear. Jennifer, a small woman, stood nearby, a dazed, happy expression on her face, an expression quite familiar by now to those who had watched a succession of freshly minted Diamondbacks and their wives and fathers and mothers parade before the press.

Andy and Jennifer were religious people, who worked with a ministry that took players to foreign countries where they taught both baseball and Christianity. It was just after one such mission to Costa Rica that Benes learned that he was going to the Diamond-backs.

"When I learned it was Phoenix," Andy recalled, "after being on that mission, I can honestly say that it brought tears to my eyes knowing I was going to be in a place where my kids, my family, could be happy."

Above, the roof was being tested that day—actually, half the roof, for the other half was retracted and not moving today—and it slid smoothly, rapidly, quietly into position. Far below, on the ground, the sod was being rolled in long strips in the outfield by one of those motorized giant metal wheels usually spotted on the highway pressing asphalt into place on the road.

All around, it was a busy day.

Though Andy Benes was the automatic choice for the starting pitcher on the big opening day, Willie Blair was slated for this smaller opening day.

Blair's first pitch was a ball to Ray Durham. He redeemed himself by striking out Durham, and then he also struck out Chicago's $55-million slugger, Albert Belle, to the "Oohhhs" of the appreciative crowd.

Frank Thomas, the great White Sox hitter, was third up and promptly spoiled Blair's perfect game with a line-drive single into the outfield. Thomas's single was hailed as the first hit ever in TEP, another mark in a game of unending, numbing firsts, all saluted by representatives from the local media, from a column down the front page of the *Republic*'s sports section to an immediate mention by broadcasters on the scene.

Blair got out of the inning without further unpleasantness, and then the Diamondbacks were up.

"Leading off for your Arizona Diamondbacks," declared the stadium announcer, "center fielder Devon White!"

White took the first pitch. It was a ball, yes, the first ball ever taken by a DB. Devon swung at the next pitch, sending it deep to center for a long out.

While some of the White Sox were standing in their dugout, every Diamondback was on his feet, leaning against the railing, not only enthusiastic but showing it.

Dwayne Murphy was in the first-base coach's box, and Brian Butterfield was at third. Butterfield had just gained a tiny measure of fame when a story on television had revealed him to be the premier fungo batsman of his time. A fungo bat was a narrow bat suited to knocking grounders for infield practice. Evidently, Butterfield knew how to place ball after ball just where he wanted it, an invaluable ability in a coach.

Jay Bell walked, earning applause from the fans.

Jorge Fabregas, the catcher rudely discarded by the White Sox, especially intent on having a good game against his former team, lifted a ball into the outfield for an out.

Two down.

Matt Williams stepped to the plate, the crowd cheering a step short of wildly. In a flash, the count was two and oh. Williams was ahead and prepared for a pitch down the pipe. Matt reared back and swung mightily. He missed. The crowd gasped.

Two and one. Three and one.

Ball four. Another walk.

Sadly, that was it for the inning. Brent Brede, whose unfamiliar name elicited minimal response from the audience, hit a dribbler back to the pitcher, who easily threw him out, stranding Bell and Williams on base.

The star third baseman and star shortstop remained on the field, talking and smiling. As protocol demanded, a teammate—in this case Tony Batista, the second baseman—brought them their gloves.

While the teams changed sides, the public-address system broadcast a Nissan ad. "What do you get when you put the Arizona Diamondbacks with the number one selling import truck?"

Something good, evidently, but there was no time to await the response because Jerry Colangelo was striding up the stairs to the upper deck where the press awaited. The press box was pretty typical, as far as press boxes went. One row raised behind the first, long tables with chairs and phones. Free local calls, free soft drinks, a free meal before the game, a first-class view behind home plate—the press had it pretty good. The only fly in the ointment, at least from a

251

fan's point of view, was the glass that enclosed the room. It allowed the reporters to concentrate on their working and talking, not to mention their eating and drinking.

Next to the press box was a series of rooms for TV and radio broadcasters. Colangelo quickly trod through the pressroom, responding to greetings from a number of media types with a quick wave and hello. Colangelo was on his way to a couple of quick interviews with his favorite media personalities—official Diamondback broadcasters.

Thom Brennaman and Bob Brenly were wearing identical winter-weight Diamondback jackets, colors and designs all over the place, which had come in handy since the window was open and the wind was blowing inside. Thom was doing the play-by-play and Bob the analysis for Fox Sports Arizona, which was televising the game regionally.

Just as it was spring training for the players, so it was for the broadcasters. Everybody needed the chance to hone his skills before the season started for real.

They were glad to see Colangelo, and the owner quickly jumped into the mix. "It's good to see you people working," he said. "I've been signing your checks for two years now."

Everybody chuckled at Colangelo's little jest. Second baseman Tony Batista beat out a ground ball to safely reach first base.

"There's our first base hit!" Jerry Colangelo pronounced.

Brennaman asked Colangelo what kind of a pitcher he had been in his youth.

"Steady," Colangelo replied, recalling that he had a "fair fastball" and a "pretty good curveball."

Greg Schulte and Rod Allen were waiting next door, handling the radio broadcast back to Phoenix. The window was closed and the temperature in the room was decidedly more reasonable. Hot or cold, Colangelo was ready for prime time.

"I think people in baseball look at this," he said, referring to TEP, "the twenty-acre facility, as the finest in baseball."

Schulte commented that, whether it was TEP or any other aspect of the franchise, the Diamondbacks weren't a typical expansion team.

"I don't think anything I've ever done has been typical," Colangelo said.

Colangelo shook hands all around and walked back to his seat outside.

Back in the main pressroom, the initial thrill of the new had worn off, replaced by the half-cynical, half-passionate banter that marked any gathering of journalists.

An anonymous voice piped into the room just for the media's benefit relentlessly reported each first, the significant and the significantly less so. This business of firsts eventually got to one radio producer, who, after a White Sox pitcher mistakenly stepped off the bag and automatically advanced the runners, loudly proclaimed, "That's the first balk at Tucson Electric Park," earning a laugh from his colleagues.

Willie Blair was back in the clubhouse, his outing over for the night. The anonymous voice informed the media that, after Blair had enjoyed a decent interval in the locker room, they could troop down for a chat with him.

Blair stood in the middle of a circle of microphones and notepads and answered question after question. He often answered the same question twice, or variations on the same question many times, as reporters wandered in, got their thirty seconds, and were replaced by another quote-hungry crew. Blair spoke calmly and intelligently, and for as long as it took.

"It is a big deal," Willie said, "because it's our first game. But I have to keep in perspective it's just the first game of spring training."

Other ballplayers were wandering around the locker room, eating or showering or dressing. Whatever they were doing, they demonstrated absolutely no interest in the media show and stayed away from the circle surrounding their teammate.

Amy Bender was in the mix, along with her camera operator, grabbing a few seconds of videotape magic for her archives. Around the room, some of the players, accustomed to the press intrusions in their formerly male-only sanctuary, kept their towels secured around their waist until they slipped on their shorts. Other players didn't care and got dressed in the usual manner, female reporter present or not.

Amy responded in kind, utterly disinterested in the dressing habits of the players. Once again, if a girl wanted to play with the boys, this was the way it was going to be.

"What did you get Belle on?" a reporter asked Blair about the first-inning strikeout.

253

"A bad slider. It was a slider that backed in on him, and fortunately, he missed it. He could have hit that thing a long way."

In the midst of Blair's press appearance, Albert Belle made up for that mistake in the top of the fourth, the game on view on all of the televisions mounted around the Diamondback locker room. With one out, Belle pounded a double. Robin Ventura walked, and then Ruben Sierra hit a single to left, giving Belle the opportunity to not only score, but—ta da!—score the first run in TEP history.

One inning later, Albert Belle smacked a home run, the first . . . oh, never mind.

Chicago had scored four and Arizona none midway through the game. That would change in the bottom of the fifth.

It went like this: Devon White walked. Chris Jones was put in to run for him. Jay Bell singled to left. Hanley Frias took his place on base. Jorge Fabregas walked. Mike Stoner ran for him. Matt Williams came to the plate with the bases loaded and no outs.

The people were yelling encouragement, expecting Matt Williams to do what Matt Williams did exceptionally well: produce.

The ump called the first pitch a ball. Williams popped up the next one high and foul.

Contact. It was a start.

Williams straightened it out with his ensuing swing. The ball traveled fast and deep, over the head of the center fielder, bouncing next to the 405-feet sign.

Two runs scored, and Buck sent in a pinch runner for Williams, waiting on second base.

Williams might have gotten the Diamondbacks back in the game, but this was a spring training game, and it was time for him to sit down.

Mike Stoner scored on another balk, and then Travis Lee added a fourth run with a single to right.

In an interview before the game, Matt Williams had said of Travis Lee, with tongue at least halfway in cheek, "He doesn't look like he hits the ball real hard, but it keeps going."

The White Sox scored off a solo homer by Jeff Abbott in the top of the seventh, but the Diamondbacks tied it back up in the bottom half of the same inning on Tony Batista's double, driving in Tom Wilson.

The Diamondbacks scored once more in the ninth after Kelly Stinnett got to first after being hit by a pitch, Hensley Meulens singled, and Edwin Diaz stroked a sacrifice fly to left.

Win or lose, it was always nice to win, it was terrific to win. However, lest anyone forget, winning wasn't necessarily the point. One veteran made no bones about why he was here.

"The hit was no big deal," Williams told the press. "It doesn't go on the back of a baseball card, anyway."

In case anyone missed the point, Williams said, "I'm just trying to get in shape. I'm just trying to get ready for the season."

Jorge Fabregas might also have been a vet, but he couldn't hide his glee at the outcome: "I'd be lying if I said I didn't want to win this one a little more."

The catcher had acquitted himself well, singling in the third, walking, and then setting up a run in the fifth. He also picked a White Sox runner off first with a perfect strike.

Despite the triumphant comeback, the team that won this game wouldn't be the team that took the field a month hence. Twenty-three-year-old Edwin Diaz, the man who had hit the fly ball that had won the game, had only played in twenty games above the Double-A level. He was the fourth second baseman in camp, behind Tony Batista, Andy Stankiewicz, and Hanley Frias.

Even so, on this night he was one of the stars. On this night, Edwin Diaz had notched a place for himself in the rapidly growing pantheon of Diamondback firsts—he had hit the first game-winning shot.

As excited as Diaz and the other Diamondbacks might have been this evening, perhaps even more excited—or at least they acted as though they were more excited—were the television folks who had driven down from Phoenix to cover the big event. The valley's Fox station, Channel 10, had established a beachhead on TEP's concourse in order to anchor its 9 P.M. broadcast from the stadium. Channel 10's anchors evidently thought of themselves as amusing individuals, because they spent an astonishing amount of time swapping what they judged to be wry observations and droll asides while delivering the news.

A theory gaining popularity among those who think about these matters is that local news is no longer about news but entertainment, a diversion from troubling issues and complicated stories, a frivolous exercise in photogenically grim car crashes, quickly solvable consumer frauds, grateful lottery winners, adoring celebrity gossip, and, for a spot of actual information, weather and sports.

Nine o'clock arrived and the anchors made it clear from the top that this was going to be an all-Diamondback news hour, apart from a few painlessly brief detours back to Phoenix for a check on those annoying Iraqis or economists or whoever else was upsetting the delightful status quo.

Fox local news proved true to its vow, as story after story was about Diamondback baseball, in all its varied aspects. There was a report about the glories of TEP, followed by a rehash on how some fans lined up early for the game, then to a sports correspondent for a recap of the game so far, over to a man who was plunked in the eye with a foul ball, on to some Arizonans who had waited their whole lives for baseball to stake its claim in the state, then a shift to the time-honored man-on-the-scene interviewing fans (who, though he was standing only fifty feet from the anchor booth, was deemed more on-the-scene because he had the field as his backdrop), then back to the sports correspondent for some more actual baseball stuff, then a return to Phoenix not because of some bothersome international crisis, but for an update on the progress of Bank One Ballpark.

Back to the anchors, just in time for the male news reader to tell the female news reader about the rumor that the national anthem would be sung on opening day by an all-star lineup of rock stars, including local resident Alice Cooper.

The female anchor shook her head in suitable amazement. "Boy," she said, "you can tell they're going whole hog."

The crowd starting leaving before the game was finished. It was cold, it was late, and it was spring training, so the impulse on the fans' part to suffer for the team was muted.

Fox Sports Arizona rebroadcast the game later that same night.

The franchise might have been in business for a couple of years already, but now the team was here. This might only have been spring training, the appetizer before the main course, but it was baseball. Not talk about franchise fees or corporate sponsorship or realignment or logos or drafts—not even talk about baseball—but of boys and men in uniform, fielding and hitting and running and catching and throwing.

Baseball. It was really here.

Chapter 21

The Games Go On

The Diamondbacks continued to win. By the time they journeyed north from Tucson for their first valley appearance, they had won three games and lost none. In an exceedingly rare instance of official DB humor, the press office's handout, called "Diamond-Facts," which provided the media with interview snippets and figures from spring training, stated that "the 3-0 start for the Diamondbacks is the best in franchise history."

Just the day before the team arrived in Phoenix, the Diamondbacks had once again come from behind to beat the White Sox, this time scoring three runs in the ninth to win 7-6. Even though it had been a sunny Sunday afternoon, the crowd was hardly more than half the size of that at the inaugural event.

Nonetheless, the Diamondbacks were still a healthy draw, pulling in more people than all but a handful of teams. Counting up almost two weeks' worth of spring training, the Diamondbacks had played six games at home, averaging 6,565 fans. They had done almost as well on the road, averaging 6,347 paying customers after eight games.

Of the thirty major league teams, only four could top the DBs' total at home: the New York Yankees, the Chicago Cubs, and the Atlanta Braves. The Yankees, in earning the number one position, averaged a tremendous 9,680 fans through seven contests.

Nobody had surpassed the Diamondbacks on the road, but then it had to be admitted that they had a distinct advantage over almost all of the other clubs in that they were never the visiting team, not really, not in Arizona's Cactus League. Only the Diamondbacks' fellow expansion mates, the Tampa Bay Devil Rays, and the Florida Marlins, both training in the Grapefruit League with twenty other teams, could match Arizona for the home-field advantage, and neither club's attendance figures came close.

Now the Diamondbacks were taking the field against the Milwaukee Brewers, and they were meeting in the Brewers' new stadium. The Maryvale Baseball Park, on Phoenix's west side, was another terrific facility, with all the requisite amenities: seats near the field, good sight lines for every fan, concession stands aplenty, adequate parking.

Each day of spring season was a feast for baseball fans. Almost every team played each day, from late February to late March, some in the afternoon and some at night. The dedicated fan could—and many did—travel from stadium to stadium, attending game after game. On this day, not too far up the road, the Seattle Mariners were battling the Oakland A's at the Peoria Stadium. Three-quarters of the seats were filled, and the lawn area beyond the outfield walls was covered with blankets and bodies as Randy Johnson walked to the mound to start the game.

The crowd at Peoria fairly well matched the size of the crowd at Maryvale, and on the same day the Mariners' best pitcher was working, so was the Diamondbacks'. It was Andy Benes's first appearance as a DB. Benes threw for two innings, and he came to the park with modest objectives. "I had two goals today," Benes later told the press. "The first was to be solid over the mound, have good balance and mechanics, and the second was to try not to get my middle infielders killed."

Benes pitched well enough to give up just three hits, one run, and no fatalities. He also picked off Marquis Grissom in the first inning, and Darien Jackson in the second.

"That's why I gave up those hits," Benes said, "so I could practice my pickoff move."

Roland Hemond brought one of his five children to the game, a son, and also his grandson and his niece—a busman's holiday, of sorts. He stood near the concession stands and shook hands and chatted with a succession of old friends and colleagues who happened to pass by.

Travis Lee was walking up to the plate. He had already hit a single to score a run. A writer asked Roland what he thought of Travis's progress.

"He's done everything we've asked of him and more," he replied. "He's only going to keep getting better. Just watch him."

As if on cue, the pitcher leaned back and heaved, and Lee swung and connected. The ball hurried over the left-field wall for a home run.

The crowd cheered and Roland beamed. "What did I tell you?" Then Roland laughed; he might have been good, but nobody was that good.

The Diamondbacks beat the Brewers, 7–4.

The team returned to Tucson the next day. The Diamondbacks played the San Diego Padres and lost. The DBs scored twice in the first inning and kept the lead until the Padres notched three runs in the third. The Diamondbacks tied it up in the fourth, but that was close as they were going to get. The Padres added two more runs in the fourth, and they were ahead to stay. The final score was 9–7.

The members of the media strolled into the locker room to get their quotes for their newspapers or radio stations or TV news segments. The Diamondbacks displayed their usual excitement at meeting the press, meaning most of those who were asked questions happily responded, while those who were not bothered by the reporters did not bother them in return.

Those who have never visited a major league locker room might be surprised to find that many of the ballplayers were far from sculpted specimens. Of course, some players were in overtly fantastic shape, big and strong, while others were lean and strong. However, many ballplayers looked like any other ordinary Joe when stripped of their uniforms.

Actually, a Phoenix physical therapist specializing in professional athletes quietly averred that baseball players were less fit than basketball, football, and hockey players. In fact, this therapist rated baseball players the least fit of any of the pros with whom he worked.

In any case, on this occasion, the media found the players and coaches quite unperturbed by the defeat.

Winning was nice, but preparing for the season was what counted.

After all, that was why they held spring training.

The Diamondbacks had split into two squads that day, with the other squad taking on the Chicago White Sox. This second team also lost, 6–4.

Arizona rebounded the next day with a 9–8 victory over the Cubs, a game in which Brian Anderson became the first Diamondback pitcher to get a hit. Anderson's triumph was all too brief as he became the first Diamondback pitcher to get himself picked off first base, by Cubs pitcher Terry Mulholland.

The next day, the Diamondbacks got picked off by the Padres, 4–0, suffering their first shutout.

The team suffered a more significant loss when Andy Stankiewicz tore some cartilage in his right knee. The injury would put Stankiewicz out of commission for four to six weeks. Since second base was one of the thinner spots for the team, Stankiewicz's injury was worrisome.

To make matters worse, Hanley Frias, another second baseman, broke a bone in his right hand, with possible ligament damage, necessitating surgery and a couple of months of rest and rehabilitation.

Mark Davis's comeback encountered a setback as he gave up four hits and three runs in two-thirds of an inning. Davis said his arm felt fine, but he needed to work on his "mechanics."

The Diamondbacks won one, lost three in a row, then won again.

Jorge Fabregas continued to perform impressively, hitting .368. He was also working his pitchers well, confidently guiding them through their innings. This, of course, was particularly important to Fabregas because his pitcher management had been the Chicago knock—the very public knock—against him.

Jay Bell wasn't having as flashy a spring, hitting just .210, over seventy points below his 1997 season average with Kansas City. The shortstop wasn't concerned, content with how he was swinging, cognizant of the difference between spring training and the real thing. Still, Bell understood that his fat contract made him, more so than at any other time in his career, the object of curiosity and scrutiny.

While Bell and Fabregas might have been looking to the future, Mark Davis had reached the end of his road. Three days after his unsuccessful outing against the Cubs, the former Cy Young winner announced he was retiring from the game. But despite his retirement,

Davis wouldn't be going too far, for the Scottsdale native had been promised a job in the Diamondback organization.

Davis had worked himself back into shape intending to play for the Diamondbacks, and no one else. If he couldn't be on the field, then at least he would be nearby.

"I can't imagine a better scenario," he said.

On March 15, the Diamondbacks traveled to Hermosillo, Mexico, for a game against the Milwaukee Brewers. The Diamondbacks made no bones about why they had crossed the border, as explained by the bold headline across the front of the latest issue of *Diamondback Magazine*, distributed free by the thousands and conveniently printed in Spanish: *"Mi Casa Es Su Casa."*

By all accounts, it was a wonderful experience, enjoyed by all, American visitors and Mexican spectators alike. Estimates of the number of fans ranged from eleven thousand to over thirteen thousand. Either way, it was an awful lot of people buying tickets priced from $7 to $26, a lot of people from a city that was far from wealthy, to watch two teams from the United States play baseball.

The game turned out to be a pretty good one, with the score tied at 5 apiece after nine innings. Then, in the bottom of the tenth, with two outs and the bases loaded, Jorge Fabregas provided the classic ending by smacking a grand slam.

To make the moment that much more perfect, local hero and native son Karim Garcia was on third when Fabregas connected and trotted home to score the winning run.

According to Jerry Colangelo, along for the ride, most of the proceeds from the game would go to Hermosillo to help develop baseball projects for the city's youth. "That's what this is about," he told the press, "helping people in this community as well as those back home."

The managing general partner also announced that the Diamondbacks had a handshake agreement to return to Mexico and play again in the future.

"We're the ambassadors of Major League Baseball," said Buck, "and this is the way it should be."

And in the Diamondback universe, the way it should be was often the way it was.

Chapter 22

Speeding into the Future

On March 19, 1998, the last full day of winter, the owners approved the sale of the Los Angeles Dodgers from Peter O'Malley to Rupert Murdoch.

Ted Turner attended the meeting in St. Petersburg, Florida, his first appearance at an owners' meeting in nine years, specifically to try to stop Murdoch.

Turner had once compared his fellow media mogul to Adolf Hitler, stating that "like the late Führer, he controls the media for his own personal benefit." As if that weren't enough, Turner said that Murdoch was "crazed for money and power. . . . I fear him, and I don't trust him."

Rupert returned the affection in his own way. During Fox's telecast of the 1996 World Series between the Braves and the Yankees, the cameras made certain never to show Ted or wife Jane, sitting right up front near the Atlanta dugout.

Though all anticipated a fiery performance from the "Mouth from the South" at the meeting, Turner remained calm and logical, laying out the possible legal conflicts of interest, and wondering whether Murdoch would be a partner with the other owners, all in under five minutes.

The only deviation from this legalistic approach was Ted's wondering whether Murdoch was really a baseball fan, and how often he attended games. That would have been a good question to ask many of Turner's fellow owners, if anyone had cared, if it mattered in this corporate sports world.

In any event, Rupert Murdoch wasn't available to answer the query because he didn't show up for the meeting, instead dispatching representatives to seal the deal.

The final vote was fourteen National League teams in favor, with the Braves against and the New York Mets abstaining, and thirteen American League teams concurring and the Chicago White Sox dissenting.

The O'Malley family had owned the Dodgers since 1950, first in Brooklyn before moving the team west to Los Angeles in 1957.

But all that was finished. The Fox Group, which already had national television and cable contracts with MLB, and full or partial local rights to games involving twenty-two of the thirty clubs, was taking over from the O'Malleys.

Murdoch and Fox were getting the Dodgers, Dodger Stadium, three hundred acres surrounding the ballpark in downtown L.A., and training complexes in Vero Beach, Florida, and the Dominican Republic.

Peter O'Malley got some $350 million.

The era of family ownership in Major League Baseball was over.

Baseball wasn't through with the day's excitement. A *Newsday* report revealed that Cablevision, which owned the New York Knicks of the NBA and the New York Rangers of the NHL, was talking to George Steinbrenner about buying the Yankees.

Cablevision, through its MSG Network, was in the tenth year of a twelve-year, $486-million cable TV deal with the Yankees.

"We've talking about a continuing relationship with them," Steinbrenner told the Long Island–based newspaper. "Their TV contract with us is up in two years, and there are all sorts of rumors flying around because of that. There is nothing definitive."

Definitive could cost Cablevision considerably more than $500 million.

Steinbrenner denied that any deal had been struck. He declined further comment.

Steinbrenner, who owned 55 percent of the most storied franchise in sports, and his partners had purchased the Yankees from CBS in 1973 for about $10 million.

In the meanwhile, some people were thinking about the upcoming baseball season—the season on the field, not in the back rooms and boardrooms. *Sports Illustrated* was on the stands with its baseball preview issue.

The magazine picked the Diamondbacks to finish last in their tough division, which wasn't much of a shock. More interestingly, *SI* rated the teams according to their abilities and prospects. The first group, called "Tanned, Focused and Loaded," included the seven best teams in baseball—the Braves, Yankees, Orioles, Indians, Dodgers, Cardinals, and Mariners. The second group was named "Close but No Cigars," followed by "Right Roster, Wrong Division," then "Talent Challenged." The Diamondbacks were in this last contingent, along with their fellow expansion mates, the Devil Rays, and four other clubs.

Four ranks down wasn't bad for Arizona, inasmuch as two other categories awaited below. "Clueless" contained four teams—the Cubs, Reds, Phillies, and Royals—and "Not Even Trying" had five members—the White Sox, Expos, Twins, A's, and of course, Marlins.

Thus, according to the learned *Sports Illustrated*, the Arizona Diamondbacks, before they had even taken the field, were judged more accomplished than at least nine other teams in baseball.

The good news didn't stop there. In *SI*'s team-by-team analysis, the mag predicted, "The Diamondbacks won't be good, but they will be better than Tampa Bay."

So that made ten teams ranked behind Arizona.

Though these rankings were based on the abilities of the players on the teams, the payrolls of the teams told the story as definitively as batting averages and earned run averages. Those in that first group, constituting the elite, spent tens of millions more than other teams in baseball. The Orioles rated number one on this dubious list, with a payroll topping $70 million—$70,408,134, to be exact. The Yankees were second at over $63 million, the Braves third at $59.5 million, the Indians fourth at $58.5 million, the Cardinals sixth at $52.5 million, the Mariners seventh at $52.1 million.

That meant that the teams judged best by *Sports Illustrated* occupied six of the first seven payroll spots. (The management of the Dodgers, the final top team, had a bargain on its hands, being twelfth out of thirty, paying salaries that totaled $47.5 million. On the other hand, the Rangers, according to *SI*, weren't getting their money's worth, being fifth on the dollar list at $54.7 million, but way down in the "Talent Challenged" category, along with the Diamondbacks.)

At the other end of the scale, money and talent and prospects also marched together in lockstep. The clubs placed in *Sports Illustrated*'s worst two classes, "Clueless" and "Not Even Trying," spent not only less than the better teams, but remarkably less. The Expos were at the very bottom, the thirtieth position, with combined salaries worth $9.2 million. Greg Maddux earned more by himself than the entire Montreal team, as did Albert Belle and Gary Sheffield. Travis Lee's bonus was $800,000 more than the Expos' payroll.

The Diamondbacks, for all the controversy over their vaunted bonuses and fat contracts, ranked twenty-third on the list, with a payroll of $30,266,500. Thirty million was right where Diamondback officials had always said they intended to be, even before the November expansion draft.

Every spot on the payroll list from eighteen to thirty, save one, was safely in the hands of the teams with the worst prospects. (The Pirates, not ranked too high themselves, had reversed positions with the White Sox on the money list.)

Though it had yet to be demonstrated that the 1998 season would unfold as *Sports Illustrated* and other experts predicted, this stratification of talent and expectation and hope based on the wealth of the individual clubs could not bode well for baseball's future. If money dominated the game and determined the standings before the season began, then the level playing field, so vital to any league's competition, was rendered a sham. The small-market franchises, permanently bereft of huge TV contracts and other sources of revenue outside ticket sales, would be granted permanent second-class status. Before too long, this would discourage and disgust the fans of those deprived teams and ultimately destroy the professional game.

"If you're not spending fifty million dollars," averred Expos GM Jim Beattie, "then you ought to cut way back. That middle ground is quicksand. I'm not sure why anyone would want to be there."

If the general manager of a baseball team—a team spending $40 million less than what the GM himself said was necessary to compete in MLB, a team that, according to his logic, had essentially conceded before the first pitch was thrown—wondered why anyone in baseball "would want to be there," then why would any of his team's fans want to be there either?

On Friday, March 20, the Diamondbacks returned to Phoenix to play the Oakland A's and the San Francisco Giants. Arizona lost to the A's Friday night in front of over ten thousand fans at Phoenix Municipal. The 5–3 defeat was the team's fourth in a row, dropping the Diamondbacks' record to 12-13 and sliding the club below .500 for the first time in spring training.

Neither the dip nor the losing streak generated any undue media or public consternation, partly because this was still spring training, and partly because a more significant event in Diamondback history occurred that same day.

For on March 20, Bank One Ballpark was dedicated.

The media was assembled for lunch in the concourse of the stadium. Workers rushed back and forth, laboring to complete the building and its many pieces, while the members of the press were treated to hamburgers and hot dogs.

From the concourse, one could look right onto the field. This was quite different from most stadiums, where cement supports and metal poles and other obstructions blocked the view of a fan buying food or a hat or just walking around.

And from the concourse, it was evident that the field was lovely and the entire ballpark glorious.

The next item on the media's menu was a tour of the ballpark. Diamondback representatives split the reporters, camera operators, and writers into small, manageable groups and led them around the stadium. The home team's dugout was the first stop, a spacious, carpeted area fitted with a long bench constructed of rows of polished wooden planks, gracefully rolled over.

It looked to be as nice a dugout as a dugout could be.

A tunnel ran behind the dugout, leading to a hallway opening into several chambers, including a pair of indoor batting cages, in case anybody needed some warming up during a game. The hallway progressed to a few stairs, which ended at the Diamondbacks' locker room, an immense room, a singularly impressive room.

Forty lockers lined the chamber's perimeter. They resembled dressing tables more than lockers, with individual cubicles equipped with chairs and a tabletop facing the wall. Beneath the tabletop were drawers, and several feet above was a closed cabinet. Hangers were already in place on a rod attached to the underside of the cabinet, ready and waiting.

After dressing—by locker room standards—in relative privacy and rare comfort, each Diamondback before making a public appearance could check his visage in the mirror implanted on the side of every cubicle.

Catchers were granted even larger lockers, in deference to their additional equipment. As already noted, these three larger lockers were deliberately scattered around the room, so the catchers, who were necessarily and basically endlessly competing, didn't have to dress and undress every day on top of each other. Moving away from the lockers and toward the center of the chamber, two long couches, with four cushions per, were arrayed on either side of the room. The couches of deep Diamondback purple were covered in either leather or synthetic leather—most likely the latter—though no one on the scene knew the answer. Two curved wooden counters provided the players with a place to rest their elbows or eat, while watching one of the six large televisions hanging above their heads.

In the middle of the room and the middle of the carpeted floor was etched the Diamondback logo.

Continuing on the tour, the next series of rooms held toilets and urinals and showers and whirlpools and saunas and a giant hot tub. One somewhat interesting note: four adult-size urinals were joined by one set lower to the ground, which was either for young sons visiting their fathers or for catchers used to squatting.

The exercise room at the end of the hall contained state-of-the-art Cybex machines, with purple seats, free weights, and six stationary bicycles, two treadmills, and three steppers, all the aerobics machines manufactured by Star Trac.

More televisions were arrayed throughout these halls and rooms. Televisions were a beloved accessory everywhere in the stadium, from the locker room to the concourses to the JumboTron in the scoreboard. No one, from fan to player, would have a legitimate reason to miss a moment of the action, if the Diamondbacks had anything to do with it.

Around and around the tour wandered, examining the pool— available for rent at $4,000 per game—with its fountains and hot tub and changing rooms and fine sight lines from the water, then up the escalators to the luxury suites, and then even higher to the upper deck.

The suites were almost completed, with their wet bars and stools and bathrooms with the nickel-plated fixtures. They had excellent vantage points, to be sure, especially the seats located just outside the suite, which placed the suiteholder actually inside the stadium with the fans. Nevertheless, the suites that the members of this media contingent inspected didn't seem to strike anyone's fancy. Perhaps when the game was in full bloom and the stadium was filled with people, the glamour of the suites' exclusiveness would become more apparent. Now, however, without guards checking passes and waiters hustling for drinks and friends and associates basking in their quarantine from the rest of the spectators, the suites, all pretty much the same, reminded one observer of an airport lounge or an extremely clean studio apartment. (The only question was where the apartment would be located; the modern decor and color scheme suggested L.A., while the rolled-down metal shade was definitely NYC).

The upper level offered a terrific panorama, gained by the stadium's climbing more upward than outward, a design probably determined by the priorities of the retractable roof. This meant that the fans looked down rather directly on the field, which was tremendous, as long as one didn't mind heights.

The media folk trod back down to the terra firma of the main concourse, where they idled for a spell until Jerry Colangelo arrived to conduct the next stage of the press tour. The concourse was busy with scores of guests, who had been invited to see what had been built, or perhaps where they would sit, a far cry from the strict-visiting—or more exactly, the no-visiting—rules imposed during construction.

All these people slowed Colangelo, who had to stop every few yards to shake somebody's hand or exchange a few words with a well-wisher. Eventually, Colangelo, accompanied by Rich Dozer, made it to the press area, where Jerry was impeded once again, by several impromptu radio interviews. One of the interviews was for a Mexican station and conducted with the services of a translator, which definitely put a halt to Colangelo's advance.

Whether in English or Spanish, it was rather daunting to listen to Colangelo answer questions, because he was asked the same questions, over and over. This had become a large, exhausting part of Colangelo's daily routine for years, ever since he had become involved in the baseball fandango, the same core group of reporters peppering him with the same core group of questions. So it went today, yet again, his being asked how he felt, what he wanted to say to the public, how BOB compared to other stadiums, was he satisfied, was he reflective, was he proud?

As always, Colangelo answered all the questions in full, the salesman ceaselessly selling, the visionary devoted to his vision.

And did he think there was a problem with corporations buying sports teams and running the sports universe?

"Those who bemoan the corporatization of sports," replied Colangelo, "are living in the past. And when you look at the Murdochs and Turners, maybe the only way to compete is to bring together the entire community, like we've done here."

As he spoke, work continued around him. Young Mexican girls were busily filling up spray bottles with pinkish cleansing fluid, loading up the cleaning carts. Twenty feet away, a painter, perched on a ladder, painted a Miller Lite logo over a doorway. To his left, a man was giving instructions to a band of popcorn and soda vendors on the order of battle come opening day.

Momentarily free of encumbrances, Colangelo ushered the media down the stands toward the field. Standing before the visitors' dugout on the third-base side, he had the press take seats around him.

Colangelo talked about how much work had been done, and how much remained to be done. "Those who have seen the almost finished product think it is magnificent and well worth it," Jerry declared.

Nonetheless, El Niño and its persistent winter rains, unprecedented for Arizona, had finally disrupted the construction timetable. The crews were working overtime to catch up, but by this date, with eleven days to go to opening day, it was clear that not everything would be finished. Colangelo confirmed that the Cox Clubhouse, the kid's playground, would require a few more weeks before it would be open for business.

These setbacks did not diminish Colangelo's delight in his stadium. In fact, Colangelo said, there is "fear and envy on the part of some baseball owners when they see our ballpark, and our market and potential."

Along with the delays, the stadium's price tag had jumped sharply. Ongoing design changes and a rise in the cost of steel had added first millions, then tens of millions, to the bill, which ultimately reached $355 million. To cover these expenses, Colangelo had called upon his investors to pony up another $29 million. Though the investors had contractually committed to contributing an extra 20 percent over their initial capital outlay if the Diamondbacks needed the money, many of the investors were unhappily surprised by the demand.

Other problems had popped up in different areas along the way. A consultant for Maricopa County had abruptly quit, saying he was being turned into a "political scapegoat" when a furor arose over the county's practice of "borrowing" funds from Cactus League revenues to pay expenses due to the stadium's construction. While this was hardly a scandal and had nothing to do with the Diamondbacks anyway, every dubious issue or situation only made those who had doubts about the stadium and the tax and all the rest doubt that much more.

The back-and-forth negotiations between the county and the team over the formal stadium lease and revenue splits from nonbaseball events caused some controversy. The first agreement allocated approximately 95 percent of profits to the Diamondbacks, leaving such a small amount for the county that, after paying off a fifteen-year construction loan, the remaining share was virtually negligible. The county would not share in revenue from concessions, TV and radio contracts, national licensing, and other income sources. The agreement left many with a bad taste, and the two sides tried again, and again, and the county's percentages were raised, though surely not enough for the deal's critics.

Regardless of the figures, the fact remained that in Major League Baseball, most teams kept virtually all the profits generated by their home stadiums. In that light, county representatives were jubilant over the final contract.

Thus was the state of professional sports in America: the franchises decided, and the communities followed along or they were cut out, abandoned for more accommodating pastures.

Back in BOB, banks of lights were placed along both the first- and third-base foul lines, as the groundskeeping crew sought to help the grass take deep root and grow stronger. The Diamondbacks had given the University of California at Riverside a $160,000 grant to research and develop a grass that would thrive in the minimal natural light offered by the stadium, tolerate the Arizona summer, and withstand the pounding of baseball.

A Japanese hybrid named De Anza zoysia, which flourished in the shade longer than other grasses, was eventually chosen. The Diamondbacks paid Arizona State University to lay down some of the zoysia, to test it out on one of the college's practice fields. The grass performed pretty well, though it was by no means the sort of unqualified success that guaranteed that the zoysia would prosper in Bank One Ballpark.

The stadium's field was prepared in layers. Sand covered the foundation of gravel. Drainage and watering pipes snaked through the sand, along with one hundred sprinkler heads. The zoysia, cut into long strips, was pressed on top, row after row until the field was covered.

After years of research and trial runs and evaluation, the De Anza zoysia was still an experiment. The grass would definitely start the season looking good; how it ended the long campaign remained to be revealed.

Colangelo pointed out several of the retro touches, the red brick and limestone, the green metal and lacy arches. A dirt path, the same tawny color as the base paths, connected home plate to the pitcher's mound. Colangelo said this path, once a common sight, hadn't been incorporated into a ballfield's design in a hundred years. Another old-fashioned feature was the narrow warning track in the outfield, which gave way to an unexpected strip of grass before stopping at the wall.

"Each day there's tremendous progress," Colangelo said. "There's a lot of pride."

The notion of pride cropped up frequently when Colangelo spoke. He talked about the rotunda in the entrance of the ballpark, a large, open, round area, near the shops and the ticket booths, with escalators climbing up and down the stadium's levels. The rotunda was more than a transit site; rather, it was intended as a central gathering place for people at the ballpark. Upon the floor of the rotunda, visible from any level of the stadium, was an enormous mosaic of the state of Arizona, a multicolored glory. The names of thirty-two Arizona cities encircled the map. "What I wanted to do was to create pride," explained Colangelo. "Pride from being from the state of Arizona."

Pride to Colangelo wasn't a one-way street—merely a matter of Jerry enjoying his pride in his accomplishments—but an organic component of life, necessary to the health and growth of both individuals and communities.

Colangelo had more to say about the rotunda, but it was time for the real show. He said that the music had been selected for four contingencies: when the Diamondbacks won, when the Diamondbacks lost, and when the roof was opened and when the roof was shut. The media was to be treated to an aural examination of the latter two instances.

"I heard the music for the first time and it's tremendous," Jerry said.

With that, Colangelo signaled to Scott Brubaker, who was standing nearby, armed with a walkie-talkie, who relayed the message to someone in the control booth, who commenced with both the music and the roof closing.

The music started first, huge crashing sounds of construction or maybe thunder booming from the stadium's loudspeaker system. The roof was moving in steady fashion, its half dozen movable parts expanding like a humongous accordion. It was an astonishing sight, the roof unfolding so smoothly, so improbably, impossibly smoothly.

The music reached a crescendo, lush with percussion and trumpets and perhaps a heavenly chorus peeking through the noise. It was hard to tell, with so many different and frequently discordant sounds, and with attention so drawn to the roof itself, the two sides drawing together, each movable part extending to its limit, the other parts still advancing, blocking out the sun, shutting off the sky, still reaching.

The music rose, both ominous and joyful, like the approach of Armageddon, or perhaps Judgment Day, and just before the two sides of the roof met at the center, more thunder erupted, and then it was shut.

The exhibition had transfixed the audience, and the women and men of the press broke out in applause. Colangelo smiled broadly, his enjoyment in the spectacle apparent.

Even so, Colangelo quickly returned to the rotunda, returning to the point he had been making before the closing of the roof. He wanted the media to know that the room around the map was taken: the names of another fifty-five Arizona cities would be etched on plaques and placed around the rotunda. And that wasn't all; the entire rotunda was an ongoing art project. On the ground level, a muralist had been contracted to paint the history of sport, "from the ancient Greeks to the Arizona Diamondbacks," to quote Colangelo. The higher level would be devoted to murals relating the history of Arizona.

Now the walls were bare gray concrete. The murals would take time, but, assured Colangelo, they would be great when completed.

Colangelo paused, as some additional information was relayed to him. It turned out that the boys up in the control booth had gotten it backward, playing the opening music instead of the closing music.

No one, not even Jerry Colangelo, seemed to mind.

The people controlling the scoreboard were trying out various pictures and schemes and information pages. A Sony JumboTron, a high-definition, monster-size television, thirty feet by forty feet, just like the one overlooking Times Square, played footage of baseball bloopers—professional ballplayers bobbling balls, dropping balls, kicking balls, running into walls, falling over railings, falling into dugouts. Across from the JumboTron was the message board where the names and statistics of Diamondback players were being displayed, each for a few seconds, as would happen when a DB came to bat. Another message board spread wide across the scoreboard was practicing different kinds of notes, announcing home runs and strikeouts, accompanied by vivid animation.

The last scoreboard element was an Arizona Diamondback logo in green and red, spinning slowly against a black screen. The logo appeared to be three-dimensional, floating on the scoreboard.

Colangelo called over John Wasson, the project manager for Bank One Ballpark, introducing him as "my first hire," stating that he had "relied on him," and that Wasson knew this place better than anyone else—even better than Jerry Colangelo.

Wasson's job couldn't have been easy. Building a stadium was not only a long and difficult task, it was dangerous. Daniel Weber, age thirty-eight, had died when his crane touched a power line and he was electrocuted. Another had broken his neck when he had fallen twenty feet onto a platform sixty feet off the ground. Other workers had suffered lesser injuries.

It could have been worse. An immense crane toppled over, smashing into the ground, but mercifully missing any of the workers. Other, less lethal problems had presented themselves—a small fire igniting when a piece of hot metal tumbled into some plywood, one of the trusses almost striking a steel beam on the south tower—and Wasson and his crew had dealt with each problem as it occurred and moved on.

Colangelo offered Wasson up to the media, who asked several technical questions concerning the continuing construction. Wasson, whose gray mustache matched his gray hair, had gotten used to dealing with the press after managing so many media tours and responding to so many queries, and he replied specifically and succinctly.

While Wasson was speaking, the roof began to open again, and a bird flew inside. It dove down and then began to circle, around and around.

Colangelo invited the media over to Leinenkugel's Ballyard Brewery for a tour and free beer. Leinenkugel's was located on the stadium's main plaza, just outside the ballpark, alongside the front entrance. The restaurant/bar, or "brew pub," provided a fine example of Colangelo's skill in maximizing every financial opportunity.

Leinenkugel's was a 150-year-old, Wisconsin-based brewery, with two restaurants in the state. In 1988, Leinenkugel's was purchased by the Miller Brewing Company. Miller, of course, was a key Diamondback sponsor, and Miller Lite was the official Diamondback beer.

The Diamondbacks and Miller, through its Leinenkugel's subsidiary, decided to go into business together—business beyond Miller's multimillion-dollar investment in its club sponsorship—and build and co-own the restaurant right on the stadium grounds. Downtown Phoenix, neglected for so long, could definitely absorb another drinking and dining establishment, particularly one so identified with the ballpark, and also so close to America West Arena. Those two venues alone, with the Diamondbacks, Suns, Mercury, Coyotes, Rattlers, and all the concerts and circuses and other events booked into both places, promised a happy, sizable crowd strolling around Leinenkugel's day and night.

The brew pub opened for business that very day, handling its first lunch crowd. Now the restaurant was empty, except for the waiters and other workers, and the crowd Colangelo was leading through the doors.

Leinenkugel's was housed in a long, rectangular building, resembling a warehouse, constructed of brick and glass and complementing the ballpark in design and materials. The interior encompassed twenty thousand square feet, dominated by a pair of gigantic stainless steels tanks where the beer was being brewed, then and there. Over five thousand barrels were planned for production annually, to be served at the mahogany bar, sixty feet six inches in length—the same distance from home plate to the pitcher's mound.

Corresponding to these dimensions, a pitcher's rubber was encased in the floor at one end of the bar, while home plate could be found at the other. And this makeshift pitching path would not go unused.

Colangelo introduced the head man at Miller, who had flown in for the event, as well as the Yount brothers, who were the brewery partnership's managing partners. The Younts brought a real baseball pedigree to the enterprise: Larry was the ex-president of the Phoenix Firebirds, and Robin was the former Milwaukee Brewers' All-Star, who had played twenty years in the majors.

Colangelo said that Leinenkugel's would be a welcome addition to a booming downtown. "Ten million people annually will walk the streets of Phoenix," he said, invoking a projection familiar to anyone who had heard him speak about the future. "This is a great opportunity to offer people great choices."

The choice here was sports and beer, and food easy to carry out and eat in the ballpark. Dining at the pub could be enjoyed on either the ground floor or upstairs, indoors or outside. Whenever and wherever the Diamondbacks played, at home or away, the action would be displayed on screens throughout the restaurant. A couple of local radio stations had set up glass-enclosed studios inside the building, so when their reporters interviewed the players, patrons could sit back and watch and listen.

Sports and beer and more beer and food that didn't require utensils—now that was a choice the franchise and the beer giant were betting would be hard to resist.

Intros done, Colangelo quietly stepped outside with a mitt and a ball and the Younts, while the media concentrated on choosing from the microbrews named in honor of baseball: Warning Track Red, Home Run Honey Weiss, Bleacher Blonde Ale, Rally Red.

A few moments later, Colangelo returned. Rich Dozer announced that to properly inaugurate the joint, Jerry would throw out the first pitch. The old southpaw took his mark on the rubber, while Robin Yount crouched at home plate. Colangelo appeared uncharacteristically nervous, as he joked about people getting out of the way of an errant toss. Colangelo might have been joking, but people listened and looked and took several steps back.

Jerry reared back and let fly. The ball curved wide to the right, and Yount nabbed it without having to jump out of his catcher's stance. A cheer went up and the drinking began.

* * *

275

An organist played welcoming music, the traditional songs of baseball, while the crowd gathered for the stadium dedication ceremony just outside the brewery on the main plaza. Several rows of chairs had been deployed in front of a podium, with the names of invited guests taped to the backs of the seats. More and more people were stopping at a large glass square. Inside was a marvelous contraption, a series of levers and slides and weights and pulleys connecting levels of chimes and bells and painted figures doing this and that, all to make dozens of differently colored balls roll and spin and career and bounce through the machine. The balls triggered devices, and devices tripped the balls, causing fans to do the wave and a batter to swing and a catcher's eyes to bug out. Every gizmo seemed to act on every other mechanism, the whole instrument resembling a perpetual motion machine as it went round and round, up and down.

On top of the structure was an oil derrick, its arms swinging like a pendulum. Naturally, this wasn't a typical derrick, but a Diamond-back derrick, and it wasn't digging for oil but for baseballs, the pipeline running down into the center of the contraption below.

The whole, fabulous thing was called Based on Balls. Its creator was George Rhoads, who had conceived and built about one hundred of these "interactive autokinetic sculptures."

A couple of small boys pressed their faces against the glass, mesmerized. "Here it comes!" the older boy yelled to his brother. "Here it comes! Watch it!"

A ball passed through a snake's head—a diamondback snake, presumably—and then spiraled down through its body, until it fell through into a miniature boxing ring, where it caromed from rope to rope.

The boys waited and held their breath for the inevitable denouement, which finally occurred when the ball dropped through the hole in the corner of the ring, to the gleeful shouts of the kids. But the show didn't stop, it didn't even slow down, because that ball was skipping down four steps, banging into long rods with golf balls attached to the ends. The golf balls popped up and struck wooden boxes, producing charming notes.

The scene enchanted adults as well as children.

"I could sit here all day and watch this," the boys' mother enthused to their grandfather.

But uninterrupted viewing was not in the cards, for Thom Brennaman was at the podium and the program was about to start.

"I have been fortunate to go to all the brand-new baseball stadiums," Thom said, "and I can assure you that this will be the talk of baseball from coast to coast. There's nothing like it, I can assure you."

It was time to dedicate "our house," pronounced Thom.

Brennaman lauded Colangelo for his "vision, leadership, courage, and experience," and the audience applauded as he approached the podium. He took out his reading glasses and put them on and began speaking from a prepared text. He said that "only a strong public/private partnership could have made Bank One Ballpark possible." In the spirit of thanksgiving, Colangelo welcomed Bishop O'Brien to deliver the invocation.

The bishop went on for a while, not only giving the stadium his blessing, but going way beyond that, putting forth the hope that "this building of bricks, steel and glass would remind us to build a world of justice." While this was more than a bit of a stretch, the bishop recovered with a crowd-pleasing, big finish when he implored, "Lord, may You help us win the World Series."

Jan Brewer, representing the Board of Supervisors, spoke next. The supervisors had arrived with their own security force. Law enforcement was already present in force, with sheriff's deputies, Phoenix police, and stadium personnel. Wilcox's shooting had caused the supervisors to increase their security contingent, and so these fundamentally anonymous officials had arrived more than adequately protected from the Larry Namans of the world.

Brewer, giving the standard politician's address for such an occasion, energetically boasted about the county and the franchise in the simplistic terms of a high school cheerleader yelling that her team was number one, number one, number one!

Brewer included one awful joke, stating that until now, she had been a Milwaukee Brewers fan—get it?—but she was switching her allegiance to the Diamondbacks.

What was especially piquant about Brewer's speech was that she had won her seat by defeating Ed King in the Republican primary, running in opposition to King's support of the stadium tax. She had called King an "embarrassment" for his yes vote, trounced him 72 percent to 28, then easily beat the Democratic opponent, who never

277

had a chance in the conservative Sun City district, filled with retirees who never met a tax they didn't hate.

Brewer had already earned her anti-stadium spurs by campaigning in the state Senate against Herstam's bill authorizing the board to establish the tax.

As Chris Herstam later put it, with a small smile on his face, "She didn't sign my baseball."

Politicians have to be flexible—politics is the art of the possible—but Brewer's contortions made Houdini look stiff.

Bob Matthews, the vice chairman of Bank One, rather appropriately talked about how the ballpark was the leading edge in the redevelopment of the central city area, including new hotels and office buildings and apartments and restaurants. At the end, he offered a doggerel penned by Steve Roman, the senior vice president of marketing, who had represented the bank at the groundbreaking ceremony more than two years ago. Roman had read his poem then and suggested that Matthews, in search of something entertaining, use it again, as an expression of the circle's completion.

It was a takeoff on the baseball classic "Casey at the Bat," written by Ernest Lawrence Thayer, Harvard graduate and onetime humor columnist for the *San Francisco Examiner,* and published on June 3, 1888 which ended with matchless, unforgettable finality:

Oh, somewhere in this favored land the sun is shining bright;
The band is playing somewhere and, and somewhere hearts are
*   light,*
And somewhere men are laughing, and somewhere children
*   shout;*
But there is no joy in Mudville—mighty Casey has struck out.

Steve Roman had taken a different tack:

Long ago in Mudville, Mighty Casey sealed his fate,
When he failed to hit the final pitch, spinning towards home
*   plate;*
But here's a secret that few do know, and fewer still do tell,
The ending would be different to that tale we know so well.
Yes, Casey would have hit a homer, he'd have brought the
*   records down,*
If he had played at Bank One Ballpark, and Phoenix was his
*   hometown!*

278

While Steve Roman was undoubtedly saying that BOB would have inspired a Casey garbed in the purple and turquoise, a little rhyming boosterism, he might have been alluding to the physics of a ball in flight. Though it might have surprised most visitors to the desert, and probably most residents, too, Bank One Ballpark, over one thousand feet above sea level, had the second-highest elevation of any stadium in baseball. Only Denver's mile-high Coors Field was nearer to the stars than BOB. The higher the stadium, the thinner the air, the farther the ball traveled—physics. Humidity, which was an all-too-true Arizona-summer reality, would only cause the ball to keep sailing even farther, since water molecules offered less resistance than nonwater molecules.

Heat and humidity, not to mention a right-field wall at 334 feet, left-field wall at 330 feet, and the swimming pool about 415 feet from home plate . . . Somebody was going to hit a bunch of home runs in Bank One Ballpark. Maybe a lot of somebodies.

Anyway, Steve Roman was probably being more boosterish than scientific.

Jerry Colangelo returned to the podium and introduced some of the local dignitaries in the audience, which mainly consisted of a long list of politicos, always ready to get in on the glory. Colangelo marched down the list and momentarily paused when he came to Chris Herstam, the former state legislator whose bill authorizing Maricopa County to institute a tax to pay for the stadium had gotten this whole ball of wax rolling. "Although I'm the one who gets blamed for this," Colangelo said, "here's the guy who put the legislation in place."

The line generated a laugh, although it was really the county Board of Supervisors' implementation of the tax, and not the legislature's authorization bill, that had stirred the pot. And speaking of the board, not only were all members gathered in the audience, but Jim Bruner, too.

Colangelo led the members of the Board of Supervisors and other distinguished guests inside the stadium and onto a balcony overlooking the plaza. While Colangelo was away, Thom Brennaman assumed the hosting duties again. As planned, Thom asked the group to join him in singing, "Take Me Out to the Ball Game," to engage the crowd until Colangelo and company reemerged. And so the organist played, and Thom and the people sang:

Take me out to the ball game,
Take me out with the crowd.
Buy me some peanuts and Cracker Jack,
I don't care if I never get back,
Let me root, root, root, for the home team,
If they don't win it's a shame.
For it's one, two, three strikes, you're out,
At the old ball game.

Jack Norworth, vaudeville star and songwriter, had written the lyrics in 1908. Norworth, who also wrote "Shine On Harvest Moon," had never witnessed a major league game, but had instead gotten the idea from a poster on the subway, urging fans to ride the new trains out to the Polo Grounds to watch the New York Giants. Norworth's friend Albert Von Tilzer added the music, and together they composed baseball's favorite tune.

And Von Tilzer had nothing on his pal, because he, too, had never attended a baseball game.

"Take Me Out to the Ball Game" was an immediate hit and has remained so for the ninety years since Norworth performed it for the first time at the Amphion Theater in Brooklyn. What has been forgotten in almost a century is that the verse we sing today only constituted the chorus of the song. The original was actually a tale about baseball fan Katie Casey, and her boyfriend, and their day at the game:

Katie Casey was base ball mad,
Had the fever and had it bad;
Just to root for the home town crew,
Ev'ry sou Katie blew.
On a Saturday, her young beau
Called to see if she'd like to go,
To see a show but Miss Kate, said
"No, I'll tell you what you can do."

What Katie's boyfriend could do—as if you didn't know—was take her out to the old ball game.

The story continued for another three stanzas. Katie knew all the players' names, cheered for the home team, booed the ump, and "would root just like any man." But somewhere along the way, the tale was dropped and the immortal chorus remained.

Jerry Colangelo and Jan Brewer from the Board of Supervisors were on the stadium's second level, each holding a bottle of sparkling water wrapped in a napkin. Water was substituted for champagne, so as not to stain the stadium.

The pair smashed their bottles against the sides of the ballpark, and then Matthews from the bank and the other supervisors got to smash bottles, two by two. When the third pair swung away, streamers shot out and two bangs resounded, as loud as cannons.

That seemed to be it. The people began walking off, and the cleaning crews immediately began picking up the streamers and mopping up the water. But one last act remained to the day, and Colangelo invited the press inside the lobby of the Diamondbacks' office entry. The entry was part of the plaza, inside the gates and to the right.

The small lobby was lined with marble, from the floor to the ceiling. On the ground were listed the names of every team and the year they entered the major leagues, commencing with the Braves in 1871, the Cubs in 1874, and going on from there. In the center of the list, which was etched inside a curving pattern, was a round hole, surrounded by the words "Arizona Diamondbacks," and the year "1998."

Not too many journalists followed Colangelo into the lobby. The main show had been on the plaza, and the reporters had their stories for that night's telecast or the next morning's paper.

Colangelo was holding a small piece of marble, cut into the shape of a baseball. He said that the lobby was intended to express who the Diamondbacks were, though he didn't explain exactly what he meant.

Colangelo knelt and carefully placed the marble baseball, white with red stitches, into the hole. He rose and faced the group, which now included some Diamondbacks employees. His face was slightly flushed, and he looked excited and even a bit overwhelmed.

"It's going to change the quality of life in Arizona," Colangelo said, mentioning tax revenue, jobs, the usual slate of economic benefits. Though none of this was new, Colangelo's voice was a little fuller, a little thicker than usual.

"We have a great deal to be thankful for," continued Colangelo, fingertips pressed together as he spoke. "Living in this county, in this state, and we're blessed to be involved in this."

The ballpark was dedicated and ready for business.

Chapter 23

The Ballpark Goes Public

The next day, the Diamondbacks appeared for their last outing in Scottsdale Stadium during the 1998 preseason, matched against the San Francisco Giants. The next time the team played in the valley, it would be to end spring training with its first game in Bank One Ballpark.

It was a gorgeous day. Eighty degrees and blue skies brought out the fans, over eleven thousand strong, a stadium record. Between innings, Diamondback players stood on the dugout steps and threw packs of baseball cards to the excited crowd, the vast majority of whom would never have considered for one second buying baseball cards, but loved getting something, anything, for free, and pleaded and waved their arms at the players like seals at the zoo begging for fish. Out on the grass beyond the outfield, people were stretched everywhere, lying on the ground, young women sunning themselves in bikinis, small children playing tag, dashing between the adults, couples eating and drinking. Some people were sleeping, head tucked upon their hands.

Others—mainly teenagers—roamed the downside of the slope or stood under the few trees. They were happily missing the game in favor of flirting and sipping beers.

The teenagers weren't supposed to be drinking, but, hey, this was an afternoon enjoying Cactus League ball, and beer was going to be consumed.

The choice of beers in this park was impressive. Four Peaks Brewing out of Tempe was a local brew, and Fat Fire Amber Ale hailed from next door in Fort Collins, Colorado. Other beers, either at the concession stands or circling the seats in cases lugged by vendors, included Anchor Steam, Corona, Coors Light, and Miller Lite. All sold for $4 per, and all were doing brisk business.

Andy Benes was on the mound. From the start, he was hit hard by the Giants. Even the outs he earned were hit hard, often into the outfield. He worked five and half innings and gave up a solo home run to Barry Bonds, the All-Star's first homer in spring training. The Giants had a loyal following in Arizona, and Bonds's strike, which traveled about 440 feet, brought much of the crowd to its feet, cheering.

The Diamondbacks won, 6–2. Andy Fox, late of the Yankees, and Mike Robertson, picked up from the Philadelphia Phillies' Triple-A club, each notched three hits, including a home run apiece. Fox was going to make the club, but the situation wasn't as certain for Robertson, voted the Triple-A's best defensive first baseman the previous year. Unfortunately for Robertson, who had played in twenty-two games for the Phillies in 1997, batting .211, the Diamondbacks had Travis Lee penciled in at first base, today, tomorrow, and for years thereafter. Robertson had two things going for him: Travis needed a backup, and Robertson could also play the outfield.

The major league team was starting to shake out, as Buck and his coaches settled on players and positions. Many of those—the lucky ones—not selected were heading to Tucson, to trade their Diamondbacks' duds for Toros' togs. The rest would be dispatched to lesser minor league destinations or released outright.

Edwin Diaz, who had hit the sacrifice fly to win the Diamondbacks' first Cactus League game, went 0 for 4 against the Giants, leaving him with a .164 batting average for the spring. A couple of days later, Diaz was dispatched to the minors.

Catcher Mark Osborne, the Diamondbacks' third-round pick in the expansion draft, and infielder Danny Klassen, the franchise's seventeenth selection, were also assigned to the minors. All three young men were regarded as players who would contribute to the big club in the future. But future prospects meant a lot of work here and now, and at Tucson Electric Park, not Bank One Ballpark.

Back at BOB, the Diamondbacks hosted an "open house" for the disabled. The Americans With Disabilities Act mandated that 1 percent of the stadium spaces be wheelchair accessible. The Diamondbacks did a little better than that, and accessible seating was found in every part of the ballpark, from right up against the field to the upper deck to the picnic area.

Debra Stevens, director of public relations for SRO, Colangelo's in-house marketing and PR firm, was running this show for the stadium. She had assembled a team of volunteers, who escorted this afternoon's guests around the venue. One volunteer, skilled in sign language, was showing about twenty people the pool. About a dozen blind men and women, accompanied by family or friends, standing along the first-base front row, were listening as a volunteer detailed the outline of the field. People in wheelchairs roamed over the concourse, trying out different vantage points.

A pamphlet distributed by the Diamondbacks spelled out the features built into the stadium that would be of particular interest to the disabled. For those in wheelchairs, windows at the ticket counters were thirty-six inches tall, rendering them accessible. Service counters were also set at thirty-six inches. Condiment counters were two inches lower. Bathrooms, sinks, drinking fountains, pay phones, as well as every level of the stadium, were all made accessible.

Braille and tactile signage was placed throughout the facility. Listening devices, which amplified the ballpark's public address system, were made available, as were headsets and radios, for hooking into live broadcasts. With ten days' notice, even the services of a sign language interpreter could be arranged.

Nor were guide dogs neglected. A grassy area outside the northeast gate K was set aside for their bathroom needs.

The goal, said Debra, as people gathered around the few concession stands that were open to snack on popcorn and other ballpark fare, was to seamlessly integrate the disabled into the stadium's activities, from top to bottom.

Those who were the object of these efforts seemed as pleased as Debra with the result.

The tours for the public started the next day. The price of admission was a can of food, to be donated to a consortium of food banks. The excursions were an immediate hit as thousands upon thousand went through the gates. Local TV highlighted the ongoing parade, with stations positioning their weatherpersons in and around the stadium, as the crowds inspected every nook and cranny. The sight-seeing continued day and night. Though the tours were supposed to be done by 10 P.M., people were still inside long after, with others exiting the stadium to line up at the ticket windows, open for business.

In less than a week, the Diamondbacks claimed that more than two hundred thousand people saw what $355 million could build, while donating 106,500 pounds of canned goods. Two hundred thousand seemed on the high side, but any way one sliced it, a lot of feet had trod the stadium's concrete floors.

When the visitors weren't purchasing tickets, it was a safe bet they were spending whatever money was left over in the team shop in the rotunda. The shop was sixty-five hundred square feet of Diamondback merchandise, with some Suns, Coyotes, Rattlers, and Mercury stuff thrown into the mix.

In case anybody forgot to pick up that DB hat or purple garment bag on the way in, shops awaited on the upper level and the suite level. A special store loaded just with children's wares was located beside the Cox Clubhouse above center field.

Including all the other smaller merchandise stands, more than one hundred employees would be selling Diamondback goods on game days.

Success and sales wafted thick through the air. Alice Cooper, whose long and profitable career as a rock bad boy was belied by his devotion to the valley's golf courses, held a press event to advertise Cooper'sTown, his $2.5-million restaurant/bar/concert venue, under construction at First and Jackson.

"This downtown is going to be the greatest downtown," Mr. Cooper said, on this occasion putting away his golf clothes to once again don his trademark black attire. "This whole place is going to go pop! It's going to be crazy. And I want to be in the middle of it."

What exactly Cooper hoped to be in the middle of was still undecided. From the beginning, the fundamental question of whether professional sports and professional sports facilities returned their investment was both contentious and vexing.

A Deloitte & Touche study in 1993 predicted that the Diamond-

285

backs would produce $230 million a year in additional revenue. In 1998, a city official was predicting an annual bump of $300 million. It wasn't exactly clear on what basis the city official had reached her conclusion.

Refuting the old joke that if you placed all the economists in the world end to end, you'd never reach a conclusion, the vast majority of economists and other researchers have unequivocally decided that sports teams and stadiums are not rational financial investments for any city or community. In many ways, this analysis runs counter to the prima facie evidence of all those tickets and parking spots and hot dogs and T-shirts being sold. The fundamental flaw in this instant evidentiary conclusion is that experts know that people have only so many entertainment dollars to spend, and that whether people spend them on the Diamondbacks (or the Yankees or Broncos or Lakers, for that matter) or movies or restaurants or golf courses, people will only spend those dollars and no more. Thus, that means that sports doesn't add anything to the economy, but merely spreads the public's entertainment dollars around in a different way. In Phoenix, this would translate into people heading downtown to go out to dinner and a show or a game, instead of staying in their Scottsdale or Glendale or Mesa neighborhood to go out to dinner and a show, or some other leisure activity.

The reality of these limited disposable funds was already demonstrated within the confines of baseball itself. Prior to the 1998 Cactus League season, the Colorado Rockies had had Tucson all to themselves. Then the Diamondbacks and the White Sox moved into town, sharing TEP. Instead of three times as many fans attending games, as one might expect if each new team attracted an equal number of fans, the Rockies saw their average home audience drop 58 percent.

The Colorado decline could not definitively be blamed on the introduction of the newcomers. El Niño, which washed away the sunny, warm, inviting Arizona winter with rain and cold temperatures, undoubtedly played a part in chasing away the crowds. What percentage could be attributed to each of these factors was not necessarily provable. Nonetheless, it would seem apparent that at least the trio of teams acted to depress each other's market share.

Another element economists reckon with is the "multiplier," i.e., how the direct expenditure of money—say, renting a hotel room—results in further indirect expenditures, such as when the employees of that hotel then spend some of their salaries in the city. In this manner, one expenditure leads to another. The services that generate the greatest number of expenditures is the most efficient and most desirable. For example, the auto industry has grown to gargantuan size not only because people need to get from one place to another, but also because every vehicle purchased supports a variety of other industries, from gasoline to car components to insurance to mechanics to towing services to car washes to new-car dealers to used-car dealers to road crews, etc.

How does a sports team size up in the multiplier department? Not very well, according to most studies. The reasons for this are fairly obvious:

1. Though many jobs are created, they are frequently temporary, low-paying service positions—ushers, ticket-takers, waiters, vendors—which do not provide the sort of salaries that allow for a great deal of disposable income. Compare those jobs with positions provided by another type of employer—a manufacturer or software developer or entrepreneur—paying the same number of people an average salary of $30,000 or $60,000 or whatever amount, for a full year's work, and then see how those people earning a more reasonable wage spend their money on homes and education and clothes and restaurants and so on.

2. Some of the people who make the most money from the franchise—who, not incidentally, constitute a very limited group, such as the millionaire ballplayers and out-of-town corporate investors—live outside the community. Hence, the dollars they earn are expended somewhere else. The local multiplier in that instance is zero, because the community where the initial investment was made does not benefit at all.

3. Sports franchises across the country have not demonstrated any compelling ability to attract other corporations and industries to relocate their operations from other cities and states. On the other hand, a computer firm, for example, might very well attract other computer and high-tech firms, as they interact with one another.

4. Finally, whereas corporations generally make investments

287

based on increasing productivity or profit, public money is spent differently, with (presumably) socially desirable ends in mind. Therefore, spending taxpayer money is not a matter of choosing from among like things, the way a business sticks to its business, but from among entirely different things—a stadium or a school, more police or more roads. Which investment opportunity creates the greatest impact on the community?

This economic analysis fails to take into account competing factors, such as long-term benefits arising from increased national and international media attention on the community, and civic pride and identification through a team. Such elements can prove virtually impossible to quantify.

Any analysis of a team and a stadium's impact on a community must focus on where that stadium has been located within the community. There's a saying in the real estate business to explain the most compelling factor in judging the hard-cash worth of any property—location, location, location. The same is true with stadiums built on that same real estate. A facility built in the suburbs, where the part-time jobs (and the increased traffic) are not appreciated by the people living in the vicinity, might do nothing to spur development in the area nor emotionally involve the city from which the team and the stadium are separated. Similarly, a stadium in a neglected area of a city that remains neglected despite the presence of the stadium is not contributing to the community.

In other words, an athletic venue, whether influential or less so, remains a component of a community and exists only within the fundamental realities of that community. When Yankee Stadium was built in 1923, it was surrounded by fields and open lots, a gleaming white ballpark in the middle of not much. Eventually, the Bronx flourished, growing in population and wealth, along with the rest of New York City. Its economic success and communal development surely did not depend upon Yankee Stadium, though the stadium just as surely helped define the community to both Bronxites and the larger world. However, in more recent years, the area around Yankee Stadium has decayed to such an extent that the ballpark is virtually the only standing, ongoing enterprise around. The T-shirt businesses and bars nearby survive on revenue from game days, and fans hurry uptown and inside the stadium for the game, then rush back home immediately thereafter. Thus, putting more money into further renovating Yankee Stadium without an investment in the surrounding apartments and businesses and services is money not well spent and does nothing for the community.

In contrast, Coors Field in Denver has been widely credited with being the spur to the redevelopment of that city's moribund downtown. Such assertions pose many questions, fraught with many conflicting factors. For example, Baltimore's Camden Yards was, in many quarters, accorded comparable due for revitalizing the city's harbor area. However, though Camden Yards is a gorgeous stadium, the harbor would have undergone a renaissance with or without it, because of the breathtaking scope of the total rebuilding project.

It would seem that Bank One Ballpark and the Diamondbacks would fall into Denver's category, helping stimulate an authentic downtown renewal. Others had tried and failed to construct something meaningful in the area. Hotels and restaurants and entire retail developments, well-intentioned and well-planned, had foundered in the past couple of decades against the rocky shoals of urban ruin.

Regardless, the efforts persevered, and some enjoyed reasonable success. A citizen bond initiative in 1988 raised $100 million for a variety of public buildings, including three theaters, three museums, and a fantastic library. Heritage Square was reclaimed and would soon attract entrepreneurs such as Chris Bianco, whose Pizzeria Bianco, housed in a converted brick machine shop, was one of only eight restaurants in the entire United States to receive twenty-nine out of thirty points in a Zagat's survey. Just to the north, a private firm, the Rouse Company, put up an office and retail complex known as the Arizona Center.

So work was being done, and probably more projects would have been enticed downtown as Phoenix and the entire Valley of the Sun continued to grow more populous and more prosperous. In fact, Maricopa County's population gains placed it first in the nation for the past seven years. Even more consequential, those gains were not recorded because of retirees moving to adult-only communities, but from younger people seeking to join in the Arizona boom. So it was logical to assume that whatever development had already started would probably have been pursued, however slowly or fitfully.

At the same time, it is also true that the Diamondbacks and Bank

One Ballpark together kicked the downtown rejuvenation into high gear, leaping it forward by years or even decades. This is proved by the construction of the Westin and Doubletree hotels, and all the restaurants and bars and stores, changing the face of the city, block by block.

Debating the precise figure that the Diamondbacks will generate this year or next is of dubious value. The point is that the team and its stadium are one piece of a whole, part of the entertainment segment of a community's cultural offerings. At the bottom line, the issue is not whether professional sports belong among all those offerings, but how large a piece of that societal whole we grant professional sports. That is where the money comes into play. Allocating money is how society shows what it values—what we value. How much are we willing to spend?

Taking a different slant on the matter, how much are we willing to be blackmailed to promote sports? Though franchise owners across the country rely upon their unceasing whining about how much money they are losing to justify raising ticket prices and to demand taxpayer funds for new venues, the price of a sports franchise—all teams in all sports—is ever on the upswing. The owners of the Seattle Mariners paid a $6.25-million franchise fee in 1977. The odious Wayne Huizenga, with his wholesale rape of his own baseball team, was demanding a tidy $150 million for anyone wishing to take the burdensome Marlins off his hands. That's $55 million more than what he paid for the franchise just seven years before.

Mark Rosentraub, director of the Center for Urban Policy and the Environment at Indiana University, and author of *Major League Losers*, put the issue into cool perspective: "Unless you buy the argument that a large number of people are willing to pay ever-higher prices for a depreciating asset, you're not looking at folks who are losing money."

Not losing money for the owners isn't the point—the point is maximizing assets, and one terrific way to make the most of any property is to have someone else pay the expenses of that property. In professional sports, the greatest single expense is surely the venue. When the community pays for the venue—and the franchise profits from it—well, that's extraordinarily good business.

The standard line is that stadiums are simply too expensive for private companies to build, that a team cannot afford both the venue

290

and the payroll. In some ways, this complaint is reminiscent of how the movie business operates. Movie ticket prices keep rising, the refrain goes, because costs keep rising—particularly the cost of hiring actors. Some actors can demand $20 million per movie, and many others routinely receive $1 million or much more, which first works to raise the fees for producers, directors, writers, and others, and then drives the cost of an average film to $40 to $50 million. Instead of holding a line on these expenses, filmmakers have passed the increased expenditures on to the consumer through higher ticket prices. If people are willing to accept the higher prices, then the movie business will continue to raise prices, because Hollywood has no inclination to check its own greed.

Is baseball any different? Why not pay outrageous salaries if the public frees up the club's checkbook by picking up the tab for a ballpark? Whose team is it anyhow? Is baseball a business or a public utility, a public trust?

If baseball, and other professional sports, are deemed to occupy such a paramount role in society, then perhaps the franchises should be owned by the public. This would ensure that the team would never leave the community nor gouge and blackmail the community. This would ensure that the team would be as secure and as treasured as the public library.

Does baseball deserve this privileged status? Is baseball that important? Is any spectator sport that important?

In New York, baseball is important indeed. The mayor who showed no mercy to jaywalkers seemed to swoon in the presence of Steinbrenner. The ordinarily stern Giuliani became positively giddy when he put on his Yankee cap and jacket and got to sit in the owner's box. Thus, Giuliani, who didn't blink when facing down mobsters and foreign terrorists, could not hide his terror at the prospect, however vague, of losing the Bronx Bombers to neighboring New Jersey. This was Steinbrenner's underlying threat as he sought a new venue for his team. He made no bones about declaring Yankee Stadium not good enough, and certainly not profitable enough, for his club. Whether this was a real threat was dubious; N.J. Governor Whitman voiced serious qualms about constructing a stadium, and it was far from certain that the other baseball owners, or the world at large, would countenance the most storied franchise in sports history moving out of state.

Giuliani made some noises about helping the Yankees ditch the Bronx for Manhattan—maybe on the West Side, near the Javits Center—at a total cost that bounced between $500 million and $1 billion, one sum more extraordinary than the next.

The Yankees weren't alone in their quest for a new place to play in the Big Apple. The Mets were going to get a new stadium, with the city's financial assistance, to replace Shea Stadium. It would have luxury boxes and club seats and a retractable roof and would cost around $500 million.

Together, the two stadiums could cost, with the usual overruns and infrastructure improvements, upwards of $2 billion. The amount of that total that the taxpayers would be asked, or required, to contribute remained undetermined. Nonetheless, no sane person could doubt that it would be considerable, especially when Giuciani was simultaneously proposing to cut funding for libraries and parks, especially in a city where the public schools and hospitals were literally falling apart.

In New York, at least during Mayor Giuliani's administration, baseball is not only important, it is viewed as a civic virtue.

In San Francisco, baseball is most definitely a business. Four times since the early 1980s, voters have rejected tax plans to build the Giants a needed new stadium. Finally, by 1992, the owners of the franchise threatened to shift the club to Florida. Solutions were proffered and tried, but they were all stopgap and ultimately unsuccessful. In the midst of all this, a new ownership group took over and pledged to keep the Giants in town. The new group's solution: build the stadium with private money.

Another vote was held, and this time the citizens of San Francisco were basically asked to rezone the area by the water called China Basin, less than two miles from Fisherman's Wharf, permitting the construction of a ballpark on the land. The vote was readily approved.

The money came next, and the money equaled $306 million. The owners started selling. They sold the naming rights to the ballpark to Pacific Bell for $50 million for twenty years. Other corporations contributed $35 million, receiving various considerations. Chevron, for example, received the right to sell tickets at their stations, in addition to advertising spots during the games. Additionally, a corporate logo would grace left field, a special logo in which the *h* in

Chevron would light up to acknowledge a hit, and the *e* would do the same for an error.

The franchise also sold luxury suites and club seats, and exclusive concession rights. In short, they did everything that every other franchise has tried to do.

The one unusual fund-raising technique was selling charter-seat licenses, a fancy—and expensive—way of peddling an option that grants the lifetime right to buy a season ticket for a specific seat. The franchise offered up 13,700 of the best seats for licenses, with prices ranging from $1,200 to $5,500. Twelve thousand, worth some $50 million, were sold in twenty months, leaving the team with two years to sell the rest before the stadium's completion in April 2000.

The franchise required another $170 million, and Peter Magowan, the managing general partner, and Larry Baer, the chief operating officer, borrowed the sum from several insurance companies experienced in short-term construction loans.

Pacific Bell Park, the first privately financed baseball stadium in more than thirty-five years, built on eleven acres of city land leased to the Giants for fair-market value, was on its way to becoming a reality. It will be one of the "new classics," old-style ballparks with modern amenities, including waiter service at the club seats, real restaurants, a business conference center, extrawide concourses, and unobstructed sight lines. An especially intriguing innovation will be a children's learning center, open year-round and connected to California's schools and libraries by computers provided through Pacific Bell's $100 million Education First program.

"We're in a situation where we didn't have much of a choice," said Stacie Walters, director of public affairs for the club, referring to the private financing, and that reality was the key. The Giants didn't have a choice: they either raised the money themselves or they left town.

The Giants possessed certain advantages over the Diamondbacks in their stadium financing plans. As the fifth-largest media market in the country, San Francisco could count on a huge annual income from TV rights. Then there was the small matter of the $130 million franchise fee and the other costs of starting the Diamondbacks from scratch, costs the Giants did not have to worry about.

So it could be done, a franchise could survive and even prosper without the assistance of the taxpayers. Perhaps it wouldn't work everywhere, perhaps not in larger cities where the mayor was besotted with baseball, nor in smaller cities with less lucrative television contracts and limited sources of revenue. Perhaps not in Phoenix. Nevertheless, when the conditions were right, it could be done.

Like almost everything else in life, it comes down to a choice: Is baseball a business or a public trust? How much is a franchise worth to a community?

The choices we make surely say more about us than about baseball.

Chapter 24

The Last Spring Training Game

The Diamondbacks traveled to Las Vegas to play a couple of games against the A's, but El Niño reared its ugly head again and both days were rained out. When it was clear the second game would be a washout, the team packed up and flew back to Phoenix to get in a workout. The change in plans resulted in an intrasquad game among the Diamondbacks, and their first chance to test out Bank One Ballpark.

One of the chief questions regarding any domed stadium is how easily, how distinctly, a fly ball can be spotted against the roof. That was quickly resolved in BOB's favor, thanks to the canopy's dark green hue highlighting the white sphere.

With just a few days before the start of the season, Showalter was getting close to choosing his major league lineup, getting the team down to the twenty-five-man limit. Reliever Hector Carrasco was waived, judged unwilling to alter his reliance on his ninety-five-mph fastball in favor of the Diamondbacks' desire for him to throw a variety of pitches. "He wasn't a fit here," said Buck.

The release surprised some. Carrasco had gone 3-0 during the spring, with a 3.86 ERA.

The club could have sent him to Tucson instead, but didn't want to be responsible for his $685,000 salary.

Carrasco was both stunned and upset. "I'm fine because I am

young," the twenty-eight-year-old said. "I have a good arm. By Monday, I'll be pitching for another team."

With Carrasco out of the picture, the team was counting on Felix Rodriguez to be the closer. Rodriguez had been a catcher in the Dodgers' system before being converted into a pitcher. Though he only had 56⅔ innings to his major league credit—and no saves—he had pitched well in the spring, notching a 1-0 record and a 2.08 ERA, while striking out 16 batters in 13 innings.

The players returned to Tucson to pack their gear and move to Phoenix. To the media, and to a man, they expressed confidence in each other and in the upcoming season.

The experts were not so sure. The vast majority of sportswriters and reporters across the country were still picking the Diamond-backs to finish last in their division, just as they had been picking them last all along, before there was Matt Williams at third or Devon White in center or Jay Bell at short. A handful of solid players and a couple of All-Stars didn't change the analysts' perception. The season was long and hard, and a team needed depth at every position to win consistently, particularly in its starting rotation and in the bullpen. That meant five starting pitchers and maybe six or seven relievers, an assemblage of talent that was rare to find in a universe of thirty major league clubs.

The simple fact was, pitching was a tough business, and there were only so many good ones. The Braves had more than anybody else, and the Yankees and Red Sox and Dodgers and a few other clubs teams had divided many of the rest amongst themselves, which didn't leave a whole bunch for the Diamondbacks. The tall, skinny young guns Arizona had plucked right out of high school, such as Nick Bierbrodt and John Patterson, or had discovered on the rough fields of Latin America, were years away from reaching their potential and making the big club. The Diamondbacks would have to hope that Benes and Blair, their top duo, played great, and that the rest of the rotation—Adamson, Anderson, and Suppan—also produced. Before the season was over, maybe some other guys would stand out, guys such as Cory Lidle, the former Met, who was waiting for his shoulder to heal.

"I feel good about them," said Mark Connor, the pitching coach. "Our starting pitchers are going to throw a lot of strikes." Connor's expectations were grounded in reality. "It's going to be interesting.

We'll find out some things about us, and by the end of the year, we'll know what we have to do."

The recently retired Mark Davis, appearing on a postgame show as he tried out a new career as a TV commentator, probably summed up the general feeling among the professionals when he was asked by his hosting partner, a local reporter, to predict the Diamondbacks' final record. Sitting on a stool in front of the bright lights and camera, the ex-pitcher stammered, trying to select his words most carefully, evidently not yet practiced in the television craft of the bland, unblinking lie.

"I don't know if anybody would mention this," Davis said, "but you don't want to lose one hundred. Eighty-five [wins] is a goal that would be unbelievable. Sixty-three—keep it out of triple digits."

Though Davis's verbalization was a little awkward, his reasoning and his math were valid. No expansion team had ever won seventy games in its first season, so, judging by the record, losing one hundred loomed as a real possibility for the Diamondbacks. In a 162-game season, Arizona would have to win sixty-three games to avoid the century mark.

"Your number one pitcher should go eight innings," Davis explained, "number two one less, three, four, and five [pitchers] need to go six innings." The days of a pitcher's consistently working nine innings were over for most clubs and most pitchers. There were too many games and not enough strong arms. Current thinking held that if a team's starting rotation could meet the goals enumerated by Davis, then its corps of relievers should be capable of going the rest of the distance.

That was the theory.

"I do feel this is going to be a team that's going to score some runs and win some games," concluded Davis.

The local reporter took those sentiments and ran away with them. "They'll be able to do what it takes to get the job done!" he gushed.

At the bottom line: With rare exceptions, a team in this expanded, talent-diluted league won with either terrific hitting or terrific pitching. Though the Diamondbacks closed the preseason with a winning record, 16-15-1, perhaps that mark would ultimately prove not as telling as the fact that no Diamondback finished in the top ten among National League players in the offensive categories of batting average, runs batted in, slugging percentage, on-base percentage, home runs, triples, doubles, total bases, or hits. Only Devon White and David Dellucci made it into the leaders' ranks for Arizona: White ended up second in stolen bases with 7 and tied for fourth in runs scored with 16, and Dellucci tied for second in the rather more passive category of garnering walks.

The situation was even bleaker on the defensive side. No Diamondback pitchers were among the NL leaders in any category, significant or otherwise: earned run average, strikeouts, won-lost, saves.

Then again, spring training was for preparation, not for results. While the two measures overlapped for many players, they foretold nothing for many others. Similarly, managers and coaches always liked to win, but winning only counted after opening day, and they used spring training to test players and ideas, training and tuning individuals and the club, always looking to build to the regular season, to peak when it counted.

On another television program, Matt Williams added his own rather cautious assessment of the club: "I think we have guys who will throw strikes, who will keep us in the games. Their job is to keep us in the games, so we can score some runs."

And in yet another interview, Buck Showalter sounded more like Davis and Williams than any local reporter when asked about his expectations for the Diamondbacks—for his Diamondbacks: "Major League Baseball already has a high bar. I just hope that someday people think that having the Diamondbacks in baseball is a good thing."

In fact, at this stage, many people in baseball did not think the Diamondbacks were such a happy addition to the MLB family. George Steinbrenner's overt dislike for Colangelo and his free-spending, free-speaking ways was a familiar topic of discussion in the great metropolis's media. A profile of Colangelo in the *New York Times Magazine* in late March repeated Steinbrenner's contention that Jerry looked "like a fool" for his expensive acquisitions not once, not twice, but three times. The magazine also mentioned Colangelo's riposte that Steinbrenner's anger started when Arizona recruited Buck Showalter. "My signing Buck was a killer for George," said Jerry.

Steinbrenner wasn't the only owner, nor the only person in baseball, who was rooting against the Diamondbacks. A columnist in the *New York Post,* just before the start of the season, named the ten individuals he chose for baseball's 1998 "hot seat," listing Buck Showalter and Jerry Colangelo as numbers seven and eight, stating, "Now they get to show if they are really geniuses. . . . Already there have been charges of tampering and covertly attempting to film Rockies' practice. The baseball world wants to see them fail."

The tampering to which the columnist referred was the Bernie Williams case, or noncase, a load of innuendo supplied by an annoyed Steinbrenner interested in stirring up some trouble. The covert-filming business was another story.

It seemed that the Diamondbacks' new video coordinator was caught taping the Rockies from the center-field camera well during a Cactus League game. The employee returned the next night and tried the same thing, with the same result—ejection by security guards.

The guy changed clothes and did it again.

Though every game is broadcast once the season starts, and teams commonly videotape their opponents at their own arenas through the spring, taping at the competition's home field in the preseason without express permission was considered a serious violation of baseball etiquette.

Arizona officials claimed the whole incident was much ado about nothing, an unintentional error by a new employee who didn't know the rules. Buck Showalter phoned Don Baylor, the Rockies' manager, to explain and apologize, then it was Joe Garagiola Jr.'s turn to make amends.

Baylor was not impressed. He told National League president Len Coleman, and he told the press. "I wouldn't have thought of stooping to that level," grumped Baylor. "I wonder what they'll have at Bank One Ballpark; they might have the clubhouse bugged. I can't put that past them considering the crap they've tried this spring."

The big gala was Saturday night. Fourteen hundred people spent $500 each to attend the black-tie affair at the ballpark.

Unfortunately for the partygoers, the rain had started in the morning and only gotten worse as the sun went down and evening fell. By the time the cars and limousines pulled up at BOB, the night was simply nasty, cold, and wet.

Most people parked in the adjoining garage, reserved during the games for the suiteholders and other preferred ticketholders. It appeared to be a perfect solution, allowing the bejeweled, high-heeled, made-up guests to avoid the rain.

Misfortune struck once more when the folks coming to the party discovered that the connection between the garage and the ballpark was a covered but open walkway three very tall stories above the ground, whipped by wind and water. Attendants were waiting with umbrellas, which didn't help much as the wind hurled the deluge sideways. By the time the guests crossed the canyon, hair was snarled and splayed, shoes were soggy and squeaking, clothes were crinkled and wrinkled.

Some of the women were in special distress, shivering in skimpy dresses and open-toed high heels, slaves to fashion, defiant of El Niño.

The event was cosponsored by the Phoenix Symphony and the team, with the symphony receiving the bulk of the proceeds, and the Arizona Diamondbacks Charities in second position.

The guests were led downstairs from the suiteholders' level to the main concourse. Beyond the concourse, a stage had been erected over the infield, in anticipation of a performance by the symphony.

This was the Phoenix elite's night out, or night in, actually, since the roof on the stadium was shut due to the inclement weather. Shutting the roof didn't necessarily keep out the rain. Leaks sprung here and there, which was actually a lucky break, giving the builders a chance to catch them now instead of during a game.

From the beginning of the franchise, the Diamondbacks had demonstrated they knew how to throw a party, and tonight was no exception. The festivities began with an hour of cocktails and hors d'oeuvres, the latter served by waiters carrying trays strapped around their necks, like vendors at the park hawking beer.

After finishing the squares of tuna, topped with caviar and served on tiny pancakes, and similar delicacies, the revelers were shepherded to seats over the third-base dugout, in front of the stage. Men and women were infinitely warmer and more comfortable now, as the champagne and other lubricants took effect.

Two young boys, dressed in old-style baseball uniforms, opened the night with a spirited treatment of "Who's on First."

The lads' performance only covered the most famous stanzas of Bud Abbott and Lou Costello's comedic sonnet. A complete rendering could be found on "Abbott & Costello's Homepage" on the Internet, presented for the public's enjoyment by Bud's and Lou's families, in conjunction with the entertainers' fan club. The entire routine, when printed off the screen, filled four and one-quarter single-spaced pages. The structure was classic: the setup laying out the premise, the lines and jokes constructing a hilarious artifice, every phrase and sentence connected and overlapping and interdependent.

Every right-thinking American knew the flow of the act, as the conversation spun round and round again:

Costello: What's the guy's name on first base?

Abbott: No. What is on second.

Costello: I'm not asking you who's on second.

Abbott: Who's on first.

Costello: I don't know.

Abbott: He's on third, we're not talking about him.

Costello: Now how did I get on third base?

Abbott: Why, you mentioned his name.

Costello: If I mentioned the third baseman's name, who did I say is playing third?

Abbott: No. Who's playing first.

Costello: What's on base?

Abbott: What's on second.

Costello: I don't know.

Abbott: He's on third.

Costello. There I go, back on third again!

Back at the gala, Jerry Colangelo welcomed his guests. "I made a deal," Colangelo declared. "It can rain today, and we'll have sunny weather on Tuesday."

Colangelo directed attention to the JumboTron. Buck, in uniform, materialized on the screen to explain the rules for the night's activities. "Listen or you'll get sent to the minors," Showalter warned. The guests were divided into ten "teams" and would be escorted around the stadium by "umps" and "managers," who would lead them to a variety of restaurants and stations organized for their dining pleasure, enjoying one course at each stop. This staggered system, along with some prizes awarded along the way, would keep the people moving and entertained.

After dining, the celebrants would return to the stands, and an orchestral presentation. The symphony would be debuting a special composition by Patrick Williams, entitled "Here Come the Diamondbacks," followed by musical accompaniment to the ubiquitous Thom Brennaman, reading some choice excerpts from baseball's literary canon.

"Play hard," concluded Buck, still up on the screen, "play fair, and play ball."

The people were taken away in their teams, roaming through the empty stadium in search of fine food and excitement.

As previously mentioned, the Arizona Diamondbacks Charities represented the franchise tonight, seeking to begin raising money for its coffers. This charitable organization was a new endeavor for the team and came under the jurisdiction of Craig Pletenik, director of public affairs. Pletenik had been the general manager of the Phoenix Firebirds for nine years, which meant he had learned to wear a variety of hats during his tenure in the minors. Where a big league GM oversaw a multitude of departments, staffed with directors and assistants and secretaries, his minor league counterpart was often fortunate if he could count on assistance from a bare-bones support staff.

Pletenik had not only become an expert in many fields, from baseball to administrative matters, he had also mastered the art of making the most of very little. In the minors, charitable donations were restricted, by financial necessity, to handing out free tickets to children and other worthy recipients.

Craig was in another playground now. His job was to concentrate on the Diamondbacks Charities, which had big plans, intent on matching the long-running success of its sister organization, the Suns Charities, which annually distributed hundreds of thousands of dollars to organizations dedicated to helping kids.

Pletenik understood that charity was not just an honorable endeavor, it was also important public relations for the team. "The stadium was built by taxpayer money," he noted, "and everybody feels the team is in the public domain. If you want the people to buy your hats and jackets and come to your games, you better be a part of the community."

Director of Public Affairs Pletenik still had tickets to hand out, two hundred per game, divided into blocs of twenty-five each. At least that was the scheme, not yet ready for implementation as opening day neared and seats were scarce. Regardless, Craig and the Diamondbacks had other avenues for their altruism. Demand by charities, hospitals, and other institutions and foundations for personal appearances by players was already intense. One of Pletenik and his staff's prime tasks was determining each player's philanthropic interest, matching those interests to the appropriate groups or causes, and scheduling those matches. Some players, such as Andy Benes and Jay Bell, were already deeply involved in their own charitable organizations, while others did nothing and probably preferred it that way.

As had been widely advertised, Diamondbacks were expected to be part of the community, and they were expected to contribute. To date, Craig claimed that he hadn't encountered any Diamondbacks who refused to participate in his community relations program. Some of the big, strong players had expressed a squeamishness about frequenting hospitals or dealing with sick children, so Pletenik found them other audiences to address and other places to visit.

The work of the Diamondbacks Charities was just beginning, and tonight was one small step in building the necessary war chest. It was the classic modern charity event, employed in behalf of causes in every city, an elaborate party that allowed the guests to feel that their eating and drinking and dancing was a real contribution to society.

A few more hours of merriment, and then the gala was last night's news, and it was time to get back to the Diamondbacks and bats and balls. Bank One Ballpark was about to receive its baseball baptism, for Sunday was the last spring training game, and it was happening in BOB.

This was a sort of dress rehearsal for everyone involved with the stadium, from groundskeepers to concessionaires, ushers to broadcasters, maintenance crews to security, not to mention the players and coaches, too.

The umpires had a few things of their own to decide. They had been huddling with Buck and the Diamondbacks to determine what was fair territory and what was foul. The outfield wall was not one smooth, unbroken half-circle, but a jumble of angles and differing heights, in the style of urban parks crammed into the available space. That meant that the umps had to settle beforehand how to call a fly ball, for example, that knocked against the overhang in center, where picnickers sat overlooking the field, and bounced back onto the grass.

After much consultation, officialdom arrived at a consensus, an agreement with a multitude of codicils. If a ball hit the black pole above the fence in center, or to the right of the yellow line in right-center, or to the left of the yellow line in left-center, or above the yellow line in the "batter's eyes," and bounced back onto the field, it was a home run. However, if the ball hit the center-field wall or the girders or the face of the overhang between the yellow lines or the yellow line, it was still in play.

It was kind of complicated, but it was surely smarter to figure this out now, calmly and rationally, rather than in the heat of battle, with a couple of screaming managers and tens of thousands of upset fans demanding justice and blood.

Arizona was facing another miserable day, courtesy of El Niño, cold and wet. The winter wasn't supposed to be like this, not at all, it was supposed to be warm and sunny, which was why this game was slated for a 5:05 P.M. start. That was early for Phoenix as the summer approached; to beat the heat and allow the roof to be opened and the air-conditioning to be shut off, almost every Diamondbacks regular-season game was set to begin at 7:05 P.M. The five-minute lag was for radio and television, giving the announcers an opportunity to properly set the scene and introduce the players before the action began.

The late start must have seemed like the clever thing to do, and undoubtedly it would turn out so as El Niño wore itself out and the proper course of nature reasserted its sovereignty. However, in the meantime, it was bundle up and play—or watch—ball.

The house was a sellout; more than a sellout, actually, when the media passes and standing-room tickets were included, 49,198 human beings, showing up for a preseason contest.

All these fans heading downtown guaranteed an unfamiliar crush of cars. The city's huge parking lot directly across from the stadium didn't have one wall up yet, and the other garages were busy raising their rates. Adding to the mess, the Diamondbacks were bumping up against the Suns, both teams playing Sunday. The basketball game would be through around three-thirty, leaving a gap of an hour and half between the two contests and maybe allowing enough time for one group of fans to depart before the next descended upon downtown.

Maybe.

Though this potential problem had been a source of concern for some time, it seemed that only a few weeks before the start of the season did the city actually decide that something, for better or worse, had to be done.

The first suggestion from the city, supported by the mayor of Phoenix, was utterly predictable and tiresomely unimaginative: let Phoenix foot the bill.

A bus shuttle system was devised. People would park at outlying lots or malls and hop a bus for the trip downtown. The city would pick up the tab for the first ninety days, priced at $57,000.

While it is a city's job to provide transportation in and out of its central district, this did seem a bit odd. The Diamondbacks were an attraction, not a burden, and a profitable plan utilizing private or public companies, benefiting the city, should have been far beyond the talking stage months ago.

But, of course, nothing was done, and then it was almost too late. The scramble to find a solution resulted in this most unsatisfactory proposal.

E. J. Montini, the *Republic* columnist who had tangled with Colangelo over the food-banning incident, talked to Mayor Skip Rimsza, he of the triplets' fathering fame, about the bus plan.

"For me," said Skip, "it is a very close call. I know that with baseball we have this facility that's going to have this tremendous synergy downtown and we haven't done anything to facilitate it."

Montini pointed out that the ballpark was built with $238 million in taxpayer funds.

"That was the county," the mayor responded.

Since the majority of the county's population resided within Phoenix's borders, the mayor's distinction lacked a certain punch.

"Initially, I didn't like the idea," stated Skip. "Then, hearing the arguments on the other side, hearing about how little we've done for baseball and how it's going to add all this synergy to downtown, I said okay.'"

Apart from all that taxpayer money, Phoenix had welcomed BOB in so many ways large and small, including excusing the stadium from what was ordinarily required of any business establishment moving into town, namely, that it provide parking for its customer base.

This mayoral nonsense highlighted yet another fine example of tortured bureaucratic logic: the indefensible lack of public transportation in Phoenix.

The public was as unenthused as the columnist about shelling out even this small additional amount, which inspired the politicians to arrive with impressive rapidity at another proposition. Corporations were induced to fund the shuttle for two or three months, the exact length of service as yet undetermined. For its $5,000, each company would receive advertising on the sides of the city buses that would ferry fans from two locations, north and west, to the ballpark and back. Riders would kick in a couple of bucks for the trip, helping defray expenses.

This temporary resolution would hopefully hold until private bus companies responded to the city's belated request for bids on a long-term fix.

The garages and parking lots were not overly concerned that the shuttle was going to cut into their business, a confidence that was confirmed by their sharply rising prices. Tracts of every kind—restaurant, office, vacant—were itching to get a piece of the spoils. Depending on location, prices ranged from $5 to $20. A parking lot across the street from the ballpark jumped its tariff from a buck and a quarter to an Andrew Jackson.

That spelled a sixteenfold price hike. Though the Diamondbacks had yet to prove that they could compete with the other big clubs, Phoenix was definitely ready for the major leagues.

The crowd came early, eager to see both the stadium and the players in action.

The Diamondbacks were warming up, taking batting practice, smacking the easy pitches around the field. Some fans gathered at the left-field and right-field walls, hoping that somebody would pop one into the stands. Matt Williams stood in the box and promptly delivered, banging three pitches high and deep and out of left field. Each time he belted the ball, the group at the wall cheered and attracted a few more members.

A pair of Diamondback press reps escorted a small boy and his father down to the field, near the dugout. The boy was not in good health.

One press rep called over Arizona players as they walked by, one by one. The Diamondbacks had apparently been told about this child beforehand and stepped over without question. Jay Bell was first. He approached the twelve-year-old and conversed with him, bending nearer to the boy, more intimately, comfortably. The child handed Bell a Diamondback license plate, which he autographed. The shortstop spent a couple of minutes with the boy, then said good-bye and went through the dugout and into the clubhouse. Andy Fox walked over next, followed by Damian Miller, Brent Brede, Hensley Meulens, Tony Batista, and Brian Anderson.

When the players had disappeared into the clubhouse, the boy was asked if baseball was his favorite sport.

"No," he said. "Soccer is my favorite."

Even so, he was unable to name any leading soccer players, and that dichotomy expressed much of the current situation and probable future for American sports. Soccer was conquering the playgrounds of the nation, but the professional game had failed to make any significant inroads.

Baseball had a lot of work to do, in so many ways, to reestablish itself in the leading spot in the American sports pantheon, and if any single player was striving to achieve that, it was Jay Bell. To the casual observer, Bell seemed to sign more autographs than any other ballplayer on the team. And now he reappeared on the dugout steps, alone among the Diamondbacks, as kids and some adults clamored for his attention.

Interviewed just the other day on television, Jay Bell was asked about the proper way to approach a player for a signature. The shortstop had given this real consideration and replied that the autograph seeker should always come prepared with his own writing instrument, patiently wait for the player to finish his exercise or practice or whatever he was doing—remember, the ballfield is his office—and then approach with respect and courtesy.

Bell stressed that he expected children to address any adult, ballplayer or otherwise, with a civility not always seen in modern society.

The valley's youngsters had either seen the show or been properly brought up by their parents, because most of them called—called, not shouted—not "Hey!" or "Jay!" or "Over here!" but "Mr. Bell! Mr. Bell!" Jay Bell looked over the crowd slightly above him with a not unkind severity and approved the next petitioner's request with a nod.

The kids knew the routine, tossing Jay a ball or hat and then a pen, though most favored the Sharpie, a permanent marker. Bell caught all of the balls and hats, but he dropped a notably high percentage of those Sharpies, especially for a shortstop.

The Diamondbacks hadn't planned any ceremonies for this game, saving the show for opening day, only two days away. Still, the club did have one memorable event on the agenda, a performance by four-year-old Austin Burke, singing the national anthem. Austin was cute and full-throated, and the crowd appreciated his effort, though one had to pause and wonder exactly why a four-year-old was singing the national anthem in a baseball stadium before thousands of people.

Arizona lost 3–0 to the White Sox. The big guns for the Diamondbacks had a bad night with the bat. Matt Williams and Devon White both made four trips to the plate, and both came away empty. Jay Bell notched one hit, and so did Travis Lee.

Jerry Colangelo was in the locker room after the game. He didn't seem bothered by the loss. He didn't seem to be thinking about anything except Tuesday. Somebody asked him how he imagined he would feel on opening day.

"It will be hard to describe," he said. "I'm a very emotional person."

Despite his personal reticence, Colangelo had no difficulty in describing what it would be like for just about everybody else. "When that moment arrives," he continued, "our lives in this state will change forever, with the quality of life, and future generations enjoying Major League Baseball."

The ballpark's overseers were conducting their own one-day version of spring training, giving the facility a test drive. BOB performed pretty well, aside from the mostly minor glitches, which ran the gamut from more leaks in the roof to toilets that wouldn't stop flushing to concession stands that ran out of food or never opened at all. The shower in the umpires' dressing room had no hot water. The electronic scoreboard had trouble getting unstuck, unable to show either ball-and-strike count or the score until the game was almost over. The lines for everything—food, merchandise, money— were too long. Many of the televisions strung around the main concourse weren't hooked up. Several ticket numbers led people to seats that didn't exist or at least weren't yet bolted into place.

And even though the night was unseasonably, uncomfortably cold, the air-conditioning seemed to be chugging out even colder air.

Before the game, Scott Brubaker had leaned against the railing in front of the Diamondbacks' dugout and chatted into a walkie-talkie with the boys upstairs, discussing the public address system. The PA was echoing around the stadium, the words bouncing off the concrete floors and steel roof and all the beams and supports and rooms and grass between, boomeranging around that enormous empty space. In many areas around the stadium, it was virtually incomprehensible.

They tweaked it this way and that, but it was questionable if much could be done. The stadium was splendid, but the truth was and would always be that it was so much better, aesthetically and practically, with the roof open. As several critics noted, viewed from the outside, the roof did bear a strong resemblance to an aircraft hangar, even with the giant Bank One Ballpark logos plastered on top and on the sides.

That aircraft hangar look might have been unavoidable, given the demands of the design, but the graphics adorning the outside were another matter. Six huge panels on the north face of the ballpark— three on either side of the scoreboard—slid open like French doors to let in the sun. With the roof unfolded and the panels unlatched, the ballpark seemed delightfully wide open to the natural world.

At the same time, when the panels were shut, the effect wasn't quite as delightful.

The corporate emblems of the "building partners"—America West Airlines, APS, Miller Brewing, Nissan, US West, and Circle K/ UNOCAL—were stretched across their interior faces. Marketing rather than taste ruled this decision, just as smaller banners and plaques were hung around and throughout the entire stadium representing many of the lesser Diamondback sponsors.

On the other side, the panels' exteriors were adorned with gigantic graphics, each sixty-four feet by fifty-eight feet, in yellow, green, orange, and red, designed to resemble mosaic murals. The murals depicted, from east to west, a pitcher from windup to release, a batter standing and swinging, a runner racing around the bases, a third baseman snagging a grounder, a second baseman in the midst of turning a double play, and an outfielder catching a fly. Each exercise was delineated in a series of three positions, one activity and one athlete per panel, the first panel leading to the next and then the next, drawn to give the impression of motion.

The art critic for the *Republic* succinctly captured the essence of this montage: "One thinks immediately of the *Charlie's Angels* title image, with its overlapped silhouettes. In some funkier places, such a design might seem hip and retro, but in BOB, it merely seems sadly out-of-date."

In other words, the more often the panels were open, the better.

Monday dawned and the work continued. The leaks were plugged, the toilets repaired, the concessions stocked, the wiring connected, the missing seats riveted to the floor.

Not everything would be ready. The largest unfinished project remained the playground for the kids beside the picnic area, which would require several more weeks.

In the midst of the ongoing construction, a caravan of trucks pulled up to the stadium, carrying fifty thousand purple seat cushions. Every man, woman, and child entering the ballpark would be handed a seat cushion to commemorate the inaugural game. Along with the cushions emblazoned with the big *A*, the date, and major sponsors' logos—those six building partners again—each fan would receive a limited-edition commemorative disk, coupons for discounts for airfare and lube jobs, and a plastic ticketholder. The ticketholders would come in handy because the tickets for the first game would be the best souvenir of them all, a plastic-coated hologram, which, when one's eyes roamed across its front, revealed Bank One Ballpark's roof opening, allowing a baseball to escape and fly out, growing whiter and rounder and larger.

This was Gina Giallonardo's project, in her role as Diamondback marketing manager. This promotion (and they were all promotions, of course, paid for by one sponsor or another) was only the first of fifty-one planned for the baseball season, reputedly more than any other team. AutoZone was giving away batting gloves, Cox Communications baseball caps, Circle K snakeskin treat bags, Discount Tire fanny packs, America West Airlines mousepads, Gila River Casino visors, the Tobacco Education Prevention Program baseball bats. Many companies, including most of those above, were represented on more than one occasion. Pepsi was good for two games—schedule magnets and equipment bags—and McDonald's was dispensing mini-helmets in April, yo-yos in July, and baseball cards in August.

Gina had come to the Diamondbacks after a post-college stint working in Paris, and then a return home to spend three years handling communications for the Red Cross. Based in Phoenix, she had been dispatched to Oklahoma City to deal with the press in the aftermath of the terrorist bombing.

Interested in a change, Gina landed a press job with the Phoenix Super Bowl host committee when the game landed in town in 1996. Football led to baseball, and here she was, selecting promotional gifts and gathering them together. But those were only the first steps. Now, before tomorrow, the dozens of boxes containing the cushions needed to be stowed, and the other freebies packaged into plastic bags.

Exceedingly competent, Gina had the situation under control. Bodies were required, many bodies. And they came forth, from APS and Bank One, scores of volunteers, ready to pack and stack. The volunteers (some of whom said they had taken a personal day, while others claimed they were on company time) were happy to be there, working hard, for the benefit of BOB and the Diamondbacks. It was a touch strange, in fact, all this volunteering, not in the service of a charity or school or religious institution, but a great, big, extremely profitable corporation.

For their part, none of the volunteers seemed to find anything peculiar in the situation.

Anyway, there was precious little time for reflection: opening day was tomorrow.

Chapter 25

At Last

Arizona Highway 51 sweeps down through the mountains of the northeast valley, bringing those who live in Scottsdale and Paradise Valley and a good part of Phoenix to the downtown area. The highway is broad and fast and bends one way and back, following the landscape.

As the road curves to the east, the stadium suddenly appears in the distance. Though still far away, the ballpark looms large, seemingly outsized, broader and bigger, when compared to the high-rise offices and hotels of the central city set off to the west.

When the roof is closed, the effect is that much more dramatic, as the sun's reflection off the steel canopy can be stunning, almost blinding. Today, El Niño has granted the valley, or maybe the Arizona Diamondbacks, a break, a day of sunshine sandwiched between waves of storm-laden clouds. That means the roof is open and the grass is finally receiving the light and warmth it needs to thrive.

This is a day for baseball.

The crowd starts arriving hours before the gates open. No specific reason exists to be there, no special entertainment has been announced, but they come anyway. An excitement rapidly builds in the plaza before the main entrance, an excitement that is unveeringly insistent. This is it, this is the day, this is the culmination of years of talk and taxes, conjecture and controversy, publicity and passion, work and more work.

After today, the *Arizona Republic* will no longer devote its entire front page to baseball, nor will any Phoenix television stations allot an entire hour to the team, instead returning to their versions of the real world.

After today, the speculation about the players and the stadium and the strategy and the money will be over.

After today, none of the political wrangling and business maneuvering and media hyping will matter.

After today, it will be all about baseball.

About forty people have slept outside BOB, before a separate gate on the northeast side of the stadium, determined to assure themselves of one of the 350 dollar tickets. Everyone knows the rules: one ticket per person, used then and there, and nobody leaves—or, more accurately, nobody who leaves gets back inside.

These forty people are soon joined by a hundred more, and then hundreds more after that. The tickets will not go on sale for hours.

One can skip the line and the cheap seats and aim for the scalpers, who are ready to deal. The newspapers have been carrying the ads for weeks, placed by professional brokers, season-ticket holders, and just plain folks smart enough to have gotten in line and bought a couple of ducats for the big game. Naturally, those tickets will cost a little more than four bits—maybe $999 more per green seat—but there's no waiting on line.

By 2 P.M., concession stands are open on the plaza, doing a brisk business in T-shirts, hats, and baseballs, with "Inaugural Day, March 31, 1998" stenciled or stamped across them. Depending on the style of the item (and there are so many styles from which to choose), a hat can cost $28, a ball $8, and a T-shirt virtually any price, though nothing cheap. On this sort of once-in-a-lifetime occasion, the rush to buy the perfect souvenir, or any souvenir, becomes irresistible for many people, and many people are buying everything in sight.

What they don't know, or don't want to know, is that the franchise will keep producing the inaugural hats and T-shirts and baseballs as long as its fans will keep buying them.

And the jewel in the merchandising department's crown, the team shop off the rotunda, behind those shut gates and turnstiles, chockfull of every imaginable (and unimaginable) item, won't even open for three more hours.

This is not to say that absolutely no one gets inside the shop. Billy Crystal is escorted through the doors, the only visitor as the young staff dashes about, hurriedly hanging jackets and sweatshirts and the rest. Crystal is glancing at polo shirts and hats, not particularly interested, killing time before the game. Noting this, a writer approaches, politely identifies himself as a member of the media, a claim verified by his press pass, pad, and pen, and compliments Crystal on a recent, flattering profile in the *New York Times* in which the actor discussed his love for baseball and his hometown Yankees. This multilayered intro doesn't require twenty seconds, and then the writer, mentioning again Crystal's ardor for the game, asks him if his investment in the Diamondbacks is more of a financial or emotional venture.

Crystal, who hasn't deigned to give the writer more than a glance to this point, finally looks up from aimlessly fingering the shirts, twists his mouth into a rather disgusted grimace, and walks away.

And that is one of the differences between bearing a television camera and a pen. Show biz protocol has invaded the ballpark.

Across the plaza at Leinenkugel's, the bar is starting to hop, as customers are getting in the mood. The upstairs is closed off, reserved for a Bank One private party. Just a few blocks away, Jackson's on Third, open for business only since Friday, has four different areas, catering to different tastes, and a total capacity of fourteen hundred people. Patrons are dancing in the darkened club space to the right, others are seated and sipping in quieter environs to the left, while others are huddled around the main bar in the expanse between, watching the TVs hanging above the bar, tuned to the games already on the air.

But the busiest spot is the patio in front, where beer is sold out of tubs packed with ice and an express menu of hamburgers and the like doesn't waste anybody's time on food. The music is loud, the customers are laughing, the waitresses are young and pretty and scurrying to and fro, and the patio is jammed.

Jackson's is doing great and intends to do great with or without baseball. Its business hours are eleven in the morning to eleven at night—and maybe later, depending on the crowd. The sports bar cum restaurant will soon be joined by more bars and more restaurants on the street, all hoping to get a piece of the new downtown action.

The roads and avenues surrounding the ballpark are filled with

Phoenicians who are lost in their own central city, stumbling north and south, east and west, requesting directions of other Phoenicians who are equally lost.

Not every local is descending on the stadium. Art Kaufman, the tax protester, remains at home, still laboring to get the money returned to those he views as its rightful owners. Still, he intends to watch at least part of the game on television.

One of Kaufman's bêtes noires will be in attendance in BOB, and she will not be alone. In appreciation of Maricopa County's efforts on behalf of the stadium and the team, the Diamondbacks have reserved one hundred tickets for sale to the Board of Supervisors and other county employees. In a flash, Mary Rose Wilcox has snapped up fifty of the ducats, leaving her fellow supervisors angry and shocked.

Mary Rose refuses to apologize or make amends, first citing the needs of her "huge" family, and then thrusting her martyr status to the fore. "You know the hell I went through," she says, referring to the bullet in her butt.

Withholding comment, the Diamondbacks have provided the county with another twenty tickets, which have presumably been kept out of Mary Rose's reach.

Roland Hemond is pacing around the stadium. He awoke at six this morning, still, after all his years in baseball, too excited to sleep and too nervous to eat breakfast on opening day. "If you don't get some degree of butterflies," he says, "then you're not alive."

He recalls another opening day, back in 1953, when he was with the Braves. The Braves began life as the Boston Red Stockings back in 1871 and were the only franchise to have had a team on the playing field in every season of professional league baseball. After the better part of a century in Boston, the team fell on hard times, on the diamond and in the stands, and the owners decided to relocate the club to Milwaukee. This was their coming-out party in the new town, and Roland and everybody else anxiously waited to see what would happen.

The Braves were up against the St. Louis Cardinals. The crowd was loud and enthused, the contest fiercely played, and the score tied heading into the ninth inning. The ninth led to the tenth, then the eleventh, the new fans screaming for the Braves to pull it out. A rookie, Billy Bruton, came to bat for the home team, and socked a ball deep to center field. The outfielder dashed back, running onto the warning track, and raised his glove. The ball glanced off the top of the mitt and over the wall for a home run. Bruton circled the bases, the victory setting off a delirious celebration in the stadium, punctuating the Braves' move with an exclamation point.

"Wouldn't it be something if we had a game like that today?" Roland says. "Though I'll settle for any kind of win."

Roland says he's off to find his family, roaming around somewhere inside the ballpark, well represented by his wife, four of his five children (the fifth is flying in tomorrow), two grandsons, and one granddaughter. Before he departs, he adds one more fact about that game played so long ago.

"The funny thing was," he says, "that was Bruton's only home run of the year."

Roland starts relating some of the other details of Bruton's twelve-season career with Milwaukee and Detroit, but then he can't stand still any longer and has to get going with the big day.

Back outside on the plaza, the crowds are massing against the gates, while small booths throughout the area, set up by radio stations, a newspaper, an oil company, a bank credit card, and other corporations eager for the public's attention, are playing music and handing out stickers, posters, and other trinkets. They have been doing terrific business for hours, but people are now intent on entering BOB.

Again, on the other side of those gates, workers are pushing the boxes filled with cushions and the other gifts into position. Camera operators and photographers are gathering around the gates, waiting for the first fans to charge into the stadium.

Rich Dozer is there, and so is Scott Brubaker. There's nothing left for them to do except watch and smile and cheer, for the day will take on its own priorities and urgency and flow forward as events demand. While Rich confers with a ticket-taker, Scott walks up to the gate and raises his arm in an effort to excite a roar from the crowd. Since the crowd is already humming like an agitated hive, this is easily accomplished, and Scott, delighted with his mastery of the audience, repeats the process twice more.

It is three minutes to 5 P.M., two minutes to, one minute, and then it is here, it is time, and the locks are undone and the gates opened. But wait, one of the gates is still shut, and the older women serving as ticket-takers are not strong enough to pull apart the latch. While fans to the right pour into the ballpark, those stuck behind the closed gates impatiently press forward, as though the others are getting ahead of them. This, of course, makes no sense, as everybody has assigned seats, but that's crowd mentality for you, all id and no ego.

Finally, the latch gives way, a spirited yell sounds, and then everyone is hurrying through the turnstiles and streaming into and through Bank One Ballpark, pursuing different avenues—toward the field, the bathrooms, the food stands, the team shop—in the same manner that surging water finds every crack and path to penetrate.

The team shop off the rotunda is inundated with almost frantic shoppers. Despite anticipation of the demand, the actual onslaught, the deluge of this tangle of humanity, is staggering, and the young staff looks stunned.

One Diamondback T-shirt has a large American flag sketched on its front, except bats take the place of stripes, and baseballs substitute for stars. Beneath the flag is the legend "It's as American as you get."

The Diamondbacks are on the field, in the midst of batting practice. The Colorado Rockies are gathering outside their dugout, preparing to stretch en masse.

The Diamondbacks are wearing their cream uniforms with the purple pinstripes, purple caps on their heads. The Diamondback *A* on the hats is a bit smaller than the original lettering had been, a change initiated by Buck after he observed at the end of last summer that the *A* was so large, it curled over at the top of the cap. Finding this esthetically displeasing, Showalter ordered the alteration, and production and merchandising and whoever else promptly responded.

Buck is surrounded by reporters, talking about the maturity of his players, veterans and youngsters, and the maturity of their expectations for themselves and for the season. Showalter has never, not for a second, at least not publicly, joined in the increasingly rosy speculation about the team's prospects. It is obviously important to the manager that his players understand—more than understand, intellectually and emotionally internalize—that the campaign ahead will be long and arduous, requiring an even-tempered, constant dedication, permitting neither isolated victories nor defeats to overwhelm the club's consistent professionalism.

Karim Garcia is in the batting cage. He and Matt Williams wear their stockings in the old-fashioned manner, pulled up high on the calf. Garcia smashes a couple of balls into the right-field stands as the crowd that has already gathered there yells its appreciation.

The Rockies are skipping to the side and then skipping back again. The line is ragged and the effort casual. The team collapses to the grass and stretches this way and that.

Reporters are everywhere. On behalf of news organizations across the country, hundreds have requested and received press credentials for this historic occasion. Knots of them are clustered around the foul lines, outfield to home plate to outfield, watching the players and talking to each other about the college-basketball playoffs and Phoenix hotels and their families and the weather. Many of these men—and the journalists are mainly middle-aged men, with the stomachs to prove it—know each other from covering major sporting events, and they catch up on their lives and jokes and opinions.

It is easy to divide the newspaper writers from the TV correspondents. The TV types tend to be younger, thinner, and more hirsute than their colleagues, or counterparts, in the writing corps. The writers are dressed in jeans and polo shirts, or slacks and sweaters. With dismaying frequency, they are a bit on the unkempt side, to put it politely. On the other hand, the TV types are garbed in their freshly pressed suits, preferably gray or blue pin-striped. Their hair is also freshly pressed, also with chemicals, into submission.

While the TV types also took notes, they didn't have to take as many, given the constraints of a ten- or thirty- or sixty-second spot, allowing them more time to attend to their grooming.

Edwin Diaz is in the cage and hits one past the right-field wall. Matt Williams and a couple of other Diamondbacks are leaning against the cage, waiting their turns. Williams gives an exaggerated "Oohhh" to mark Diaz's shot, garnering smirks from his mates.

Behind the cage, near the seats, in front of the netting, a batting tee bids upon any batter who wishes to check his swing one last time. A batboy tarries next to a basket of balls. The balls look hard-worn, and the batboy says that these balls have made their way down the ladder, beginning their careers in the bright gleam of spring training games, then, as the scuffs and knocks took their toll, being demoted to practice days, then down to this tee.

And when they're done here, the batboy explains, and they're all beaten up, they're sent down to the minors.

About thirty waiters and waitresses, attired in white shirts, black

318

bow ties, and black vests, are gathered together in the lower stands. They review one last time the handheld computers issued to them, which will transmit the food orders and accept the credit card charges of those ensconced in the $50 section, a sizable region extending from dugout to dugout, around home plate, encompassing all the rows from the first walkway to the field. These fans (who also have reserved parking spaces in the adjoining garage) can have a shrimp cocktail ($8.75), a Polish sausage ($4.50), or a Diamondbacks Dog ($4.25), without budging from their extrawide seats with extralong legroom.

This segregation by ticket price is not a new feature in ballparks. However, the many levels of separation, from luxury boxes to club seats to regular seats to bleachers, are no longer just a function of preferable perspectives, but entail a whole host of differing levels of service and privilege. Nor are these differences discretely hidden; everybody can see the waiters hustling about, and men and women splashing around in the pool, and corporate execs reclining in their boxes. Discretion is an antiquated concept; the current mode is to celebrate one's wealth and power and prominence as publicly as possible.

Despite this striation of rank, as distinct as the geologic lines in the Grand Canyon, the stadium feels intimate and close, everybody in the same place, everybody one for all, and all for the Diamondbacks.

About ten members of the grounds crew are lined up near the visitors' dugout, rakes and hoes in hand, outfitted in tuxedos and sneakers for the occasion. Photographers are gathered before the grinning groundskeepers, snapping away for prosperity. The grounds crew breaks for various positions on the diamond. One man spreads dirt around home plate with his hands, smoothing it down, again by hand, then another smacks it with a metal square attached to a pole. It's a funny juxtaposition, the tuxes and the dirt, and the photographers furiously record the scene.

The organist plays *"Charge!"* and the fountains in the pool spurt high in the air. The seats are beginning to fill up. A surprising number of babies are in attendance, carried around the stadium by their parents.

Amy Bender is to the left of home plate, talking to her producer and camera operator, preparing for her first Diamondbacks pregame show. She is wearing a purple gown. This was not her idea, but a decree from Scott Brubaker, marketer impulse on overdrive, for all on-air personalities to dress to the nines—and maybe well into double digits—tonight.

Amy doesn't own formal attire and was accorded a fifty-buck budget to procure a frock. That budget said a lot about what it's like being a woman in a relentlessly male industry.

Nevertheless, Amy journeyed unto the malls and stores to discover a dress, some dress, any dress, when lightning—in the form of Loehmann's—struck. There it was, within the walls of the discount cathedral, a gown, and purple, Diamondback purple at that, and for the grand sum of—thunder and lightning, please—$35. That left Amy with $15 to buy a pair of shoes. More than enough.

So here she is, decked out and ready to get the show under way. And the show is getting nearer, as the crowd fills up the stadium, and the buzz from the fans increases. Many walk down to the low wall dividing the stands from the field, to get as near as permissible to the diamond, to the grass, and to the players.

The photographers are crammed behind a rope into a relatively small space between home plate and the Diamondbacks' dugout, as teenage boys in white shirts and black pants run out from the right-field bullpen carrying white benches. They split into two groups, aligning their benches in single rows along each foul line, home to first, and home to third. Following the boys, preteen girls in purple jerseys and white shirts, bearing streamers on sticks, run into the outfield. The boys run off.

It's showtime.

The JumboTron comes alive. Black-and-white footage of Lou Gehrig appears on the screen, and the crowd hears the Yankee Iron Man say, "Today, I consider myself the luckiest man alive." Gehrig gives way to Bobby Thompson hitting his pennant-winning home run for the New York Giants, and then a series of stellar baseball memories: Hank Aaron's 715th homer, Pete Rose's 4,192nd base hit, Dodger Kirk Gibson's World Series dinger, Joe Carter's similar feat for the Blue Jays, Cal Ripkin's 2,131st consecutive game. Each episode in the continuum that is such an essential part of baseball is cheered by the assemblage.

And now the Diamondbacks are ready to join that proud history, and the giant screen reels through DB highlights: Buck meeting the press as the new manager, the stadium groundbreaking, Travis's spin at the podium, the franchise officially entering the National League, then, in quick order, Bell, White, and Williams on the stage, pulling

320

on the Arizona jersey and cap and becoming Diamondbacks. Every face, every fact, gets applause, with the loudest saved for Matt Williams.

"Ladies and gentlemen," calls the public address announcer, "welcome to the big leagues!"

The crowd is bellowing in response as an Indian in traditional garb quietly walks to the microphone on the infield grass. In giving Bank One Ballpark a blessing—"I ask that the Creator provide the courage and the wisdom," the usual sort of thing, same as any religious blessing, praying that the stadium be used well by generations to come—he veers toward politics, congratulating the team for not employing a "racially based mascot" nor anything "that is derogatory to native people."

That said, he spreads his arms wide, revealing his cape to be an American Indian Movement flag. The fans, giddy with baseball and the stadium, don't seem to notice or care about politics, especially not on this night, and courteously applaud as the Indian departs.

Not an instant is lost, and the girls already on the field are running about waving their streamers, while others extend lengths of material in purple and turquoise and copper, creating wheels and other patterns. A song entitled "Welcome" plays. It's halftime at the Super Bowl, cut down to local size, hokey, but kind of sweet.

Gov. Jane Hull gets her time at the microphone on the grass and welcomes the crowd "to the greatest opening day in history, and welcome to the greatest ballpark!"

The cheers that greet that remark are undeniably missing when she follows up with an allegedly hipper reference: "If I were to put it in my grandchildren's words, 'This place is awesome!'"

She's lost the fans now, even when she invokes the name of Matt Williams, relating her grandkids' dream of catching one of the third baseman's home runs.

She paces away and is replaced by Jan Brewer from the Board of Supervisors. She is either extremely nervous or can't adjust to the microphone, because she reads from prepared notes as if she had just learned to read. The banality of her speech is enlivened by the bizarreness of her delivery.

Len Coleman, the rather urbane president of the National League, is next. "Welcome to the senior circuit," he says. A few more words and then he's finished, brief and to the point. "Congratulations and good luck."

One more speaker remains, and the announcer introduces "the man whose vision brought Arizona its own field of dreams."

Jerry Colangelo receives a standing ovation. He is genuinely touched, one more unforgettable moment in a three-year mountain of moments, each building upon and besting those that came before.

"Tonight's game is one of the most significant days in Arizona," Colangelo begins. He thanks many people, including Chris Herstam, present and past supervisors Mary Rose Wilcox, Jim Bruner, and Ed King, Governors Rose Mofford and Fife Symington, Dwight Patterson, the city of Phoenix. The rapid recitation of these mainly political names elicits meager enthusiasm from the people of the valley, who love the result but have not loved the process. Colangelo continues his thank-yous and finally hits upon a more popular acknowledgment—"the Maricopa County taxpayers, who shared in this joint venture with the Arizona Diamondbacks"—garnering more cheers, and then finishes with his wife, Joan, and family, and the "men and women who took part in building Bank One Ballpark."

The formalities over, Colangelo announces that, at that very instant, two unsuspecting children are being plucked out of their seats to throw out the first ball. It's been an ongoing Arizona mystery: Who would receive this honor? Which local or national dignitary from the long roll call to choose? Joe DiMaggio, Barry Goldwater, President Clinton—or Jerry Colangelo?

Diamondback officials weren't talking, which only caused the media to continue stoking speculation, which only caused Diamondback officials to guard their silence even more vigilently.

Now the secret is out, and the correct answer is Richard and Ashley Volpe, six-year-old twins. "Hours ago," Colangelo says, "they didn't know they'd be getting into the game. Tonight they'll be taking part in history.

"Dreams really do come true!"

While a DB functionary was fetching the kids from their $5.50 seats, the ceremonies proceeded. A host of baseball notables— Harmon Killebrew, Ryne Sandberg, Bert Campaneris, Joe Garagiola Sr., Frank Robinson, Robin Yount, Eddie Leon, Floyd Bannister, Jim Lefevbre, and Don Baylor, in his Colorado Rockies uniform—are introduced, to help two other special guests, Willie Mays, one of the greatest and most beloved ballplayers of them all, and Joe Black, a star of the old Negro Leagues prior to joining the Brooklyn Dodgers, unveil a tribute to Jackie Robinson in left field. Mays and Black, who roomed with Robinson way back when and is now a community-relations official with the Diamondbacks, pull down a drape to reveal a jersey numbered 42, Robinson's number, painted on the wall.

Sharon Robinson, Jackie's daughter, receives a replica of the jersey, already framed, from Colangelo and Coleman, along with the declaration that no Diamondback will ever wear the number of the first black man to break the major league's color barrier.

The preteen girls begin dancing and jumping again. While they are kicking up a storm, à la Rockettes, to the strains of "You've Gotta Have Heart" from the Broadway show *Damn Yankees*, former vice president Dan Quayle and wife Marilyn show up and take seats a couple of rows behind Colangelo.

Not only do you need to have heart to play, the announcer tells the audience, but you need first base, and second and third, too. With that, three rappellers slide down ropes fastened to the roof, one by one, to deliver the bases.

The roof, accompanied by the musical arrangement that clashes and cries, commences to open. The crowd erupts, amazed and enraptured, for it truly is an astonishing sight, almost otherworldly, more closely resembling the underside of an alien spacecraft initiating some maneuver than anything having to do with baseball.

Fireworks explode, and then the Rockies are arrayed along the first-base foul line. Their names are read over the loudspeaker with alacrity, and the Arizona audience does not respond with excessive enthusiasm.

Enough of the visitors; it's time for the home team. The music swells and the JumboTron bursts alive with an animated snake, a diamondback, naturally, that is curled in the desert, coiled around a baseball. The snake squeezes the ball, which shoots out of its embrace, into the sky, and inside BOB. The ball bounces off the walls and the fountains, until it rolls onto the mound and to a stop inside the mouth of the diamondback, which gives a fearsome rattle.

The animation is startlingly crisp, the colors perfect, and the crowd eats it up with a roar. The Diamondbacks are called out, players, coaches, and trainers, minus the starting lineup, and they stand along the third-base line, each taking a step forward as his name is read aloud.

Now it's time for the opening day lineup, preceded by their manager, and Buck Showalter quickly jogs out of the dugout. He runs down the line, pumped and ready for the season, greeting his

Diamondbacks by banging his fist into theirs. A couple of the DBs are clearly caught off-guard by the fervor of Buck's salutation, and their hands suffer for it.

The starters are summoned to the field according to the batting order: Devon White leading off, followed by Jay Bell, Travis Lee, Matt Williams in the cleanup spot, Brent Brede, Karim Garcia, Jorge Fabregas, Edwin Diaz, and Andy Benes.

Everyone in the great state of Arizona has known all along that White would bat in the number one slot, and that Williams would hit fourth. The other places, however, have been up for grabs. Buck has picked Lee for the third spot, a crucial position in any batting order, but feels that the rookie can handle the pressure, just as he has quietly and efficiently handled every other challenge thrown at him.

That leaves Bell at number two, which should constitute a solid, major league, front four. After that, things are not so clear. Showalter has selected Brent Brede for the fifth spot. Brede, who will patrol left field, has enjoyed a productive spring, batting .324 with 2 home runs. Karim Garcia, the second rookie in the lineup, will take right field and hit sixth, Jorge Fabregas is the seventh man in the order, Edwin Diaz is eighth, and Andy Benes is ninth. Diaz is something of the Cinderella story of the team, at the bottom of the depth chart for second base when spring training began, and the unlikely hero of the first exhibition game with his sacrifice fly in the ninth inning. The injuries to Andy Stankiewicz and Hanley Frias have given Diaz more opportunity to show his stuff, and Buck has decided, just the day before, to go with a hunch and bring Diaz up from Triple A and give him the start for opening day.

Baseball, like all sports, is a zero-sum game. For every victory, there is a defeat, and for every promotion to the big leagues, there is a demotion. David Dellucci was informed he was being dispatched to the Tucson Toros and Triple A on Monday. It was a hell of a day for Dellucci; before learning he was busted to Tucson, he had discovered that somebody had stolen his pickup truck, along with most of his clothes, packed in the truck's cab.

Dellucci has played hard and well during spring training, impressing Showalter. "David's the type of guy who you know what you're going to get every day," Buck told the *Republic* exactly a week before sending Dellucci down to Tucson. "He brings a real sincerity to his game. There aren't a lot of pretensions. He comes to play baseball and win baseball games."

Regardless, Dellucci is an outfielder and Buck wants more infielders on the squad, and so Diaz is in and Dellucci is out.

So here are the twenty-five ballplayers, at least on this day, who constitute the 1998 Arizona Diamondbacks. Combined, their 1997 batting average is .256, with an ERA of 4.42, and an average MLB tenure of 4.7 years.

The ceremony, or ceremonies, continue. A conclave of singers and musicians stroll toward home plate to sing the national anthem. Nils Lofgren, Dave Mustaine, Robin Wilson, Rob Halford, Sam Moore, Andy West, Joni Sledge, Alice Tatum, Margo Reed: rock stars old and new, international and local, valley residents all, led by that most famed of all Arizona rockers, Alice Cooper. They perform a sweet, soulful version of the anthem, their voices merging wonderfully, charming the crowd with an entirely fresh interpretation of a song not known for being either terribly sweet or soulful.

The thrills are not finished. Five soldiers from the U.S. Air Force Wings of Blue are already hurtling through the night. Each appears suddenly, out of the night, twisting and floating toward the open roof, which suddenly doesn't seem quite as large as it did before, swaying in the windy sky, somehow finding his way to the green turf. The parachutists bear tokens: the Diamondback and National League pennants, the Arizona and U.S. flags, and the inaugural ball.

Jerry Colangelo escorts the Volpe children, first-graders from Superstition Springs Elementary School in east Mesa, to the pitcher's mound, one on each side, his hands grasping theirs. They are blond and adorable, almost lost within their Diamondback jerseys and caps. The Little Leaguers take their assignments seriously and set and hurl their balls to catchers Fabregas and Kelly Stinnett. After the celebrities and the hoopla, this might well stand as the best moment of the ceremonies, an instant of pure enthusiasm and simple joy, a dear reflection of baseball.

The show is over, the ceremonies are done. The ballplayers take the field.

Andy Benes has the ball. Thousands of cameras are raised. Benes leans back, beginning his motion, and releases the ball. An encircling white blast of flashbulbs pop as Colorado's second baseman, Mike Lansing, takes the pitch, and the umpire calls a ball.

Local historians will record that Arizona enters the professional ranks with that first pitch at 8:22 P.M. One minute later, the Diamondbacks give up their first hit, when Lansing laces a single up the middle. But that's it for the Rockies this inning. Ellis Burks, Larry Walker, (the 1997 National League MVP) & Dante Bichette—one, two, three—all ground out. The Diamondbacks close out the top half of the inning and run off the field to appreciative applause.

Devon White steps to the plate. The left-handed hitter sets himself by planting his left foot first, and then, almost gingerly, as if he's dipping into a hot bath, drawing his right forward. He waves his bat below him, only raising it when Colorado's Darryl Kile tenses to throw.

Kile is good, one of the ten best pitchers in the National League, a 19-game winner for the Astros last year. The Diamondbacks wanted the right-hander and pursued him with zeal, but Kile chose the Rockies instead, inking a three-year, $24-million deal. Arizona's inability to snare Kile was their most public failure, which turned out to be good news for Benes, subsequently signed to be the ace on the Diamondback staff.

Kile throws and White swings and misses. Strike one.

Devon takes the next pitch and the count goes to 1-1, but that's as close as he'll get this turn. White strikes out—another Diamondback first, incidentally, on a night where a ballplayer could scratch or spit himself into the record books by doing it before anybody else. Speaking of spitting, the players on both sides expectorate with uninterrupted vigor. It is quite a disgusting performance, and simply unnecessary. Most probably, the habit began when so many players chewed tobacco and had to eject the resulting, revolting bile. While a contingent of players continue to chew, others have finally learned about cancer. Joe Garagiola Sr. has emerged as baseball's most fervent missionary to convince players to forgo the dangerous practice, visiting MLB locker rooms to spread the gospel of health.

Instead of simply abandoning tobacco, many players have substituted sunflower seeds or some such other thing to occupy their mouths, allowing them not only to chew but also spit. And even a fair percentage of those who chew nothing at all enjoy spewing forth with saliva and other natural products.

Sometimes baseball is best appreciated from a safe distance.

Jay Bell taps the plate with his bat, waves it around, then hauls it far back. He looks a little knock-kneed, but comfortable. Bell sharply whacks a pitch, but the shortstop snags the ball just before it skips out of the infield and throws Bell out at first.

Travis Lee receives a nice hand as he strides into the batter's box. He stands straight, takes a couple of abbreviated swings, and stops. Once ready, bat easy and high, he hardly moves and seems calm, focused: self-possessed and imperturbable. His classic stance and fluid, fast swing remind many observers of Ken Griffey Jr., who might be the best hitter in the game.

Lee lashes Kile's first pitch through the middle into the outfield for a single, bringing the fans jumping up as one, emitting an electrified shout. History again—the first Diamondback hit.

The organist plays the series of chords denoting "Charge!" and Matt Williams digs in. He holds his bat high, hands above his cap, the end of the club waving aggressively, waggling menacingly. It is an intense, threatening stance, befitting the All-Star.

Williams swings at the first pitch and misses. Strike one. He takes the second pitch, and the ump signals strike. Strike two. Matt fouls off a pitch, then sits back as Kile throws three pitches far outside.

The count is full, 3-2. Kile lets loose a breaking ball, which Williams watches sail past for a called strike three.

The side is retired.

In the old days, peace reigned in the few minutes between innings, the normal, unmannered lull between the action. But the blessed silence has been permanently broken, as the placid pause between the action is filled with commercials and advertisements, cartoon characters and cheery actors prancing across the JumboTron, chirpy, insistent voices blaring over the public address system. Discount Tire, Shamrock Farms, Fry's Supermarkets . . . If it can be sold in Arizona, it's probably being sold here.

And not only here. While Thom Brennaman is on the radio hawking a golf community, and Jay Bell and Matt Williams do a star turn on TV for the Diamondbacks' team shops, Buck has quickly emerged as the most popular of the new boys in town to hire as corporate pitchman. He's on the radio for Basha's, a supermarket chain, rambling on a bit about "fresh produce" and the like. Buck's wicked sense of humor, delivered in his subdued Southern style, isn't really suited to either supermarket commercials or the radio, and the spot is, at best, flat.

Buck does better in a Bank One television commercial, hyping Diamondback checks and credit cards. The manager is in the midst of running errands, purchasing incidentals at a hardware store, picking up his dry cleaning, buying a TV. Of course, once each salesperson sees that Buck is paying by check, the joy over garnering Showalter's autograph precludes that check from ever being cashed. This works well for Buck as he purchases increasingly expensive items, until he gets behind the wheel of a vintage Mustang, and the salesman assures him he fully intends to deposit the check. Buck gives his version of a startled expression, and that's all, folks!

But that's for the outside world. Here in the stadium, McDonald's is selling a giant cheeseburger on the giant screen, and just for pocket change, right inside BOB.

Back on the field, Vinny Castilla faces Benes, and the third baseman singles to left. Todd Helton, a rookie who's replacing Andres Galarraga and his 41 home runs at first base, socks a hit down the left-field line. Brede chases down the ball but Helton races to second and Castilla crosses home plate.

The Rockies have scored first, but most of the fans don't appear overly upset. The crowd is so giddy with the glory of the new, with the sheer fun of this place and event, that the Rockies' run is just another journey into the dazzling unknown.

Colorado makes some more noise but doesn't score again that inning. Benes and Kile both pitch well for the next few innings, and neither side reaches home plate.

Boyd Orth, the native Phoenician who grew up without baseball, is sitting with wife Sharon in Channel 3's luxury suite. Boyd and Sharon are reclining in the suite because Channel 3, the Diamondbacks' local broadcaster, is owned by Del Lewis, Boyd's best friend since childhood.

Boyd has a commanding view of the entire scene and he's impressed. The suite's accommodations aren't bad, either, and waiters carry in strawberries dipped in chocolate and other delicacies.

Boyd likes the stadium, absolutely, he appreciates what it has already done and what it will continue to do for downtown Phoenix. "I still think the county should have represented themselves better," he says. "The county should have gotten more for its taxpayers' money."

Boyd has also had enough of the saturation press coverage and prays that, with the season under way, the media fever will subside. "When the front page is covered with Diamondbacks, is that sick?"

Boyd has had a lot of fun tonight, partaking in the total ballpark experience, which includes not just watching the action on the field, but also eating and schmoozing and sight-seeing.

On the other hand, Boyd likes to get up early, and he's had enough baseball, so it's time to go home.

Investors Tom Jorishe and Randy Suggs are not departing early. Both the car dealer and the home builder attended Sunday's Cactus League game played in BOB. Tom mixed a little business with pleasure, parking his 1998 Volkswagen Beetle outside the stadium— illegally, actually, but correctly guessing that the police would think it was supposed to be there, on exhibition. The Beetle, redesigned and reissued after decades in retirement, is the sensation of the automotive season, and Tom maximizes his visit to BOB by showing it off.

Jorishe leaves the Bug in the garage, for tonight he's concentrating on baseball. He bought season tickets over the visitors' dugout, on the first-base side, section E, row 16, and is with his wife and another couple. Tom is as happy as he can be; he loves the retractable roof, he loves the grass, he's wearing the sweatshirt he got on the road trip to Denver aboard the America West Diamondback jet almost two years ago.

Tom is realistic but enthused about the team. He's primed for the season.

"This is great," he says. "Just great."

Randy Suggs's season tickets are in the club section, a handful of rows behind Jerry Colangelo. This is the celebrity section tonight (and probably always), with Crystal and Quayle. But the biggest celeb on this occasion is Colangelo, and a constant line of autograph seekers, young and old, troop down to the front row and beseech his signature.

Randy's sitting beside his wife and his brother and another investor. Randy has longed for a team since he was a boy, when he rooted for the Yankees of Mickey Mantle and Roger Maris, in far-off New York City. Now he has his own team. He plans on being here quite often, with friends, family, and clients, a home away from home, a portable office.

"I knew Jerry Colangelo could pull it off," he says. "Anybody else may not have been able to do this."

In addition to his immense personal gratification, Suggs is sure this is good for Phoenix. "Every city needs promotional activities, and that's what this is."

329

That's responsible and adult talk, but it's a sideshow, at least tonight, to the fun on the field, and Randy knows it.

"This is tremendous," he says. "You have to be a fan."

Randy is one fellow who is definitely not splitting his season tickets with anybody else.

Former governor Rose Mofford is at the game, and so are Chris Herstam and Jim Bruner and Eddie Lynch and many others who have played a part in bringing this team and this stadium to fruition. The Arizona political and business elite are gathered in this place, along with some fifty thousand more regular citizens.

The Diamondbacks come close in the bottom of the fourth when Jay Bell walks to start the inning, and Travis Lee, after hitting two towering foul balls, cracks a double on a 2-2 pitch over third base. But the umps call it just foul, and Travis strides back to home plate to hit again and Buck races out of the dugout to protest. Of course, the complaint does no good, and Lee singles between first and second, moving Bell to third.

This should be a proper stage for some patented Matt Williams heroics, and the crowd is collectively, eagerly leaning forward. Williams cuffs the ball down to third and Bell breaks for home. He is out by a country mile at the plate, out by so much that he doesn't attempt a slide or risk a collision.

Lee is on second and Williams is on first when Brede grounds into a double play, and the Diamondbacks are out of the inning with nothing on the scoreboard to show for their efforts.

Colorado strikes hard in the top of the sixth. Dante Bichette chops the ball toward third and the ball pops out of Williams's glove as he stretches to the foul line. Bichette reaches first and the scorer generously marks it as a hit and not an error. Vinny Castilla is up next, and he knocks the first pitch over Brede's head and the left-field wall for a home run.

Rockies 3, Diamondbacks 0.

Bottom of the sixth, top of the order for Arizona. White bunts for an out, Bell strikes out, and Lee is up. Travis sends the first pitch flying over the right-field wall, scoring the Diamondbacks' first run.

As he trots around the bases, cheers pour down on him from the assemblage. On this inaugural day, he has won the appreciation of the Arizona fans.

But Lee's feat does not turn the tide. Williams pops out to center field and the Rockies bat again. Lansing singles and center fielder

330

Ellis Burks doubles to score Lansing. That's it for Benes. He walks off the mound, to polite applause, and is relieved by Clint Sodowsky.

The Rockies do not let up. Walker singles, driving in another run. Bichette pumps out a single, and Colorado has men on first and third. Castilla sets and bangs his second home run, a huge shot to center, way, way back.

Rockies 8, Diamondbacks 1.

Fans are heading for the exits. Nothing personal, but this is a school night and the game has been on for well over two hours. The whole nine innings will consume two hours and fifty minutes, which means that the game won't end until 11:12 P.M.

Losing has nothing to do with the crowd's departure. That euphoric feeling that baseball is here to stay perseveres over anything else. The Rockies score another run in the eighth, but who's counting? No one on the Arizona side of the ledger, not until Karim Garcia homers with two out in the ninth, and the remaining fans give a full-throated roar. This is the honeymoon period, and the expansion Diamondbacks know they will have to rely upon their fans' forbearance as they try and mainly lose, and try and mainly lose again.

The final score stands Colorado Rockies 9, Arizona Diamondbacks 2.

The media gather outside the home team's locker room. There's a ten-minute cooling-off period for the players before the press is permitted inside.

The doors open and the scribes and camera crews rush past the security guard. Any expectations that the media-friendly Diamondbacks will be lolling in front of their cubicles, ready to dispense quotes, are sorely disappointed, for the room is stunningly empty. Only Buck awaits the onslaught, still in uniform, arms crossed, leaning against a tabletop in the center of the clubhouse.

In an instant, the manager is surrounded by the ravenous press. Buck speaks in his studied monotone, reserved for official occasions, in such a hushed voice that the microphones and tape recorders are thrust even closer to his face to catch his words.

Buck doesn't stop talking, but he doesn't really say too much, or at least too much that can't be anticipated.

What were his impressions of the night?

"The night was a good memory for the fans and the organization."

Will the starting lineup change for tomorrow's game?

"We'll have to see, but obviously not a lot."

What did he think of Travis Lee's performance?

"He's handled every challenge that we've thrown at him."

Showalter rambles on, giving every station and reporter an opinion or an evaluation, inevitably returning to the same basic themes: the night was memorable, Travis Lee was marvelous, but the season will be long and hard, and no matter how memorable or marvelous any of tonight was, it was only one game, with 161 more on the schedule, so let's not get too excited.

Travis Lee emerges from the shower area and steps to his locker, and much of the media abandons Buck and closes in on the rookie. Travis is the story of the game, going three for four, including that first Diamondback hit and that first Diamondback home run.

Lee's performance was the brightest spot in a fairly dreadful outing. In fact, only the two rookies in the Diamondback lineup, Lee and Garcia, produced for the team, belting solo homers. Though the veterans fell seriously short—Williams went 0 for 4 at the plate, Bell, 0 for 3, with a walk, and White 1 for 4—the rookie explosion was a hopeful harbinger of happy days to come.

Lee, his hair still wet, looks stunned by the attention, but he has his answers ready, and they tend to sound an awful like Buck's responses.

Which was sweeter, the first hit or the home run?

"I was just up there trying to hit the ball hard."

More, Travis, tell us more about what it was like, but Travis didn't have much more to add.

"It's a good day to be lucky, I guess."

But the reporters keep asking, and Travis keeps talking, and he relaxes and grows more comfortable with each question. His eyes lose that hunted look, and he starts to smile, and he's still talking.

Thaddeus White, ten years old, sits in front of his dad's locker. He states he enjoyed the game and declares that his father "did okay." Devon is dressed in jeans and a sweater when he appears and doesn't appear to be in a particularly cheery mood. A reporter approaches him, but White waves him off, saying he's done answering questions for the night. White and son leave.

The clubhouse is a family affair. Cherubic Nathan Showalter, an *A* painted on one cheek, strolls about the clubhouse, as familiar with these surroundings as a grizzled vet. Jay Bell's three-year-old boy waits on his father's chair while his dad showers. He points out his miniature replica of his dad's jersey, both hanging on the cubicle's wall. The little blond fellow declares he has had a fine time at the game and, shifting gears, reveals that because his mom is away in Tampa, he gets to sleep with Daddy tonight.

Jay steps up, wrapped in a towel, and is asked about the Diamond-back first baseman. "Travis Lee comes as advertised," he says, compliments Lee's skills and poise, and requests a few moments to dress.

Bell is subdued, as is Benes, but they give the media their due. Travis has excused himself to finish dressing and now he's back, still the object of the press's attention and affection, still doling out those blandly assured answers that athletes have always doled out when they don't have anything to say or have said it for the millionth time.

How does the ballpark play?

"Same as any other ballpark."

The locker room remains deserted. The bulk of the team quietly and quickly slipped away before the media's entrance, and the press has pretty much gotten what it's going to get out of the few players who have submitted to the interrogation. Some members of the media start packing up, while others have already left to file their stories.

Jerry Colangelo enters, his eyes positively shining. No one knows better than this highly competitive man that sports are about winning and losing, but sometimes events, even in sports, transcend the usual measure of success. This is one of those events, and Colangelo clearly is aware of this exceptional moment.

The owner has a baseball with him. It is Travis Lee's home-run ball. Rich Dozer tracked down the man who retrieved the ball in the right-field seats and, with Colangelo's assent, offered a pair of season tickets for the trophy.

Later, reports will question whether the man who nabbed the ball did so by trampling over a couple of people in the disabled section in the scramble to grab the prize. Later, local Indian tribes will angrily wonder why the Diamondbacks selected a Native American who not only represented a politically contentious group, but lived in Oregon, to bless the stadium.

Later, Edwin Diaz will return to Tucson to make room for Andy Stankiewicz, whose speedy recovery from knee surgery will allow him to join the team for its first road trip. David Dellucci, the last man cut by the Diamondbacks before the season opener, will be brought up to the big club to replace Chris Jones, who will be traded to San Francisco. Dellucci's stolen truck will be recovered. The truck will be badly damaged, and all his clothes, which had been packed inside, will be gone.

Later, more changes will be made as the Diamondbacks get off to a slow start, losing their first six games before attaining their first victory—perhaps the only first that really means anything.

Later, more stadiums will be built, incorporating BOB's innovations and adding fresh ones. However they are designed, one can be certain that they will all have broad concourses, diversions and exhibits off the field, restaurants galore, and most important of all, real grass.

Later, the greatest ballpark in America, Yankee Stadium, will have to shut down for a few days when a steel expansion joint falls, crushing a seat and knocking out a row only hours before a game is to begin. The House That Ruth Built could be one step closer to demolition, as Steinbrenner and Giuliani, directly and indirectly, seize upon the opportunity to make the case for a new stadium. Testing the presidential waters, Giuliani will visit Phoenix just a few days later. While in town, he will check out Bank One Ballpark, pronounce it "absolutely terrific," and a model for a new Yankee venue. In fact, Giuliani will state his appreciation for the Arizona version of private-public partnership and happily speculate that the naming rights for a New York Yankee ballpark could reach over $100 million.

The Colosseum of Rome is still standing after two thousand years, but Yankee Stadium may be hard-pressed to make it much past its seventy-fifth birthday.

Later, Larry Naman will be convicted of attempted first-degree murder.

Later that night, the bars and restaurants in downtown Phoenix will remain open as patrons stay for hours. The team shop will keep selling until the last of the fans have emptied the shelves and emptied their wallets, around midnight. To gain some idea of how much merchandise will be sold this day, one small concession stand on the plaza outside the stadium's gates offering official Diamondback hats, T-shirts, and baseballs grosses $60,000.

Later that night, a local television station will provide the grace note on the entire media saturation coverage when it headlines a story on the utterly sane preponderance of female-to-male toilets "Potty Parody" instead of "Potty Parity."

334

But that's all later. Now, in a gesture of unprecedented corporate humility, Jerry Colangelo approaches Travis Lee and, without speeches or fireworks or fanfare, hands him his home-run ball. Lee is both astounded and touched by the generous and gracious gesture.

Let this first day end with this brief exchange. It's not a play at the plate or a grand slam in the ninth, but the moment, and all the ideas and emotions it can inspire, is indisputably part of the game, part of the sense and taste and feel of the game, one more moment in the enduring sport and abiding pageant that is baseball. There will be many more moments, many more days, that will prove just as important to baseball.

There will also be many more debates about salaries and stadiums, many more discussions about the impact on culture, the obligation of celebrity, the consolidation of big business, the globalization of markets, the impoverishment of politics. But the debates and discussions can be set aside until tomorrow, for today, this day, belongs to the simple pleasures of sport, which here and now is embodied by the promise of the Arizona Diamondbacks and the joys of baseball.